D0562689

NUCLEAR NORTH KOREA

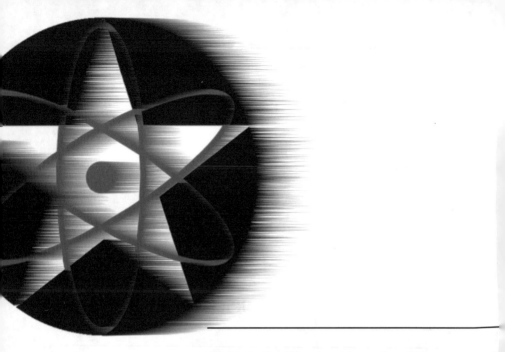

NUCLEAR

VICTOR D. CHA | DAVID C. KANG

NORTH KOREA

A DEBATE ON
ENGAGEMENT
STRATEGIES

Columbia University Press   New York

COLUMBIA UNIVERSITY PRESS

Publishers Since 1893

New York   Chichester, West Sussex

Copyright © 2003 Victor D. Cha and David C. Kang

All rights Reserved

Library of Congress Cataloging-in-Publication Data

Cha, Victor D., 1961–

Nuclear North Korea : a debate on engagement strategies /

Victor D. Cha, David C. Kang.

p.   cm.

Includes bibliographical references and index.

ISBN 0–231–13128–3

1. Nuclear warfare—Korea (North) 2. Korea (North)—Military

policy. 3. United States—Foreign relations—Korea (North)

4. Korea (North)—Foreign relations—United States.

World politics—21st century. I. Kang, David C.

(David Chan-oong), 1965– II. Title.

UA853.K7C445 2003

355'03355193—dc21

2003055063

Columbia University Press books are printed

on permanent and durable acid-free paper

Printed in the United States of America

All the citations to information derived from the

World Wide Web (URLs) were accurate at the time of

writing. Neither the authors nor Columbia University Press

are responsible for Web sites that have changed or

expired since the time of publication.

Designed by Lisa Hamm

c 10 9 8 7 6 5 4 3 2 1

To Victor's loved ones, Hyun Jung, Patrick, and Andrew

To David's loved ones, Laura and Steven

CONTENTS

ACKNOWLEDGMENTS

This was a book no one wanted. It started as a series of phone conversations about two years ago commiserating on the absence of well-informed public policy commentary on North Korea and our shared views on the widening gap between social science and area studies. We agreed then that we would try to write something together, but found very little interest in what we thought was an intriguing idea: using social science to understand better and to debate a key foreign policy issue for the United States and its allies in Asia. Our initial approaches to academic and public policy journals to do an article "set" on North Korea failed miserably. Our initial approaches to foundations and book publishers also met with little enthusiasm.

Then September 11, President Bush's "axis of evil" speech, and the October 2002 revelations of a secret uranium enrichment program made North Korea's nuclear truculence front-page news. Publishing interest in our book project spiraled upward. Some might call this an academic attempt to capitalize on a "hot button" issue. We like to believe that we foresaw a problem, stayed ahead of events (rather than reacting to them), and persevered. Thus we are gratified to have this book to show for our efforts.

This book has benefited greatly from the generous support of our friends and colleagues throughout the world. There are too many to mention here, but David Kang would like to point out in particular the intellectual guidance of Muthiah Alagappa, Peter Katzenstein, Bradley Martin, William Wohlforth, Stephen Brooks, Andrew Stigler, Mo Steinbrunner, and Mike Spirtas. Different parts of this manuscript have been presented at various seminars in the United States, Japan, and South Korea. For comments at these meetings or on different portions of the manuscript, Victor Cha

x

would like to thank Dave Asher, Kent Calder, Tom Christensen, Ed Dong, Bob Gallucci, Charles Glaser, Gideon Rose, Avery Goldstein, Mike Green, Sung-joo Han, Jim Lilley, John Mearsheimer, William Perry, Bob Myers, Denny Roy, Gil Rozman, Scott Snyder, Joel Wit, Hong-choo Hyun, and Sung-han Kim. An earlier and different version of chapter 1 first appeared in *International Security* 27.1 (2002). Christopher Whipps provided invaluable research assistance.

We are especially thankful to Columbia University Press for their special efforts at putting this book on a "crash publication schedule." Anne Routon, Peter Dimock, and Helena Schwarz were indispensable to moving this project through the various stages and ensuring its prompt publication. Leslie Bialler made the book readable to the general public. Madeleine Gruen made the general public read the book. We also thank the three anonymous reviewers who gave detailed, critical insights and suggestions, and who helped improve this book immeasurably.

Unsurprisingly, the authors would like to acknowledge each other. The field of international relations scholars working on Asia is small, and those working in Korean studies even smaller. The authors have been a great source of intellectual challenge, comradeship and support to each other over the years.

Finally, we thank our respective families, who have been a constant source of encouragement, advice, and support throughout the years.

Victor D. Cha
David C. Kang
MAY 2003

NUCLEAR NORTH KOREA

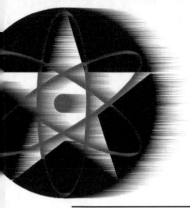

VICTOR D. CHA | DAVID C. KANG

INTRODUCTION
THE DEBATE OVER NORTH KOREA

WHAT ARE WE CONCERNED ABOUT?

Put two people in a room to discuss North Korea and three different opinions will emerge—all likely to be charged with emotion, if not outright vitriol. Why? Because the debate on the Democratic People's Republic of Korea (DPRK or North Korea) has emerged in the past decade as one of the most divisive foreign policy issues for the United States and its allies in Asia. Interested parties have disagreed vehemently over the regime's intentions and goals, and over the appropriate strategy that the United States should employ to deal with this mysterious country.

The debates over North Korea's bombshell admission in October 2002 of a second secret nuclear weapons program, their withdrawal from the Nonproliferation Treaty, and the ensuing crisis in 2003, are only the most proximate illustration of the perennial division of views on the opaque regime. Many "hawks" or hardliners assert that Pyongyang's conduct not only amounted to a violation of a series of nonproliferation agreements (i.e., Nonproliferation treaty, 1994 US-DPRK Agreed Framework, and 1992 Korean denuclearization declaration), but also revealed the fundamentally unchanged and "evil" intentions of the Kim Jong-il regime. Hence the only policy worth pursuing is isolation and containment, abandoning the "sunshine" policy of unconditional engagement made famous by former president Kim Dae-jung of the Republic of Korea (ROK or South Korea).[1] Others, more dovish, argue that North Korea's need for such a secret program, albeit in violation of standing agreements, derives from basic insecurity and fears of U.S. preemption. According to this view, chief North Korean interlocutor Kang Sok-ju's admission of the secret nuclear program is a "cry for help" to draw a reluctant Bush administration into direct talks.[2] To the hawks, the doves are weak-kneed appeasers, while doves dismiss the hawks as irresponsible ideologues.

The North Korean problem, moreover, has become intricately tied to partisan politics; rivalries between the executive branch and Congress; controversies over intelligence assessments; the viability of the nonproliferation regime; the efficacy of homeland defense; and differing assessments of the utility of deterrence versus preemption in U.S. security doctrine. That's a pretty impressive record of troublemaking for a small, closed, and arguably most backward country in the post–cold war world!

Obviously the crux of the concern over North Korea stems from the threats it poses to neighbors with its conventional military forces, ballistic missiles, and capability to produce weapons of mass destruction. North Korea boasts a 1.1 million man army in forward positions bearing down on the border separating the two Koreas (Demilitarized Zone or DMZ). It is infamously known as an aggressive exporter of ballistic missile technology to regimes like Iran and Pakistan. Its drive for nuclear weapons in earnest dates back to the 1980s, and was being pursued even before then. Many experts believe the DPRK holds one of the largest stockpiles of biological and chemical agents in the world.

At the same time that the regime empowers itself militarily, it starves its citizens at home. This combination elicits a plethora of colorful epithets about the regime and its leader Kim Jong-il. According to a former South Korean head of state, the North Korea regime "is a closed, unpredictable, irrational, bellicose group, the likes of which are hard to find."[3] According to others, the regime is "mad," "rogue," and "a country full of 'crazy' people."[4] Pyong-yang is the world's worst nightmare—an illiberal and irrational regime that is the number one proliferator of ballistic missiles and enabling technology, and is willing to sell them to anyone willing to buy them.[5]

Today's "24/7" news cycle only exacerbates the need for quick judgments and attention-grabbing headlines. For example, a major U.S.-based news magazine covered the unexpected death of the first leader of North Korea, Kim Il-sung, in July 1994, with the cover story, "The Headless Beast."[6] A *Washington Post* (December 29, 2002) op-ed contribution referred to North Korean leader Kim Jong-il as a "radioactive lunatic."[7] The cover story of *Newsweek* (January 13, 2003) carried a picture of the North Korean leader, clad in chic black, with the aphoristic caption, "Dr. Evil." Greta Van Susteren introduced a Fox News story on Kim Jong-il with the opening question, "Is he insane or simply diabolical?"[8] Mary Mc-Grory's column in the *Washington Post* (February 9, 2003) named Kim "the little madman with the passion for plutonium."[9]

The arguments about policy toward North Korea reach even higher levels of animation. Congressmen Benjamin Gilman (R, NY) and Christopher Cox (R, CA) claimed a U.S. policy of en-gagement with North Korea was the equivalent of entering "a cy-cle of extortion with North Korea" and nothing more than a "one-sided love affair."[10] While some saw engagement during the Clinton administration as one of the "unsung success stories" of American foreign policy;[11] others condemned it as "the screwiest policy that I have ever seen."[12] While some saw incentives as a re-sponsible way to try to transform the regime, outspoken figures like Senator John McCain (R, AZ) accused the Clinton adminis-tration of being "intimidated" by a puny country, and that the American president had become a "co-conspirator" with DPRK leader Kim Jong-il.[13] Moreover, some even argued that the Unit-ed States was encouraging North Korean aggression with its pol-icy of appeasement that rewarded bad behavior and "encouraged all these crazy people over in North Korea to believe we are weaklings because we are giving them everything they want."[14] Pat Buchanan, criticized both the Clinton and Bush administrations for giving Kim Jong-il a "fruit basket" and "sweet reason," rather than a "tomahawk missile."[15]

These statements are a small sample of the degree to which discussion on North Korea has become emotionally charged and ideological. Rarely does good policy that serves American and allied interests emerge from such emotional debates. Our purpose is to step back from the histrionics and offer a reasoned, rational, and logical debate on the nature of the North Korean regime and the policy that should be followed by the United States, Japan, and South Korea. Each of us have our own orientation toward the problem, ranging from more pessimistic to more optimistic assessments. Nevertheless, the debate is a genuine one. While apolitical and scholarly in nature, it has real implications for the basic foundations of different schools of debate on North Korea policy.

In this short book we take different logical paths to the same conclusion. We both argue that North Korea is neither irrational nor undeterrable. We also both argue that under most conditions in which the United States must deal with North Korea, the "default policy" toward North Korea is engagement. In other words, whether one is pessimistic or optimistic with regard to the regime's intentions, we show that some form of conditional engagement with North Korea—barring extremely deviant behavior by Pyongyang—remains the best policy for the United States. As readers will see, the caveat in the previous sentence is important. Our opinions diverge on the current North Korean nuclear crisis in large part because we assess differently the meaning of Pyongyang's recently revealed nuclear ambitions in defiance of standing agreements.[16] Nevertheless, barring such extreme behavior (or if the current crisis is somehow resolved), we both agree on engagement as the "commanding rationale" for policy.

On both sides of the policy spectrum, there are more extreme views than our own. A more hardline view sees no reason to compromise American values and negotiate with a brutal and morally repugnant dictator. This perspective sees Pyongyang as attempting to blackmail and extort concessions from the United States through threats and brinksmanship. In this view, the United States should not engage in dialogue with North Korea under any conditions. At its core, this perspective sees a more confrontational strategy as the best way to pursue a conclusion to the situation on the peninsula. By dealing with dictators in a principled and determined manner, it is believed that the U.S. is more likely to see positive results.

At the other extreme, there are those who view North Korea as essentially a victim of great-power politics. In this view, the United States has consistently overlooked the wholehearted attempts of the North to reform its system. Often, those espousing this view are willing to overlook the North Korean regime's obvious faults in favor of concentrating on the human rights needs of its citizens. This perspective views carrots as more worthwhile than sticks, and emphasizes the responsibility that the world's most powerful nation has in resolving crises through negotiation.

We make no attempt here to cover the entire spectrum of possible perspectives on North Korea. Rather, we set forth as clearly as possible what our arguments are, and how we arrived at the conclusions that we have. This allows us not only to be precise about the sources of our policy prescriptions, but also to show that they derive from serious study of the issues at hand, and not necessarily from any predetermined ideological perspective.

As noted above, the majority of discussion on North Korea is informed only by newspaper op-eds and punditry that feeds the cable news cycle. What emerges is an uninformed and unrefined public policy debate based on caricature-like arguments from the Hard Left and Hard Right. In January 2003 CNBC's *Kudlow and Cramer* show made at least three factual errors in a two-minute report. This debate benefits no one (except the talking head proponents of those arguments), moreover, it underestimate the stakes of this foreign policy problem for the United States and its allies. *Newsweek* cover stories that paint DPRK leader Kim Jong-il in a Dr. Strangelove-like fictional way belie the true dangers at hand.

A former commander of U.S. forces in Korea, General Gary Luck, offered a sober but succinct estimate of the bottom line if things go badly awry on the Korean peninsula: "one million and one trillion." That is, the costs of going to war over North Korea's nuclear program would amount to one million casualties and one trillion dollars in estimated industrial damage and lost business.[17]

These stakes are far too high to base a public policy debate on pundits and op-ed contributors. Through this book we try to give substance to the debate. Along the way we refute a number of misconceptions and faulty thinking that surrounds the discussion of North Korea. Among them, we show that North Korea is complex but not complicated—i.e., its actions and behavior—no matter how deplorable—are comprehensible. And because they are understandable (as opposed to irrational), there is a basis for diplomacy.

WHAT'S OUR SCHOLARLY CONCERN?

This book is more than the application of scholarship to policy, however. It constitutes an attempt to synthesize the best elements of Korean studies with social scientific argumentation. Intellectually, the study of Korean politics is subject to the same tensions inherent in the field of political science and indeed, throughout the social sciences. There have been increasing debates in the past decade over whether area studies constitutes a legitimate field of study in the social sciences. As rational choice, game-theory, quantitative methods become far more commonplace in the field, scholars who spend years studying the politics of one country in great detail have had a harder time justifying their research. Whether this is accurate or not is beside the point, the issue is that the gatekeepers in political science are increasingly valuing work that is driven by "hard" methodological or theoretical principles, and not valuing work that is deeply textured or nuanced.

This issue falls over the entire field of political science and its relationship to area studies subfields like that concerning Korea. Controversy over deep knowledge versus rational choice, or area studies versus quantitative methods, has affected international security studies, comparative politics, and other fields.[18] This book will not address this issue per se other than to point out its existence, and try to offer a work that views the disciplinary push to be methodologically rigorous and theoretically clear as only strengthening area studies by providing better analytic tools for scholars. In reality, there is a trade-off between the enormous time and energy required to learn about a foreign country and the investment required to learn methodological tools. As such, the standards for scholarship in the field of political science as a whole are rising: one must have language competency, area knowledge, and firm theoretical and methodological tools.

As this tension continues, there are increased demands on Koreanists. If Jack Snyder once held out the standard of empirical richness, theoretical rigor, and policy relevance for research in the field of Soviet studies, these standards are exponentially more demanding of Asia/Korea specialists.[19] They must have deep intimate knowledge of Korea to be taken seriously by Koreans and other Asia specialists. But they increasingly find that this knowledge is of little use in advancing their careers. And these scholars are increasingly facing a trade-off. On the one hand, these scholars must decide whether to potentially alienate the area specialists by focusing their energies on attending political science conferences and publishing in mainstream international relations and foreign policy journals. On the other hand, in order to continue to learn about Korea, gain access to fellowships and funding for Korean studies, and to be invited to major conferences, they need to devote energy to building ties with the area specialists. This can be a difficult row to hoe.

With this book, we aspire to produce scholarship on Korea that is empirically rich, analytically rigorous, and policy-relevant. Those of us with deep knowledge of an area have a duty to inform public debate over important public policy issues. We also have a duty to think as clearly and rigorously as possible, laying out logic, arguments, and evidence as self-consciously as possible. We hope that this book is a step in the right direction.

WHAT HAVE OTHERS SAID (AND NOT SAID)?

The literature on North Korean politics and security written in English remains small, but some of the work is quite good. Books and monographs on the contemporary aspects of the DPRK fall roughly into three categories. One set of empirically rich, single-authored works delves deeply into specific aspects of the North Korean society, economy, leadership,or military.[20] A second set of recent and useful empirical studies of the 1994 nuclear crisis seeks to induce propositions about North Korean negotiating behavior, and beyond this, the strategy, intentions, and future of the regime.[21] A third set of edited works looks at North Korea's foreign policy and domestic politics.[22] But there is a glaring hole. Much of this scholarly literature, though relevant to the real-world policy dilemmas and near-war crises created by North Korea, remained largely unread and unreferenced in the public policy debates.[23] As Leon Sigal's comprehensive study of the 1994 nuclear crisis noted, much of the scholarship on Korea by professors "tended to be marginalized in the policy debate, both by the other experts and by U.S. officials."[24] Instead what dominated the debate on North Korea was a plethora of short editorials, opinion pieces, and two-page "think-tank" policy briefs that lacked depth, were politically- or ideologically-motivated, and went forgotten the day after they were read.

The preceding overview of the literature therefore illuminates the gap we try to fill with this book. Policy debates on North Korea are based on a *papier mâché* version of the DPRK as a "rogue, irrational" state. Moreover, these debates are informed more by partisan recriminations about who screwed up the policy than by North Korean behavior. "Area specialists" who actually know something about North Korea are spectacularly incapable of communicating with the public and policymakers in a useful manner. And political scientists operate at a level of generality about generic state behavior that is equally unhelpful. Add to this the fact that the Pyongyang government's behavior makes a black box look transparent, and we are left with a policy and scholarly chasm.

Given this, one could conceivably imagine the United States and its allies sliding into a crisis, if not war, with everyone left wondering why there was not serious study of strategy toward North Korea beyond the op-ed pages of newspapers. Some of the literature described above tries to induce the diplomatic and strategy lessons learned from past crises with the North Korea. Nevertheless, still missing is a single work that: 1) offers a framework about how to think about policy toward North Korea; 2) systematically analyzes the assumptions behind different arguments about the DPRK leadership; 3) derives rigorously a spectrum of interpretations of North Korean grand strategy; and 4) that features BOTH dovish and hawkish assessments in direct debate.[25] Our goal is to show the diversity of opinions, and show the conceptually rigorous and empirically rich dialogue that can occur among scholars that could be useful for the public policy community.

OUR PLAN?

The book is organized into two main sections and somewhat differently than a typical book. In chapters 1 and 2, we present our contrasting arguments and lay out the logic behind them. This shows that we can have a serious, rigorous and insightful discussion about North Korea free from hyperbole. In chapters 3 and 4, we respond to each other's initial statements, refuting the other's arguments and substantiating our own viewpoints based on additional evidence or logic. In chapter 5, we apply each of our "models" to the 2003 crisis with North Korea's violations of their international nuclear nonproliferation violations. We have a vigorous debate about the meaning of Pyongyang's latest bouts of intransigence and what should be done by the United States and its allies.

Chapter 6 is a collaborative effort to distill from the preceding chapters a longer-term outlook for United States policy on the Korean peninsula. It should come as no surprise to readers that just as policy debates on North Korea are wanting, so are serious grand strategies on the American position in East Asia. Arguably the future viability of the American alliances network in the region hinges in good part on how the Korean question is resolved. Yet, both historically and currently, U.S. policy toward the Korean peninsula has been ad hoc, reactive, and derivative of the alliance with Japan.

Arguably, this "benign ignorance" formula has worked despite its flaws. Both Japan and South Korea's security was preserved and their prosperity was bolstered beyond anyone's wildest expectations when these alliances were formed respectively in 1951 and 1953. Some might therefore say, "why change what has proven successful?" But these neglectful policies toward Korea took place against the backdrop of the cold war when a overbearing and proximate Soviet threat managed to unite allies and dampen down fissures and resentments within the alliance.

As events surrounding the 2002 presidential elections in South Korea showed clearly, the alliance, from an American perspective, cannot simply be taken for granted anymore. To even casual observers, a sequence of developments at the end of 2002 and beginning of 2003 that started with a fatal traffic accident, led to fundamental questioning of the U.S.-South Korea alliance's worthiness on both sides of the Pacific. The death of two South Korean schoolgirls in a vehicular accident during U.S. military exercises engendered a groundswell of publicly expressed resentments in Seoul toward the U.S. military footprint in Korea. These televised "anti-American" demonstrations on CNN—complete with burnings of the American flag—in combination with US-ROK divisions on policy toward North Korea helped to foist an unconventional politician, Roh Moo-hyun, to the presidency over a perceived "pro-American" candidate. Meanwhile in the United States, anger at South Korea's perceived "ungratefulness" for the American security guarantee to Korea led many pundits and prominent journalists to call for the withdrawal of U.S. troops.[26] Many experts might debate the direct causality among these events, but no one would disagree with the startling pace of these events: One day, experts were talking about the tragic death of two schoolgirls hit by a U.S. army vehicle; only weeks later, this snowballed into angry discussions about pulling out U.S. forces from the peninsula.[27] The point is that without a well-thought-out vision for the alliance that is not simply premised on a DPRK threat, not simply derivative of Japan, and not eternally based on an older "Korean war generation" of supporters, the alliance, and in turn the U.S. position in Asia, could crumble as events outpace it. The US-South Korea alliance, celebrating its fiftieth anniversary in 2003, does not have luxury of languishing for a decade in search of a post–cold war rationale for existence. In this vein, our final chapter envisions the commanding rationales behind future U.S. strategy in Asia that incorporates Korea in a proactive and contextual way.

VICTOR D. CHA

WEAK BUT STILL THREATENING

1

THE PUZZLE: GETTING AT THE NORTH KOREA PROBLEM

[The DPRK regime] is about as unpalatable a diplomatic partner as
one can imagine, making Iraq look like a democracy.

—*Nicholas Kristof*[1]

I would describe [Kim Jong-il] as a very good listener and a good interlocutor. He strikes me as very decisive and practical and serious.

—*Madeleine Albright*[2]

The opacity of North Korea has not discouraged any number of
judgments about the regime's nature and its intentions. Indeed, the
variations in the DPRK's demeanor over the past few years raise
more questions about this mysterious and isolated regime than
they answer. In 2000, Pyongyang embarked on a diplomatic offensive that included the normalization of relations with many Euro-
pean Union countries, the unprecedented June 2000 summit between North and South Korean leaders Kim Jong-il and Kim
Dae-jung and exchange visits of high-level envoys with the United
States (General Jo Myong-nok's visit to Washington in August and
Secretary Albright's trip to Pyongyang in October). Shortly after

14

these events, the DPRK's more intransigent face emerged in 2001–2002 with the dispatch of spy ships in Japanese waters, fiery rhetoric about the United States, feverish work on a new nuclear weapons program (then secretly aided by Pakistan), and a deadly provocation against South Korean naval vessels. By mid-2002, however, Pyongyang's mulishness turned pliant as it undertook major new economic reforms, re-engaged with South Korea, and achieved a unprecedented breakthrough summit with Japanese leader Koizumi Junichiro (September 2002). Then in October 2002 revelations of a secret nuclear weapons program in North Korea in violation of nonproliferation agreements set Pyongyang back in the direction of brinkmanship.[3]

How do we make sense of these two faces in North Korea? Has the DPRK truly been in reform mode after a long period of uncertainty dating back to Kim Il-sung's death in 1994? Do recent events suggest a "new" Kim Jong-il who has been fundamentally misunderstood by the outside world? Has the path of engagement undertaken by the United States, the Republic of Korea (ROK or South Korea), and Japan since 1993 been validated or undercut by North Korean behavior? What, if any, is the larger strategy of influence behind American engagement with the DPRK?

Policymakers in Washington, Seoul, and Tokyo wrestle over these questions and dichotomous images of North Korea. At the core of these debates are differing assessments of whether the conditions for effective engagement are present in the DPRK case. Although the Bush administration rhetorically advocates engagement with North Korea, there is a healthy dose of skepticism, expressed at the highest levels, about the ultimate success of this process. According to this view, one needs to distinguish between tactics and intentions in assessing recent DPRK behavior. There is no denying that Pyongyang's opening contacts with the outside world reflect a change in diplomatic *tactics* for the purpose of gaining the food and economic aid necessary to keep the debilitated regime afloat. However, there is nothing in DPRK behavior (e.g., drawdowns in its threatening military posture) thus far consonant with or indicative of a deeper and more fundamental change in the nature of the regime and its *intentions*. Hence engagement is at best ill-advised and at worst dangerous as it will revive a regime still bent on overturning the status quo on the peninsula.

By contrast, those in Seoul favoring engagement agree that recent DPRK behavior represents tactical changes for the purpose of the regime's survival, but they *believe* that such behavior in fact reflects a fundamental change in Pyongyang's intentions (with further concessions by the North awaiting larger carrots from the West). Those less willing to accept this "true believer" proposition still welcome the mere tactical changes in DPRK behavior because these changes, in conjunction with engagement's carrots, are seen to eventually result in a positive and peaceful transformation of regime's character and its intentions.

The dilemma regarding North Korea for the United States and its allies in Seoul and Tokyo is clear: Absent more empirical evidence, this debate about true change in the DPRK's intentions remains unresolved. Nevertheless policy—which is presumably based on some assessment of the regime's intentions—must still be made. "True believers" willing to advocate engagement without concrete evidence are criticized for entering the realm of "theology." Those hardcore skeptics opposed to engagement are criticized for not giving diplomacy a chance. Moreover, the stakes of this policy choice are high, involving nuclear and missile proliferation and the potential for renewed conflict on the peninsula.

In my initial statement, I try to address this policy dilemma. I agree with the skeptics that policymakers would be ill-advised at present to posit major change in DPRK intentions. Absent changes in the military situation on the ground that go beyond "smile summitry" and political atmospherics over the past few years, and given the history of DPRK revisionist intentions on the peninsula, it is difficult to assume that tactical warming by Pyongyang carries deeper meaning. However, such skepticism does *not* preclude engagement as the chosen policy by the United States and its allies. On the contrary, for reasons having to do with the changing nature of the DPRK threat since the end of the cold war, I argue that the appropriate policy even for "hawks" in Washington, Seoul, and Tokyo on North Korea remains engagement.[4]

Three points substantiate this argument. First, deterrence and robust defense capabilities (i.e., containment) remain the cornerstone of US-ROK-Japan security on the Korean peninsula, and these will remain integral to any new policy vis-à-vis the DPRK. The policy choice is therefore not between containment and some other policy, but how this military capability should be complemented diplomatically. In other words, should the policy be containment-plus-diplomatic isolation (i.e., benign neglect); containment-plus-coercion; or containment-plus-engagement?

Second, there is a "hawk" rationale for engagement. The three primary "theories" put forward by advocates of engagement have no credibility with hardliners. These are the "insecurity spiral" argument, which basically says we should engage Pyongyang because it is misunderstood; the "collapse" argument, which sees engagement as preventing regime entropy; and the "irrationality" argument, which calls for engagement to create predictability in DPRK behavior.[5] Hawks reject all rationales because: 1) they do not believe that rogue regimes are reformable (which is the presumed outcome of engagement advocates); 2) they chafe at the notion of supporting such a morally reprehensible regime; and 3) they believe engagement (or appeasement) creates moral hazard incentives for other regimes to "act crazy."

I put forth a preventive defense rationale for engagement. In short, hawks should engage Pyongyang not because the regime is crazy, near-collapse, or misunderstood, but because engagement avoids the crystallization of conditions under which *Pyongyang could calculate hostility as a "rational" course of action even if victory were impossible.*[6] In other words, the real danger with regard to the DPRK threat is that in spite of an objective military balance unfavorable to the regime, the North could still choose to initiate conflict or other forms of hostile behavior as a wholly logical policy—i.e., that there is still a "rational" option to be belligerent. In this sense, engagement is a form of preventive defense—actions taken by the United States and its allies to prevent the emergence of potentially dangerous and conflictual situations.[7]

Third, engagement remains the "default" policy on the peninsula. Many hardliners may view the preventive defense rationale for engaging the DPRK as merely window-dressing for appeasement. They would argue that we are rewarding this rogue regime for its bad behavior; moreover, engagement-advocates are pursuing this policy for lack of a clear alternative, and without a responsible exit strategy. I make a number of sub-arguments as to why engagement, while gaining a window on the degree of change in DPRK intentions, is also simultaneously laying the groundwork for punishment if necessary.[8] In this sense, engagement is not in lieu of the exit strategy—it is the exit strategy. In short, regardless of whether one is a "hawk" or "dove" on North Korea, the optimal policy is engagement.[9]

WHY NORTH KOREA IS THREATENING

Conventionally the arguments against peace on the Korean peninsula have been the irrationality of the DPRK and the potential that the regime will collapse. The first derives from the opacity of the regime and the perceived recklessness and unpredictability of the leadership. North Korea has done "crazy" things in the past, and despite its weakened state, it still possesses the wherewithal (i.e., forward deployed forces, heavy artillery, long-range missiles, and nuclear-biological-chemical [NBC] potential) to do terrible things again. The second argument held sway particularly in the early 1990s when the DPRK started to register negative economic growth and revealed the extent of its chronic food and energy shortages. These conditions coupled with the uncertain political transition after the death of Kim Il-sung in 1994 raised serious concerns about a Romania-type collapse of the regime, sending ripples of instability throughout the region.[10]

As regional and military experts have argued, however, a premeditated all-out assault by North Korea seems unlikely.[11] The

American security guarantee to the ROK is firm; Beijing and Moscow do not support aggression by Pyongyang; moreover, the military balance on the peninsula favors the combined U.S.-ROK forces in terms of quality and firepower. In short, the conditions that prompted Kim Il-sung to exploit windows of vulnerability in June 1950 are now tightly shut. While a renewal of hostilities would no doubt be bloody, in the end a US-ROK alliance would prevail—one that would result in the extinction of the North Korean state.

In regard to the scenario in which the regime collapses, the DPRK survived despite the many premature eulogies to it written in the early 1990s, and it has "muddled through" largely because no party, including South Korea, wanted to deal with its collapse and expensive absorption. Food aid from China and international relief agencies, and interim fuel sources from the United States kept the regime on "life-support" in a crippled but less ominous state.[12]

The logic of both of these counter-arguments to the conventional wisdom are powerful and persuasive. Implicit is the view that North Korean behavior still adheres to a basic sanity regarding its survival; North Korea is indeed not "crazy," and US-ROK efforts to convey deterrent threats are understood in Pyongyang. The scenario in which the regime collapses is, while certainly plausible, nevertheless unlikely, because the internal and external conditions that would assign a high probability to such a collapse are lacking. Moreover, such a scenario still leaves unanswered the question of what circumstances or actions by Pyongyang might trigger such an event.

I argue that the threat to the Korean peace stems neither from the regime's irrationality, collapse, nor even a second DPRK invasion and all-out war. Instead, North Korea could perceive some use of limited force as a rational and optimal choice even when there is little or no hope of victory. The danger is not that the regime will commit suicide knowingly, but that it will encounter situations where belligerent "lashing out" or "striking first" is the best and only policy—the unintended consequence of which (given likely U.S. and ROK military responses) is suicide and/or collapse.

The logic of preemptive and preventive action, borrowed from international relations theory, suggests conditions under which the recourse to hostility can be a rational act even if objective factors weigh against victory.[13] *Preemption* occurs when a state perceives aggression by another as imminent and acts first to forestall the impending attack. *Preventive* action occurs when a state is motivated to attack first, or otherwise suffer increasing inferiority in capabilities vis-à-vis the opponent over time. Though preemptive and preventive motivations represent two discrete paths to conflict,[14] they are similar in a number of respects. First, they are motivated by fear more than aggression. Belligerent actions are undertaken largely as a result of closing windows of opportunity or expanding windows of vulnerability brought on by relative power shifts.[15] Second, both are acts of anticipation. The decision to preempt or prevent hinges as much on misperception and images of the adversary as on the objective military situation. Insecurity spirals and reciprocal fears of surprise attack can cause security-seeking states to "fall" into conflict out of survival even in the absence of aggressive intentions. Third, both types of belligerency stem from a fundamental dissatisfaction with the status quo. States do an expected-utility calculation in which the costs of the current situation are higher than the costs of change. In the preemptive situation, maintaining the status quo means being the victim of imminent aggression. In the preventive situation, maintaining the status quo means certain inferiority and defeat in the future. In both cases, the expected costs of peace are higher than the potential costs of conflict. Winston Churchill once assessed Japan's 1941 decision to attack at Pearl Harbor as one that "could not be reconciled with reason. . . . But governments and peoples do not always take rational decisions. Sometimes they take mad decisions."[16] However, if any situation is better than the current one, states can rationally choose to fight even when there is little hope of victory.[17]

There is no denying that the "sunshine" or engagement policies of the Kim Dae-jung and Roh Moo-hyun governments in South Korea over the past half-decade have helped to move the peninsula beyond the decades of confrontation that defined it. However, as the 2003 U.S.-DPRK nuclear crisis has shown, such cooperative phases can easily wane and North Korea's situation can revert back to its former self, in which instance it is not difficult to imagine North Korea succumbing to this preemptive logic of striking first. While fears of an imminent South Korean attack are not a salient preemptive/preventive motivation for Pyongyang today,[18] the yawning deficit in capabilities vis-à-vis the South undoubtedly raises anticipatory fears of extinction-through-absorption in North Korean eyes. Throughout the first three decades of the cold war, the two regimes faced off as relative equals with each buttressed by security guarantees from its great-power patrons. From the early 1960s to 1970s, North Korean GNP per capita and conventional military capabilities rivaled if not surpassed that of its southern counterpart.[19] Parity entitled each regime to privilege its particular vision of unification, which essentially meant domination of one over the other. Parity also entitled each to legitimize any dialogue with the other as a step toward this ultimate goal of hegemonic unification.

By the 1990s, however, what emerged was an enormous and insurmountable gap between the two countries. Annual 8 percent growth in the ROK (before the financial crisis) versus successive years of 2–3 percent negative growth in the North resulted in a $400 billion southern GDP—15–20 times that of the DPRK. Although Pyongyang clings to *juche* (self-reliance) and visions of hegemonic unification, even staunch ideologues like Hwang Jang-yop admitted after defecting in 1997 that a communist revolution in the South is no longer a viable DPRK objective.[20] In a similar vein, a low-key but very significant event at the September 1998 session of the Supreme People's Assembly (1st session, 10th term) was abolition of the Unification Committee.[21] Propaganda emanating out of Pyongyang under Kim Jong-il, while still promoting strict adherence to "revolutionary traditions," increasingly admits that "existing theories" may not be sufficient to deal with new problems and developments. Indeed, revisions of the DPRK constitution in 1998 deleted phrases relating to Marxist-Leninism and proletarian dictatorship. Russian observers note that among the core principles that have made up the *juche* ideology, emphasis has shifted recently from universal "communization" to "self-dependency" as the ultimate revolutionary goal.[22] Moreover, in moments of candor, DPRK propaganda itself acknowledges how national goals have changed. A government-run *Nodong Sinmun* newspaper editorial stated bluntly, "The masses' independent demands grow higher ceaselessly with the times as the revolution develops. . . . Should the regime fail to strengthen and develop fast enough to meet the masses' incessantly growing independent demands, the people would turn their back on it and eventually it would collapse."[23] Kim Jong-Il openly admitted the need for change, "self-reliance should not be intepreted as meaning that we will not import what others have because we will import selectively."[24] As one expert noted, "[t]hirty years ago a very different verdict on the national strategies of the two Koreas might have been rendered. . . . [T]he North Korean goal of enforcing a Socialist unification upon the South was no mere pipedream."[25] Now, Pyongyang's end game has changed from one of hegemonic unification to basic survival, avoiding collapse, and avoiding dominance by the South, precisely the type of fears behind a preventive lashing-out type action.

THE ABSENCE OF MITIGATING FACTORS

Many of the theoretical factors that mitigate the motivations for striking first are absent in the North. For example, if a state operates with long time horizons (viewing a disadvantageous position vis-à-vis the adversary as only temporary), this can reduce the urgency to act. Internal military buildups or accretion of power through new external alliances also reduce the need to deal with widening windows of vulnerability through preemption/prevention. The collapse of the USSR, however, has invalidated any Marxist-Leninist notions that, with patience, socialist regimes would eventually witness capitalist countries collapsing over their own contradictions. Power accretion through alliances or internal balancing is not feasible for Pyongyang, given the effective security and economic abandonment by Moscow and Beijing in 1990 and 1992. The North has also been relatively unsuccessful in attempts to drive a wedge in ROK relations with the United States and Japan over the nuclear issue or a peace process on the peninsula. The absence of China and Russia as allies also removes impediments to North Korean contemplation of preventive/preemptive action. The unwritten purpose of alliances on both sides of the DMZ during the cold war was to restrain the two combatants from entrapping the superpowers into another war as much as supporting them.[26] Such constraints are effectively gone; as one Chinese official observed, "The North Koreans don't listen to us . . . they don't listen to anyone."[27]

The prolonged economic crisis afflicting the ROK economy and the general ambivalence prevalent among younger generations of South Koreans about a costly unification with the North may marginally raise hopes among Pyongyang's leadership that they can muddle through. A January 2003 poll found that as high as 66 percent of South Koreans believed unification should be achieved at a slow, deliberate, and planned pace. Moreover, that any consideration of such an exercise should be postponed for a minimum of ten years.[28] But any Northern aspirations of closing the gap with the South have been thoroughly erased. If anything, the aggregate effects of DPRK negative economic growth, yearly food shortfalls, energy shortages, and an increasingly confident and militarily growing South Korea have shortened rather than lengthened the North's time horizon.[29] Despite the ROK's economic problems, the collapse of the 1994 Agreed Framework (which was to provide the North with ROK-financed nuclear energy reactors) and domestic scandals in Seoul over side-payments of some $200 million by South Korean officials during the Kim Dae-jung administration to obtain the June 2000 summit with Kim Jong-il, successive ROK governments remain committed to being the primary financial backer for any new energy and economic rehabilitation projects for North Korea. Seoul is also the only source of large-scale support to remedy the North's agricultural deficiencies and chronic food shortages. The current atmosphere of rapprochement between the two Koreas may somewhat assuage Pyongyang's anxieties about this dependence (indeed, this may have been a contributing motivation for the North's opening). However, if relations backslide even slightly to their prior condition, from Pyongyang's vantage point, the prospect of having to rely on its primary rival for future energy and food sustenance would render the status quo an unbearable and losing proposition.

History shows that preemptive/preventive situations have also been ameliorated when the two parties are liberal democracies, when they want to avoid the reputational costs of being branded the aggressor, and when they have defensive, rather than offense-based, military doctrines.[30] Again, in spite of the DPRK's recent diplomatic overtures to the outside world, longer-term trends in Pyongyang do not hint at any of these conditions. Given past acts of state-sponsored terrorism, and rogue acts in violation of international nonproliferation and human rights norms, reputational concerns do not appear to factor into Pyongyang's policy calculations, effectively removing any additional stigma attached to lashing out or being perceived as the aggressor. Barring some unforeseen internal transformation, North Korea will remain the type of illiberal state which history has shown not to be averse to initiating preventive hostility. And most ominous, the North's forward deployments of artillery, tanks, and personnel along the demilitarized zone—which have not abated despite the recent inter-Korean thaw—reflect a preemption-friendly belief in offense having the advantage.[31] Moreover, even a benign interpretation of the North's deployments as defensively intended does not mitigate preemptive or preventive incentives to act. On the contrary, as demonstrated in a Korean war gaming scenario on *ABC's Nightline* with Ted Koppel, inferior forces deployed offensively (but for defensive reasons) are extremely prone to "use them or lose them" motivations if conflict appears imminent.[32]

Finally, if motivations to strike first are to be compelling, the envisioned outcome must be perceived as having a higher utility than doing nothing. The preemptor may exaggerate or idealize the utility of this alternative, but one must exist, otherwise, the choice of striking first amounts to suicide. For example, in the Pacific war case, the Japanese option was a surprise attack dealing initial heavy losses to the American Pacific fleet, combined with a quick strike into the Southwest Pacific, that would deter the Americans from undertaking a protracted and costly war in Asia. Although this plan was ill-conceived, without the belief that this non-status-quo outcome carried a higher expected utility than doing nothing, the Japanese attack on Pearl Harbor would have been conscious suicide.

There has to be a story that a North Korean can tell herself as to why the alternative to non-action is rational. Ominously, one can envision a spectrum of such stories. At one end, Pyongyang could follow a "coercive bargaining" strategy that derives from the preemptive/preventive logic. This strategy does not advocate all-out war. Rather it utilizes deliberate, limited acts of violence to create small crises and then negotiates down from the heightened state of tension to a bargaining outcome more to the North's advantage than the status quo. The logic of striking first is essentially one of leveraging a status quo that Pyongyang does not have a stake in. At the worst-case end of the spectrum, through long-range artillery barrages, missile strikes, or chemical weapons attacks deliberately non-American in target and short of all-out war, the North could seek to hold Seoul hostage with the hope of renegotiating a new status quo.[33] Again, the relevant point here is not the objective feasibility of "winning" with such an action, but the belief in North Korea that acting is better than doing nothing, and that doing nothing promises slow and certain death.

"DOUBLE-OR-NOTHING" LOGIC

A typical response to the preemptive/preventive logic I ascribe to North Korea is disbelief on the simple grounds that Pyongyang knows full well that if it were to initiate any aggression on the peninsula, the United States and the ROK would retaliate with overwhelming force and with the highly probable objective of regime termination (i.e., not just repelling an attack).[34] Thus, given these odds, Kim Jong-il—if he is a right-minded gambler—will not strike first, preferring the certain gains of regime survival. Right?

Wrong. The logic described above assumes a gains-motivated basis for action, and does not account for more risky inclinations by states as their situation deteriorates. As behavioral and decisionmaking theories applied to international relations have found, states do not make choices on the basis of profit and loss; they are context dependent.[35] Three tenets of prospect theory illuminate the North Korean case. First, how states "frame" a situation or "encode" a decision can drastically affect choice. For example, if I play golf expecting to shoot 10 strokes below my handicap, but shoot only five strokes below, I see this as an inferior outcome rather than a positive improvement in my game. On the other hand, if I play with no prior expectations of a final score, and achieve the same five-below performance, my assessment of this outcome is substantially different. In both cases, the "frame of reference" determines the evaluation regardless of the objective equivalence of the two situations. Second, states are generally averse to losses ("endowment effect"); they value what they have more than what they can achieve. For this reason, states generally fight harder to defend territory they already possess more than they would have done to acquire that same territory from an enemy. Schoolyard fights break out to defend reputations, not to increase them. The endowment effect was implicit in the domino theory of the cold war because the motivation to fight in the periphery was more to avoid losing a chain of small allies to the enemy rather than seeking new states bandwagoning in one's favor.[36] Third, certain outcomes weigh more heavily in states' calculations than probable ones (certainty effect). This does not mean states always prefer certain outcomes to uncertain ones, but that their behavior is primarily motivated by the pursuit of certain gains or the avoidance of certain losses.[37]

Loss-aversion and "framing" can give rise to risk-acceptant behavior entirely different from that based on gains-motivated, expected-utility calculations. As political scientist Janice Stein notes, the degree of risk political leaders are willing to incur over a policy is starkly different depending on the context: "Because people are generally averse to loss, whether an outcome is treated as a gain or a loss has a significant impact on the choice they make. Indeed, when an identical outcome is re-framed as a loss rather than a gain, people reverse their preference and make a different choice."[38] An illustration of the risky choice thesis is gambling. A risky "double-or-nothing" bet looks bad to a gambler with pocketed winnings; this same strategy, however, looks increasingly appealing to one who is down to her last few dollars. In sum, the "decision frame" is critical to choice. This frame, in turn, is determined by the identification of a reference point and the coding of decisions in terms of gains or losses.[39]

ACTUALIZING PREEMPTIVE/PREVENTIVE SITUATIONS

Prospect theory specifies the conditions under which preemptive or preventive action can occur among similarly situated states.[40] There is general agreement that a preemptive or preventive situation is one in which the future occurrence of a situation is deemed unacceptable. The theory is unclear, however, on the causal mechanism that leads some states to act under objective preemptive/preventive conditions. Some scholars have focused on the offense-defense balance as the key determinant; others on hostile images of the adversary; and others on regime type.[41] Empirical studies have found, however, that many of these factors are not sufficient to explain why some states strike first.[42]

Incorporating the framing of choice and decisions, one can deduce more specified propositions about the occurrence of preemption/prevention among similarly situated states (see table 1.1).

An examination of the table shows that if a state is potentially a target of attack but frames the situation as a "winning" one, then

TABLE 1.1 Actualization of Preemptive/Preventive Action.

	HOW DO STATES FRAME THE STATUS QUO?		
	DOMAIN OF GAINS	NEUTRAL	DOMAIN OF LOSSES
Preemptive or Preventive Situation with Offense Having the Advantage	*Cell 1* Unlikely (indeterminate)	*Cell 3* Likely	*Cell 5* Very high
Preemptive or Preventive Situation with Defense Having the Advantage	*Cell 2* Very unlikely	*Cell 4* Unlikely	*Cell 6* High

it will generally be risk-averse to preemptive or preventive actions. Even though such actions offer the possibility of larger gains, the motivating factor for nonaction is the threat that such actions pose to current holdings. This incentive for nonaction would be reinforced by beliefs in defense having the advantage (cell 2).[43] If a state is contemplating preemptive/preventive action and frames the situation as "neutral" (i.e., either through discrete or cumulative encoding, it sees the status quo as a nonlosing one), then it is still unlikely to take the risky choice of striking first and jeopardizing current holdings. The disincentive to act in this situation is marginally less than if framed in the domain of wins and thus less determinate. The critical factor determining choice in this situation is the offense-defense balance. If conquest is perceived as easy, then the occurrence of preemption/prevention is more likely (cell 3). If conquest is difficult, then preemption or prevention is unlikely (cell 4).

If a state perceives itself to be the potential target of attack and frames the situation in the domain of losses, then the likelihood of preemptive/preventive action is high (cell 6). Time horizons are short; moreover, loss aversion in a losing situation results in risk-acceptant behavior akin to an "anything-to-stop-the-bleeding" mentality. A state is willing to accept the risk of preemptive/preventive war, which carries probable but substantially disastrous losses in order to avoid near-certain losses in the present. The incentive to act is exponentially reinforced if offense is perceived to be advantageous (cell 5). Jack Levy rightly points out a problem here regarding relative risk assessments. Whether a risk-acceptant state in the domain of losses sees war or doing nothing as more risky is not easily determinable.[44] While not wholly resolving this problem, I argue that one important criterion is the severity of the domain of losses. If a state sees itself in the domain of losses but hovers just above a subsistence level, then it may be marginally more risk averse (i.e., choose a minimax strategy) and willing to take certain losses provided they do not result in outcomes below the subsistence level. If the state is already below the subsistence level and in the domain of continuing losses, however, loss aversion, risk acceptance, and the incentive to act becomes acute.[45]

NORTH KOREA'S DECISIONAL FRAME

A priori indicators by which to designate North Korea's decisional frame are: (1) those ideational objectives that legitimate and celebrate the national identity, (2) state of material well-being (i.e., economic and military), (3) standing in the international community, and (4) availability of allies.[46] An important barometer of a changing frame of reference is the perspective on time. If a nation feels that time is on its side (i.e., that decisional frame indicators have positive values—ideational objectives being attained; satisfactory economic and military strength; garnering some external support), then a state is not in the domain of losses.

No matter which way Kim Jong-il may slice it, North Korea's decisional frame on the Korean peninsula is a losing one (cells 5 or 6).[47] The Dear Leader's reference point could be the status quo, in which case notwithstanding the slow trickle of aid and support from the outside world, the widening economic gap between North and South would leave him in a rapidly "losing" situation. Or, his reference point could be a future aspiration point such as unification with northern dominance—in which case the losing situation is more acute. Although North Korea faced this window of vulnerability with the South during the cold war, the motivation for preventive action was less salient as the situation was not nearly so desperate then.[48] Through the mid-1970s, the Central Intelligence Agency calculated GNP per capita for the two Koreas as roughly equal.[49] Pyongyang's *juche* ideology had standing in the international community and won it membership in the Non-Aligned Movement while ROK applications were rejected (because of U.S. forces in Korea). The North had a sizeable military with quantitative edges over the South. DPRK infiltration of the South was so extensive that Kim Il-sung confidently stated in 1977 that he could insert or extract units anywhere, anytime (a claim that U.S. Forces in Korea confidentially conceded as true).[50] In addition, from Pyongyang's perspective, the ROK hardly looked the model of stability in the 1960–70s: Its presidents were exiled, overthrown by coup, or assassinated, and its external security guarantees looked, at best, tenuous based on ambivalent actions by successive U.S. administrations from Johnson to Carter.[51] By contrast, the North's livelihood was fully ensured by the security and economic patronage of the Soviet Union and China.

Pyongyang therefore had the impression that with time, gaps could be closed. North Korea's decisional frame was at worst neutral, and more often than not in the domain of wins (cells 2 or 4). Recently released documents from East German archives of confidential discussions between Erich Honecker and Kim Il-sung in December 1977 provide a rare window on Kim's private views.[52] Kim expressed extreme confidence in the longevity of the DPRK regime. The economic gap favoring the South was not a concern because ROK general-turned-president Park Chung-hee's un-popular authoritarian rule and U.S. President Jimmy Carter's conviction, announced in 1977, to withdraw all U.S. forces from the peninsula would eventually lead the South Korean people to choose *juche*.[53] The communization of the Korean peninsula, the North Korean leader continued, would then lay the conditions for "stimulating the revolution in Japan."[54] As Don Oberdorfer recounts, Kim was so confident of the South's eventual demise that there was little the North needed to do to encourage this out-come even after the opportunity created by the assassination of ROK president Park by his chief of intelligence. DPRK time horizons were long.

> [T]wo days after Park's assassination, Kim Il-sung addressed a military meeting, drawing a stark contrast between South Ko-rea, "one half of our territory . . . under the occupation of the U.S. imperialists and reactionaries, landlords and capitalists," and the DPRK, where "our people are enjoying a happy life . . . without any worries about food, clothing, medical treatment and education." Kim announced, "There is no better 'paradise' and no better 'land of perfect bliss' than our country. . . . While approving the elimination of 'traitor' Park Chung hee, the North Korean leader cautiously told the military assembly, "We must *wait and see what change this will bring about* in the rev-olutionary situation in South Korea. (Emphasis added.)[55]

The situation dramatically changed, however, in the 1990s. Per-ceptions of the status quo as a losing one became apparent between 1989 and 1994. During this time, the Soviet Union collapsed, Chi-na normalized relations with South Korea, Kim Il-sung died, and the cumulative effects of decaying infrastructure, poor harvests, and energy shortages, manifest in consecutive years of negative economic growth were beginning to take their toll. German unifi-cation had deep psychological and material impacts on North Ko-rean confidence as Honecker's GDR had been a close ally and consistent economic supporter. Abandonment of subsidized trade and security patronage by China in 1992 and Russia in 1990 took place at a time when fuel shortages were undermining military readiness. Western visitors to the Chinese border in 1997 reported increased self-help barter activities by local and provincial DPRK authorities, in defiance of the central government's control and directives.[56] A steady stream of diplomatic defections led Pyongyang to recall 12 ambassadors from foreign missions in 1997–98. And at home, a growing number of public executions of prominent party officials suggest divisions in elite leadership circles.[57] These trends were unheard of during the cold war; moreover, the instances increased dramatically since 1993 according to South Korea legislative reports.[58] As one expert observed:

> By 1993, North Korea was a country without a national strategy. To be more precise, it had a national strategy—the same one it always had—but this was almost completely irrelevant to the problems at hand. The pressing problem at hand was regime survival.[59]

Noted Korea specialist Bruce Cumings put it more graphically:

> Kim Il-sung's death came amid dire war threats [from the West] and inaugurated an unending stream of calamities: floods in 1995 and 1996, drought in 1997, even a tidal wave killing hundreds as August ended . . . Pyongyang is in a triage mode right now, helping where it can, denying when it must, . . . This crisis is terrible, by far the worst since the Korean war."[60]

Signs of the status quo viewed in the domain of losses are abundant. First, there is outright acknowledgment in DPRK statements that the status quo is substantially worse than any past reference point. Statements talk about "returning" to economic levels of the past (and then growing beyond these levels).[61] Second, themes of change and reform have proliferated in North Korean propaganda; whereas Kim's speeches in 1997 carried messages of continuity (e.g., maintaining certain "revolutionary traditions"), increasingly these were couched in conditional language that "reserv[es] the right for creative development" as the North experiences the "trials and tribulations in our construction of socialism."[62] Public statements are more desperate in tone, showing a clear need for change. As the government-run *Nodong Sinmun* newspaper stated in a 2001 New Year's editorial, " . . . the most important task to be accomplished with priority, precisely, is to effect fundamental innovations in the ideological viewpoint of people and their way of thinking, struggle ethos, and work attitude in such a way that meets the requirements of the new century. . . . It is impossible to advance the revolution even a step further if we should get complacent with our past achievements or be enslaved to outdated ideas and stick to the outmoded style and attitude in our work."[63] Third, anecdotal evidence reinforces the notion that the status quo is a losing one. Highlighting Kim Jong-il's formal power ascension and the DPRK's 50th anniversary celebrations in September 1998 was an odd re-broadcasting of an old Kim Il-sung speech, symbolizing how celebration of the present and future could only be made with reference to better times in the past. South Korea intelligence officials reported in 1999 a massive population relocation plan in North Korea designed to expel hundreds of thousands of jobless, homeless, and hungry people who migrated to Pyongyang in recent years. The five-year plan, covering some two million citizens, was ostensibly to create a larger agricultural work force but was primarily to prevent urban unrest in the capital city.[64] U.S. congressional groups visiting North Korea in 1998 estimate one million dead of starvation since the early 1990s.[65] The food rationing policy's Darwinian selection-like nature well reflects increasingly short time horizons: the very young and very old are the last priorities.[66] Former DPRK ideologue Hwang Jang-yop's characterization is perhaps the most accurate and ominous: "It's like a land of darkness there. Most people think it's too painful to go on. They even think if it takes a war to bring change they are willing to start a war."[67]

Hostile actions taken by the DPRK during the 1990s clearly reflect this logic of preemptive/preventive action. A number of such actions took place in 1995 in the Joint Security Area (JSA) at the truce village of Panmunjom. They were in clear violation of the armistice. These included moving troops well beyond the mutually agreed number into the militarily sensitive JSA, removing uniform arm bands designating the forces allowed into the area, and violating the minimal arms requirements (i.e. nothing beyond side arms). In August 1998, the North test-fired a ballistic missile (Taepo-dong I) over the Sea of Japan. Pyongyang claimed this to be a satellite launch, but it was also interpreted as an attempt to demonstrate a three-stage missile capability beyond what many intelligence analysts had previously predicted possible. In December 1994, the North shot down a U.S. helicopter in the DMZ, killing one crew member and detaining the other. The incident was all the more remarkable in that it occurred a little over a month after the landmark U.S.–DPRK Agreed Framework in late October.

These were both clearly provocative and unsolicited actions, at the same time appearing devoid of a clear strategic calculation. In each case, these events were not part of a chain of escalating tensions but were isolated, almost random incidents.[68] Many saw these as reconfirming the view that the North was an unpredictable and dangerous adversary. Yet this puzzling behavior is explainable by the logic of preemptive action. In each case, Pyongyang sought to disrupt a status quo deemed highly unfavorable with the purpose of renegotiating a new status quo to its advantage. In the JSA case, this had to do with an attempt to debilitate the Military Armistice Commission (MAC) and draw the United States into direct bilateral negotiations on a peace treaty, excluding the ROK.[69] In the chopper incident, a newspaper account of the event arrived at a similar North Korean motive: "By detaining [the chopper pilot], North Korea tried—as it

34

did in the earlier nuclear negotiations—to draw the United States further into direct negotiations with Pyongyang, thus diminishing the role of South Korea." [70] In the ballistic missile case, the purpose was, in part, to overturn an emerging consensus in the expert community that the DPRK could not build missiles more advanced than their short-range No-dong class, and therefore would eventually hit a revenue ceiling on missile sales to the Middle East and South Asia as buyers would want more sophisticated products. The Taepo-dong test revealed the North's potential to manufacture three-stage missiles using solid-fuel propellants, and thus indicated a technological leap beyond all expert expectations. The missile test, in effect, disrupted the status quo by drawing attention to North Korea's more advanced ballistic missile program as a new issue of negotiation and compensation for Pyongyang. It should be remembered that the issue here is not whether these strategies are successful (in the JSAF and chopper cases, it was not, but in the Taepo-dong case, it arguably was), but that there is a calculation that sees disrupting the status quo with an act of violence as rational.

Depending on how desperate Kim Jong-il assesses the situation, one can imagine other such incidents in the future. The DPRK might lob several artillery shells into a Southern city and create chaos among the population. It might conduct a Pakistani-type nuclear detonation, declaring itself formally as a nuclear power. It might launch one chemically armed short-range missile on a Southern port or a longer-range missile on Japan, all of which would cause massive capital flight and send stock market indices into a tailspin. It might infiltrate three suicide terrorists armed with radiological "dirty" bombs (plutonium-laden fuel rods wrapped around conventional explosives) into major ROK cities (e.g., Seoul, Pusan, and Kwangju) and demand the government concede on some issue or else face the consequences. Each provocation is too minor to prompt all-out war, but serious enough to raise the incentive for Seoul and Washington to give ground and negotiate a peaceful resolution to the crisis.

IS THE SUN SHINING ON THE DPRK?

Critics might concede the applicability of this analysis to North Korea for the past fifty years, but argue that it lacks relevance given events that transpired in 2000–2001. Kim Dae-jung's sunshine policy for engaging North Korea with economic carrots and political dialogue provided the context in which Kim Jong-il agreed to hold the first inter-Korean summit in June 2000, followed by agreements on family reunions, economic cooperation, and infrastructure rejuvenation.[71] For the first time since the death of Kim Il-sung in July 1994, Pyongyang ventured beyond its traditional cold war orbit of allies, opening diplomatic relations with almost every EU country (except France and Ireland). The former nongregarious-turned-garrulous leader Kim Jong-il secured outside assistance in the form of food aid, medical and humanitarian supplies, and economic aid from international organizations and nongovernmental organizations to help the country through lean times. In the aftermath of the successful summit with Seoul, Kim Jong-il entertained the prospect of normalized political relations with the United States at the end of the Clinton administration. He engineered a breakthrough summit meeting with Japanese premier Koizumi in Pyongyang in September 2002 and with this, the potential for large amounts of economic assistance from Tokyo and the international financial institutions.[72] Pyongyang therefore favors the *current* status quo, critics might contend, in ways that render irrelevant the logic of preemptive action. It secured a level of subsistence from the outside through small diplomatic openings on its part. Moreover, it looks at these gains in absolute rather than relative terms vis-à-vis the gap with the South, hence reducing any anxieties about increasing inferiority.

There is no denying that the DPRK is in a better place after the June 2000 summit than it was between 1989 and 1998.[73] To argue that this new status quo is permanent, however, is highly questionable. First, although famine-like conditions have abated, the absence of large-scale agricultural reform initiatives means that the mere symptoms rather than the underlying causes of the food shortages are being treated by the inflow of food assistance.[74] In addition, the long–term reliability of these annual inflows by international and nongovernmental organizations is highly susceptible to donor fatigue or relegated to a lower priority by more pressing needs in Afghanistan, following the U.S. ouster of the Taliban regime, and in Iraq. Second, the attention and goodwill showered on the North in the heady years of 2000–2001 is not permanent. In particular, the provision of assistance from the ROK, United States, and Japan has been without meaningful reciprocal responses from Pyongyang; this in turn has increased domestic political pressure in all three capitols to cut off support. Finally, the combination of economic rationality in the South and the complete absence of internationally compliant legal institutions in the North implies that the initial inflow of hard currency and other economic carrots are politically and charity-based than economically sound, which makes their continuance far from reliable. Thus, what is apparent with the North's improved situation in 2000–2001 is not a new status quo, but a positive variation from the original one. This incremental change is welcome, but it is at the same time highly contingent and vulnerable to backsliding.

Arguably an important change connected with how the DPRK frames the status quo the decreased likelihood of absorption as a scenario for unification. If absorption is completely irrelevant as a potential outcome, this would ameliorate DPRK visions of the status quo as unbearable and reduce incentives for risk-taking behavior. Again a distinction must be made between permanent changes to the status quo and temporary variations from it. Although transient material conditions (i.e., DPRK's improved situation, and the ROK's economic difficulties) might favor a no-absorption outcome, what matters from a DPRK decisional frame is the longer history of the ROK's stated intentions. During the Kim Dae-jung years, these were enunciated in the "no-absorption" (or no unification) pledge of the government's sunshine policy, and the successor policy under Roh Moo-hyun.[75] But this policy is as much an aberration as it is distinct in the history of South Korean unification policy, which since the establishment of the Republic in 1948 has held up unification (with southern dominance) as the ideal objective. It is difficult to assume from a DPRK perspective that the precedent set by Kim Dae-jung (well-known as historically unique) and carried through by Roh Moo-hyun would be the permanent norm for all future governments in South Korea.[76]

THE POLICY (PREVIEWED): "HAWK ENGAGEMENT"

Contrary to the conventional logic, North Korea has perfectly rational reasons for choosing to violate the peace even if defeat is likely. Understanding the North Korean threat in terms of this logic highlights the misdirected focus of the DPRK engagement debate in Washington and Seoul. Hawks and doves oppose or support engagement according to their judgments about whether the North seeks to subvert the South or the degree to which it seeks reform. Instead, the criteria for choice should be the capacity of any strategy to circumvent situations in which the North (1) sees the status quo as an unbearable and losing situation; (2) sees an attack on it (or extinction) as imminent; or (3) sees its own threatening behavior as better than doing nothing.

In this light, coercion or isolation strategies are *not* appealing as a complement to basic deterrence/defense postures toward the DPRK (this proposition presumes that North Korea will remain within the structure of institutions and agreements that were produced by U.S.-DPRK engagement in the 1990s. If they step away from these agreements, as has been evident in the 2003 U.S.-DPRK nuclear crisis, I qualify the argument as explained in chapter 5). Noncommunication, threats, and intimidation only exacerbate preemptive/preventive situations by increasing the North's vulnerability, pushing the leadership further into framing the status quo in the domain of losses, and raising the costs of peace. On the other hand, conditional engagement (i.e., containment-plus-engagement) ameliorates preemptive/preventive situations. While maintaining necessary deterrent measures, it lengthens time horizons, reduces the threat of imminent attack, lowers the costs of the status quo, and can help change Pyongyang's frame of reference. Recent work on theories of influence concur with this basic point: "When the continuation of the status quo portends losses and is perceived as costly for a given state A, logically another state B can decrease the incentives for A to attack by adding to the value of that status quo, promising rewards for peaceful relations."[77]

DPRK behavior at the immediate end of the Cold War (1989–92) and in 1998–99 offers two significant examples that validate this line of thinking. In the former case, the conditions for preemptive/preventive action were acute. In a space of three years North Korea's worldview was fundamentally altered. The Cold War ended; the Soviet Union abandoned the North by normalizing relations with the South in 1990; China took similar actions only two years later; moreover, the economic gap with rival South Korea had become clearly insurmountable as the DPRK economy began registering negative growth rates for the first time. While the North's economy already showed signs of distress prior to 1989, the collapse of the communist bloc and termination of patron aid by Moscow and Beijing exponentially worsened the situation. For example, DPRK petroleum imports from the Soviet Union dropped by more than half between 1988 (3.4 million tons) and 1992 (1.5 million tons) after Moscow terminated subsidized sales. Similarly DPRK overall trade, three-fifths of which took place with Warsaw Pact countries, contracted by nearly 33 percent between 1988 and 1991 after hard currency terms of customs settlement became required for most transactions.[78] Statements by DPRK leadership during this period recognized the gravity of these watershed events and a status quo in the domain of losses.[79] Yet in spite of this dire situation (cells 5 or 6), the North Koreans did not lash out. This non-event stemmed from engagement initiatives taken by the United States and the ROK. During the same 1989–1992 time span, the U.S. opened a low-level direct dialogue with North Korea in Beijing (started October 1988) that yielded 18 meetings through 1991. More important, in September 1991 the Bush administration issued directives leading to the withdrawal of nuclear weapons from the Korean Peninsula and canceled the annual major U.S.-ROK joint military exercise (Team Spirit).[80] South Korea also initiated engagement with the North as part of its "nordpolitik" or Northern diplomacy under the Roh Tae-woo government and this resulted in a major set of inter-Korean agreements in 1992 on political reconciliation and denuclearization.[81] Engagement policies by the U.S. and the ROK were therefore critical to preventing the actualization of a dangerous preemptive/preventive situation.

Arguably, the recommendations made by a major U.S. review of North Korea policy in 1999, mandated by Congress and led by former Secretary of Defense William Perry, had similar effects on DPRK behavior. In December 1998, before Perry began his review, North Korea undertook a series of limited hostile acts to disrupt a status quo deemed unfeasible (the most prominent of these, as described earlier, were the JSA incursions, missile tests, and other sea incursions). All were somewhat successful status quo-altering events (from a DPRK vantage point) because they put new issues and bargaining chips on the table with the United States, South Korea, and Japan for negotiation. But with the Perry review's recommendations for the United States and its allies to pursue engagement with the North (particularly after Secretary Perry's mission to Pyongyang in June 1999), holding open the possible inflow of economic funds, humanitarian aid, and political normalization, the train of limited hostile acts by the DPRK ceased. Perry's recommendations for engagement basically moved the DPRK out of the domain of losses and into a situation where it had a stake in the status quo. How the Bush administration's North Korea policy fares in this framework will be addressed in chapter 3.

WEAK BUT STILL DANGEROUS

In sum, although the cold war and post–cold war periods both presented preventive/preemptive situations for North Korea,

40 during the cold war itself, North Korea took no actions because its decisional frame remained in the domain of gains. Despite the vulnerability gap favoring the South, time horizons were long, and survival was never in question. The situation in the post–cold war era, although superficially appearing similar, is fundamentally different. Survival has become the unwritten state objective, time is not on the North's side, and the decisional frame is firmly in the domain of losses. South Korea's sunshine policy has led to a marginal improvement in the North's conditionbut the continuance of this policy is uncertain; moreover the North has failed to institute the structural reforms in the North that the policy was intended to spur. Hence backsliding to the status quo ex ante is a distinct possiblity. Like the gambler who can't catch a break, the more North Korea frames today's situation as a losing one, the more appealing becomes the double-or-nothing option, and the greater the danger of preemptive action. Again, such an act would not be based on a rationale about winning, but one of avoiding further loss.

DAVID KANG

THREATENING, BUT DETERRENCE WORKS

2

I loathe Kim Jong-il—I've got a visceral reaction to this guy . . .
— *U.S. President George W. Bush*

We are capable of winning decisively in one [Iraq] and swiftly defeating in the case of the other [North Korea] . . . Let there be no doubt about it.
— *U.S. Secretary of Defense Donald Rumsfeld,*

Everything will be negotiable . . . our government will resolve all U.S. security concerns through the talks if your government has a will to end its hostile policy.
— *DPRK. ambassador to the U.N., Han Song-ryol, November 2002*

North Korean leader Kim Jong-il is a brutal dictator who has impoverished a nation in order to sustain a massive military machine. He presides over horrifying human rights abuses and concentration camps. Due to its bungled economic policies, as many as one million North Koreans may have died from starvation in the past decade. Kim Jong-il is a reclusive, enigmatic, callous, and some say, irrational leader. How can such a man—and such a country—have any legitimate security concerns? Shouldn't the United States and the rest of the world fear such unpredictable behavior? Isn't North Korea responsible for its own dilemma? Indeed, if North

Korea does develop a nuclear weapon, wouldn't that be the worst possible outcome—a madman with a huge gun?

These are not new concerns. Ever since the first Korean War in 1950, scholars and policymakers have been predicting a second one, started by an invasion from the North. Even in 1997, the Defense Intelligence Agency still considered a Korean war to be the primary near-term military concern of the United States, and the most recent worry is that North Korea may develop nuclear weapons, and perhaps even engage in a missile attack on the United States.[1] A good example of this approach comes from Richard Betts:

> Since the direct attack in 1950, Pyongyang has frequently demonstrated its risk propensity in more consistently reckless provocations than any other government in the world . . . Today pessimists worry about a North Korean nuclear weapons program. Would any government be more willing to do wild and crazy things with such weapons than the one that so regularly perpetrates acts like those mentioned above?[2]

This is just the latest of a long series of dark predictions about an increasingly risk-acceptant North Korea. Earlier scenarios under which scholars have expected North Korea to invade include the 1961 military coup d'état in South Korea by Park Chung-hee that followed a year of turmoil in the South, the withdrawal of 50,000 U.S. troops from South Korea under the Nixon doctrine of the early 1970s, the assassination of Park Chung-hee by his own security forces in 1979, the military coup d'état by Chun Doo-hwan in 1980, the mass demonstrations for democracy in 1986–87, and the nuclear crisis of 1992–94.[3] Whether seen as arising from preventive, preemptive, desperation, or simple aggressive motivations, the predominant perspective in the west sees North Korea as threatening and dangerous.[4]

Yet for fifty years North Korea has not come close to starting a war.

This raises a question: is North Korea as dangerous as is popularly believed?

Although accurate, the description of North Korea given at the beginning of this chapter is incomplete. Just as important to any complete picture of North Korea in 2003 is how weak it really is. In the past 15 years, the balance of power has shifted dramatically against the North. North Korea is also a tiny country that has lost its allies and faces a threatening United States. The state of New Hampshire's economy is twice as large as that of North Korea, while South Korea's economy is thirty times larger.[5] The United States is openly belligerent toward it, as the quotes at the beginning of the chapter show. With the recently announced National Security Strategy that moves the U.S. toward a stated policy of preemptive strikes, the North is worried that if it agrees to disarm and abandon its deterrent posture, the United States will move to destroy it.[6] The North deters preemptive action by the U.S. precisely because the costs of a war on the peninsula are staggeringly high. North Korea's threatening rhetoric and large army exist to deter the U.S. and convince the U.S. that the costs of war are too high.

This raises another question: does North Korea have legitimate security fears?

In a nutshell, the problem is this: the United States refuses to give security guarantees to North Korea until it proves it has dismantled its weapons program. The North refuses to disarm until it has security guarantees from the United States.

Hence, stalemate.

The key issue is whether North Korea has legitimate security concerns. If it does—and I will argue that this is the case—we can explain the pattern of North Korean behavior and also point to a solution. North Korea's nuclear weapons, missile programs, and massive conventional military deployments are aimed at deterrence and defense. If North Korea really wanted to develop nuclear weapons for offensive purposes, it would have done so long ago. Even if the North develops nuclear weapons, it will not use them because of a devastating U.S. response. The North wants a guarantee of security from the U.S., and a policy of pressure will only make North Korea feel even more insecure. Even isolation is at best a holding measure, while economic sanctions—or even economic engagement alone—will be unlikely to get North Korea to abandon its weapons program.

Without movement toward resolving the security fears of the North, progress in resolving the nuclear weapons issue will be limited. The United States and North Korea are still technically at war—the 1953 armistice was never replaced with a peace treaty. The U.S. has been unwilling to discuss even a nonaggression pact, much less a peace treaty or normalization of ties. With the U.S. calling North Korea a terrorist nation and Donald Rumsfeld discussing the possibility of war, it is no surprise that North Korea feels threatened. Upon closer examination, North Korea never had the material capabilities to be a serious contender to the U.S.-ROK alliance, and it quickly fell further behind. So the real question has not been whether North Korea would prevent or preempt as South Korea caught up, but instead why North Korea might fight as it fell farther and farther behind. To paraphrase William Wohlforth, "theorists tended to concentrate on dynamic challengers and moribund defenders. But in Korea the North was the moribund challenger, and the South was the rising defender."[7]

If North Korea was so weak, why did so many people conclude that North Korea was the likely instigator of war? Since North Korea was not powerful, scholars and policymakers hypothesized extreme psychological tendencies to North Korean leaders. That is, if the material conditions such as military or economic power did not lead logically to a conclusion of North Korean threat, then the leadership's psychology was what must matter. These ancillary and *ad hoc* psychological assumptions range from an irrational North Korean leadership to an extremely strong preference for invasion. Most theories of war focus on material conditions such as relative power, but in the case of North Korea, the real analytic lifting has been done by psychological assumptions about intent. As I will show, none of these assumptions are tenable.[8]

The explanation for a half-century of stability and peace on the Korean peninsula is actually quite simple: deterrence works. Since 1953 North Korea has faced both a determined South Korean military, and more importantly, U.S. military deployments that at their height comprised 100,000 troops and more than 100 nuclear-tipped Lance missiles aimed at North Korea. Even today the United States maintains bases in South Korea that include 38,000 troops, nuclear-capable airbases, and naval facilities that guarantee U.S. involvement in any conflict on the peninsula. While in 1950 there might have been reason for confidence in the North, the war was disastrous for the Communists, and without massive Chinese involvement North Korea would have ceased to exist. Even during the cold war, North Korea's leadership never challenged this deterrence on the peninsula. As I will show, the attempted assassinations of South Korea's authoritarian leaders during the 1970s and 1980s have stopped because they would be clearly counterproductive in a democratic South Korea, and will not begin again. Given the tension on the peninsula, small skirmishes have had the potential to spiral out of control, yet these incidents on the peninsula have been managed with care on both sides. The peninsula has been stable for fifty years because deterrence has been clear and unambigious.

The end of the cold war marked a major change in North Korea's security position. The past 15 years have seen the balance of power turn sharply against the North. What was stable deterrence during the cold war by both sides has swung quickly in favor of the West and South Korea.[19] In the 1990s North Korea lost its two cold war patrons, experienced economic and environmental crises, and fell far behind the South. Although during the cold war the North was the aggressor, this shift in power put it on the defensive. It was only when the balance began to turn against the North that it began to pursue a nuclear weapons program. Both the weapons program and the bellicose nature of its rhetoric are an attempt to continue to deter the U.S. from taking any preemptive moves against it.

North Korea has the worst public relations in the world. The North's anachronistic cold war rhetoric and seeming inability to present itself reasonably make it difficult for even impartial people in the West to make sense of its actions. This chapter is aimed at providing an explanation. As history has shown, pressure only exacerbates North Korean security fears. Since North Korea does not pose the threat many analysts think it does, the United States may be wasting resources aimed at the North, and may also be unnecessarily raising tensions throughout the region.

I want to emphasize that I am neither defending nor justifying North Korean behavior. Much of the regime's actions are abhorrent and morally indefensible. However, sound foreign policy is built upon clear and objective analysis of the conditions at hand. Emotion and ideology have often interfered with the reasoned study of North Korea, and this has led scholars and policymakers to consistently overestimate the North Korean threat and to misunderstand the motivations behind North Korea's actions.

This chapter is focused on explaining the pattern of North Korea's military and security policies. A complete picture of North Korea must also include the dramatic steps taken in the past decade to reform and open up its economy. In chapter 4 I will discuss North Korea's economy and what it tells us about their foreign policy. In this chapter I perform four tasks. First, I show why North Korea is not a threat. Second, I explain why deterrence has worked for 50 years, and show that the changing balance of power has increased North Korea's security fears. Third, I show why, even if North Korea develops a nuclear weapons capability, it will not use them, and also why North Korea is unlikely to engage in terrorism. Finally, I examine the "madman hypothesis" to show how questionable assumptions can be smuggled into the analysis of North Korea, and show why assuming irrationality is unproductive.

WHY NORTH KOREA IS NOT A MILITARY THREAT

In explaining North Korea's foreign policy, a useful place to begin is by exploring why North Korea has become weaker and what has deterred it from starting a war. North Korea chose not to attack the South during the cold war, even though it was at the height of its power and was supported by the PRC and the Soviet Union. The past 15 years have led to severe economic and military decline in North Korea, and it is now much weaker than South Korea. Intuitively, it follows that this nation is fearful of the United States.

The majority of international relations theories conclude that the source of threats is clear: power is threatening. Kenneth Waltz writes that "balance of power theory leads one to expect that states, if they are free to do so, will flock to the weaker side. The stronger, not the weaker side, threatens them. . . . Even if the powerful state's intentions are wholly benign, less powerful states will . . . interpret events differently."[10] Because states are concerned primarily with their own survival, and since states are concerned about relative power, there always exists the possibility that a strong nation may decide to begin hostilities with a weaker nation. Viewed differently, "parity preserves peace."[11] Thus a potential aggressor will not initiate a conflict if it cannot win.

Threats arise by the mere presence of capabilities. Even if a nation was peaceful when it was weak, changes in power can bring changes in goals. Robert Gilpin writes that "rising power leads to increasing ambition. Rising powers seek to enhance their security by increasing their capabilities and their control over the external environment."[12] In this sense intentions are not fixed, but instead flow from and respond to changes in capabilities. The obverse of Gilpin's argument is that as a nation's capabilities fall behind, as it grows relatively weaker, its fears about the external environment will increase. Its ambitions will lessen, and its perception of external threat will rise. A preventive war might occur if the challenger's economic and military capabilities begin to catch those of the defender. In that case, there exists the possibility that the defender will decide to fight a preventive war to keep the challenger from catching up, or that the challenger will fight after it catches up.[13]

However, there are two generic problems in applying the theories to the Korean peninsula. First, the theories predict peace if a small challenger falls farther behind the defender.[14] If a nation was deterred from attacking when it was 60 percent the size of the defender, why would it attack after it has fallen to 30 percent, or even less, of the defender's size? There are only two logical ways in which one can end up with the weaker power attacking the stronger. The first argument is well elucidated by Victor Cha in chapter 1, which I will discuss that at length in chapter 4. The

GRAPH 2.1 North Korean GNP as a percent of South Korea; 1953–2000

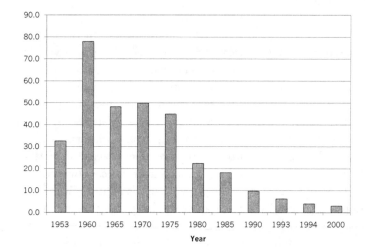

Source: Vantage Point 19, no. 3 (July 1995): 18; National Unification Board, *The Economies of South and North Korea* (Seoul: National Unification Board, 1988): 30; and *CIA World Factbook*, various years (*http://www.odci.gov/cia/publications/factbook/*).

second way is to assume that the leader is irrational.[15] I will show below why the madman theory does not make much sense.

Before that, however, I will show how absolutely weak the North actually is. The first calculation compares only North and South Korea, while the second calculation includes likely U.S. actions in these assessments. The typical approach has been to take both North and South Korea and compare them along a range of economic and military measures, and I will show that North Korea's capabilities were never preeminent over the South. More important, however, is an assessment of relative power that includes the U.S. forces that would be involved on the peninsula in event of a conflict. Scholars rarely consider this balance of forces, but this is a mistake, because any war would certainly involve the united States. Both of these measures show clearly that preventive war and power transition theories are not applicable to the Korean case.

GRAPH 2.2 Per Capita GNP of North and South Korea, 1953–1990

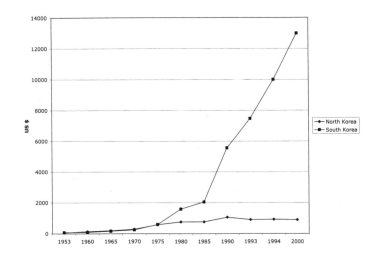

Source: Vantage Point 19, no. 3 (July 1995): 18; National Unification Board, 1988): 30; and *CIA World Fact book* (Washington, D.C.: CIA, 2001).

South Korea has always had twice the population of the North. In economic terms, North Korea was never as large as the South, and even at its closest was no more than three-quarters the size of the South. Graph 2.1 shows estimates for the gross national product (GNP) of North and South Korea from 1953 to 2000. It is clear that North Korea was never close to the South in absolute size, and indeed after 1960 rapidly began falling farther and farther behind. North Korea's GNP in 1960 was $1.52 billion, while South Korea's GNP was $1.95 billion. By 1970 North Korea had grown to $3.98 billion, while in the South GNP was $7.99 billion.

On a per capita income basis the North was never much farther ahead of the South, either. The North and South were roughly equivalent until the mid-1970s, when the South began to rapidly leave the North behind (graph 2.2). In 1960 North Korea's per capita GNP was $137 as compared to $94 in the South, and in 1970 the North's per capita income was $286 to $248 in the South.

GRAPH 2.3 Defense spending, 1967–1997 (excludes military aid and transfers from third countries)

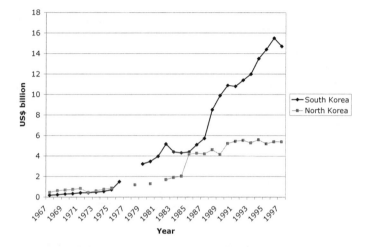

Source: IISS, *The Military Balance*, various years. (gaps in data due to incomplete or contradictory information).

However, by 1980 the North's income was $758 per capita, while the South's was $1,589, and by 1990 $1,065 to $5,569. Furthermore, in terms of preventive war, per capita income is not as important as absolute size, because small nations may be rich on a per capita basis (Singapore, Switzerland) but be militarily insignificant.

In terms of defense spending, North Korea quickly fell behind the South, spending less on defense by the mid-1970s (graph 2.3). As far back as 1977 the South was spending more than the North on defense in absolute dollar terms, $1.8 billion in the South opposed to $1 billion by the North.[16] The only measure by which the North outspent the South was on a per-capita GNP basis, which is an indicator of weakness, not strength.[17] Additionally these numbers do not include military transfers from their respective patrons. Between 1965 and 1982 North Korea received $1.5 billion in military transfers, mostly from the Soviet Union. Over the same time period South Korea received $5.1 billion from the United States.[18]

GRAPH 2.4 North and South Korean armed forces, 1962–1998

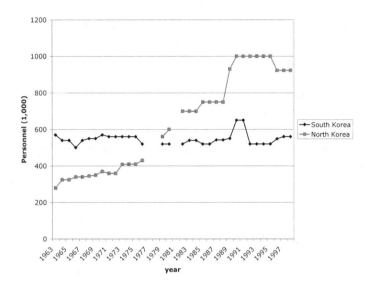

Source: IISS, *The Military Balance*, various years. (gaps in data due to incomplete or contradictory information).

Thus the most common measures of power in international relations—economic size and defense spending—show quite clearly that North Korea was never larger than South Korea, has been smaller on an absolute and per-capita basis than the South for at least 30 years, and continues to fall farther behind. Those who see North Korea as threatening need to explain why North Korea—having waited 50 years—would finally attack now that it is one-twentieth the size of the South.

In military capabilities the North and South Korea were in rough parity for the first two decades following the Korean War (1950–53), and then the North began to fall behind. Graph 2.4 shows the number of men in the armed forces from 1963 to 1998. Most interesting is that North Korea did not begin its massive expansion of its armed forces until well into the 1970s. This is most probably a response to its falling further behind the South. But for the past 30 years, North Korea's training, equipment, and overall military quality has steadily deteriorated relative to the South.

The South Korean military is better-equipped, better-trained, and more versatile with better logistics and support than the North Korean military, and some assessments suggest that this may double combat effectiveness.[19] Although the military has continued to hold pride of place in the North Korean economy, there have been increasing reports of reduced training due to the economic problems. *Joong-Ang Ilbo*, one of South Korea's major daily newspapers, quoted an unidentified Defense Ministry official as saying that North Korea's air force had made 100 training sorties per day in 1996, down from 300 to 400 before the end of 1995, and that the training maneuvers of ground troops had also been reduced to a "minimum level."[20] American military officials have noted that individual North Korean pilots take one training flight per month, compared with the 10 flights per month that U.S. pilots take.[21] This drastically degrades combat readiness.

Table 2.1 shows a comparison of weaponry in North and South Korea in 1997. The bulk of North Korea's main battle tanks are of 1950s vintage, and most of its combat aircraft were introduced before 1956. Evaluations after the Gulf War concluded that Western weaponry is at least twice, or even four-times, better than older Soviet-vintage systems.[22] By the 1990s North Korea's military was large in absolute numbers but the quality of their forces was severely degraded relative to South Korea's and the U.S. military. Michael O'Hanlon notes that: "Given the obsolescence of most North Korean equipment, however, actual capabilities of most forces would be notably less than raw numbers suggest. About half of North Korea's major weapons are of roughly 1960s design; the other half are even older."[23]

To view the North as superior in military terms is a mistake. But even more surprising about many of these accounts is that they measure the strength of the North Korean military only against that of the ROK, without including the U.S. forces, either present in Korea or those potential reinforcements. North Korea knows that it would fight the United States as well as the South, and it is wishful thinking to hope that the North Korean military

TABLE 2.1 A Comparison of North and South Korea's
Military Hardware in 1998

HARDWARE	NORTH KOREA	SOUTH KOREA	COMMENTS
Main battle tanks	3,000: T-34, T-54/55, T-62, and Type 59	2,130: 400 M-47 850 M-48 800 Type 88	T-34 are WWII vintage; T-55 introduced in 1957
			M-47 are WWII vintage; M-48 from 1952
Bombers	82 Il-28	—	
Pre-1956 fighter aircraft	107 MiG-17 159 MiG-19 130 MiG-21		
1960s fighter aircraft	46 MiG-23	130 F-4D/E	
1970s fighter aircraft	195 F-5		
1980s fighter aircraft	30 MiG-29 18 Su-7 35 Su-25	60 F-16	U.S. has 72 F-16 in Korea and 36 in Japan; U.S. also has 54 F-15 in Japan

Source: The Military Balance 1997-1998 (London: International institute for Strategic Studies, 1998); and James F. Dunigan, How to Make War (New York: Quill, 1983).

planners are so naïve as to ignore the U.S. military presence in South Korea, expecting the U.S. to pack up and go home if the North invaded. Comparisons between the South and the North that ignore the role of the United States are seriously misleading as to the real balance of power on the peninsula.[24]

In event of a full-scale conflict, the United States could reinforce the peninsula with overwhelming power. Currently 36,000 U.S. troops are stationed in Korea, including the U.S. Second infantry division and 90 combat aircraft including 72 F-16s. In addition, 36,000 troops are stationed in Japan, including the headquarters of the Seventh fleet at Yokosuka naval base, 14,000 Marines, and 90 combat aircraft. This is only the beginning, as more would soon arrive from within the United States.[25]

This economic and military comparison of North and South Korea shows that North Korea never had a lead over the South, and after the 1960s quickly began falling behind. The end of the cold war marked the beginning of a major change in North Korea's fortunes, as North Korea continued to have economic difficulties, while its allies deserted it. This situation has only become more grave in the new millennium.

North Korea is not a threat to start an unprovoked war. North Korea was never in a preeminent position relative to the South, and the real question for the pessimists is why they continue to believe that a nation that is far behind and falling farther behind might still attack. The weak may attack the strong—but the conditions under which we expect that to happen do not exist on the peninsula. Yet many people still see the situation as tense and threatening. This is true, but it is true because deterrence at its heart requires both sides to know that the other side can severely damage it.

DETERRENCE AND THE CHANGING BALANCE OF POWER

North Korea has not attacked for fifty years because deterrence works. Despite the tension that has existed on the peninsula, the balance of power has held. For more than 50 years neither side has attempted to mount a major military operation, nor has either side attempted to challenge deterrence on the peninsula.[26] Any war on the peninsula would have disastrous consequences for both sides. The tightly constricted geographic situation intensifies an already acute security dilemma between the two sides.[27] The capitals of Seoul and Pyongyang are less than 150 miles apart—closer than New York and Baltimore. Seoul is 30 miles from the de-militarized zone that separates the North and the South (DMZ), and easily within reach of North Korea's artillery tubes. One estimate calculates that a war on the Korean peninsula would cost the United States more than $60 billion and result in 3 million casualties, including 52,000 U.S. military casualties. The North, although it has numerically larger armed forces, faces a much more highly trained and capable U.S.-ROK armed forces. This led to stalemate: there was little room for barter or bargaining. The result has not been surprising: although tension is high, the balance of power has been stable. Far from being a tinderbox, both sides have moved cautiously and avoided major military mobilizations that could spiral out of control.

Why did deterrence succeed in Korea? For the first decades after the war, the U.S. deterrent made it very clear that a North Korean attack would fail. Analysts in this respect have generally missed the forest for the trees, for although they often refer to the "U.S. tripwire" and deterrent posture, they continue to ignore the deterrent and focus instead on force-levels, terrorism, or subversion by the North.[28] As the balance of power began to turn against the North, the North deterred the U.S. from attempting to crush it through massive conventional military deployments along the DMZ. North Korea already has the functional equivalent of a nuclear deterrent. North Korean threats to destroy Seoul "like a rabid dog barking at the sky, unaware of the fate about to befall it" are taken seriously in Asia and the West, leading South Korean and U.S. leaders to deal quite cautiously with North Korea. Especially because Seoul is both vulnerable to air attack and the center of South Korean life, the South Korean government is quite reluctant to escalate tensions too quickly. North Korea's military—both conventional and missile systems—exist to deter the South and the U.S. from becoming too adventurous. Rather than seeing the North in a position to invade the South, a more accurate description of the peninsular situation is uneasy standoff. Both sides are very careful, and neither side wishes to provoke a war, because all sides know the destruction it would bring.

In addition, the U.S. faces other international constraints on the use of force in the region. A major war involving the United States would most likely bring the U.S. and China nose-to-nose, a situation that neither side would like to see at this point in time. China has historically been a supportive ally of North Korea, and while China would probably not defend the North against the United States, the U.S. runs a great risk of escalation beyond its control if anything were to go wrong. Additionally, neither South Korea nor Japan would be enthusiastic about such a war, and the U.S. would risk seriously damaging its relations around the region. In the worst-case scenario, a war could spill over and involve Japan, China, Russia, and the United States, all against their best intentions. This worst-case scenario is horrifying, and all parties have shown considerable caution in discussing military options on the Korean peninsula.

What might destabilize deterrence? The main risk in such a situation is if the power of the larger party in the dyad becomes so great that the forces held for deterrence were in fact capable of pre-empting themselves. For deterrence to be stable, it requires a level of force that is adequate to make an attack senseless, but but not so high that it would make pre-emption tempting to the other side. The past 15 years have seen the balance tip steeply against the North. Simple deterrence theory would expect that North Korea would be increasingly threatened as it falls far behind the South and the United States both economically and militarily.

Whether North Korea has legitimate security concerns is the key question in attempting to explain North Korean behavior. There is considerable evidence that the United States is hostile toward the North. Rhetoric about North Korea has rarely been conciliatory and is often bellicose. Most significantly, the U.S.

and North Korea are still technically at war. The United States steadfastly refuses to discuss a nonaggression pact, or replacing the 1953 armistice with a peace treaty until the North reassures it that the nuclear programs have been stopped.

From Rumsfeld's statements about waging war on two fronts to Bush's inclusion of North Korea in the "axis of evil," to administration officials saying that other countries should impose economic sanctions, U.S. rhetoric over the past two years has been relatively confrontational. In December 2002, Secretary of State Colin Powell said that "We cannot suddenly say 'Gee, we're so scared. Let's have a negotiation because we want to appease your misbehavior.' This kind of action cannot be rewarded," while in January 2003, a senior U.S. official was quoted as saying that "First is regime change. It need not necessarily be military, but it could lead to that."[29] In addition, the administration has refused to put a nonaggression pact in writing. Given this reluctance, it is follows that the North Korean regime would interpret these signals as conveying that the use of force by the United States remains an option.

In addition, the military balance in many ways is favorable to the South and the United States. The "Nuclear Posture Review," of December 2001 specifies North Korea as an "immediate contingency," for which the United States must be prepared to respond with nuclear force. [30] As noted above, the U.S. maintains a considerable military posture in the region, with the capability to strike at North Korea. My point is not to try and pin blame on either side. Both sides are threatening and bellicose, and both sides contribute to tension in the region. Rather, I only point out that the U.S. is, indeed, threatening to the North.

Deterrence itself is threatened if one side becomes too strong. If the balance of power begins to shift, deterrence may not hold. On the peninsula, it is the United States that is gaining predominant power, and this is in turn increasing North Korean fears. Especially with the U.S. reluctant to provide any security guarantees, the North has reason to fear the changing balance of power may make it so weak that the U.S. decides to undertake military action. This is why North Korea has a nuclear weapons program.

NUCLEAR WEAPONS AND TERRORISM

The world has become alarmed in recent years not because of the North's conventional military forces, but rather because it is pursuing a nuclear weapons program combined with a ballistic missile program. The real American fear of the past decade has been that a nuclear-armed North Korea might potentially strike targets even in the United States itself. However, these weapons also serve a deterrent function. Given the weakness of North Korea compared to the South and the U.S., and their security fears that arise from that weakness, it is not surprising that the North seeks security assurances from the United States. Deterrence also means that North Korea will not use its weapons—if it actually develops them—for offensive purposes. The consequences would be annihilation by the U.S.

As noted in the previous section, for deterrence to be stable, it requires an adequate level of force to make an attack senseless, but cannot tip over into a level or type of capabilities that would make pre-emption tempting to the other side. Would the acquisition of nuclear weapons by North Korea be destabilizing to the balance of power on the peninsula? The logic of deterrence theory would argue "no," because North Korea would still be deterred by the overwhelming conventional and military power of the United States.

As the tragic events of September 2001 demonstrate, no missile shield will protect a nation against determined terrorist attacks. Yet North Korea has not engaged in terrorism for well over a decade, because their goal is not suicide and random wanton destruction, but survival. As to North Korea's missile program, this is part of their deterrence strategy. North Korea could blow up terrorist bombs in downtown Seoul or Tokyo (or Washington, D.C.) every week if they wanted to.[31] As for rogue states and their alleged plans to fire a couple of nuclear warheads at the United States, there are three basic reasons to doubt this threat. First, North Korea has not yet developed this capability—it is only feared that eventually they may do so. Second, to actually use nuclear weapons would be suicide, since any attack on the U.S.

would result in massive American retaliation, and North Korea's efforts over the past decade show that it has an intense desire to survive. Finally, why develop an expensive ballistic missile to shoot at the United States when it would be so much easier just to smuggle in a nuclear weapon? There is a difference between capabilities and intentions—while missiles will not give North Korea any more terrorist capability than they already possess, they do provide a much stronger military deterrent than could terrorist bombings.

I have two points about nuclear tensions in Korea. First, two or three crude nuclear weapons provide no offensive capability and would not significantly alter the military balance on the peninsula, although the diplomatic context may change. North Korea will be no more likely to win a war with nuclear weapons than without them. North Korea, knowing that the stakes are even greater, and that the United States could respond with nuclear weapons, might even be less likely to launch a war. Nuclear weapons confer no offensive capability. Nuclear weapons are too large and powerful to be able to confer militarily useful offensive capability. Nuclear weapons do not "fight" anything, they merely destroy. And thus they offer little offensive or defensive capability. What nuclear weapons do best is deter, for they allow the loser of a war to kill the winner.[32] Nuclear weapons hold little offensive value, but were North Korea to develop the bomb, North Korea would have a robust deterrent. North Korean diplomats have explicitly stated that they view their missiles as a deterrent against U.S. campaign of "Yugoslavian-type aggression" against the North. The NATO air war against Yugoslavia made a deep impression on Asian military planners, including Chinese and North Koreans. Some scholars have argued that North Korea is developing the bomb because they want to invade South Korea under a nuclear umbrella that insures a conventional war will be fought. However, as noted previously, conventional deterrence still holds, and there is little doubt that the North would lose a conventional war. North Korean statements, although equivocal, point out their acute awareness of their own vulnerability.[33] In

1999, a North Korean diplomat noted that "the Agreed Framework made American generals confident that the DPRK had become defenseless; the only way to correct this misperception is to develop a credible deterrent against the United States."[34]

Second, robust deterrence on the Korean peninsula has resulted from a steadfast U.S. commitment to the South. Less important to deterrence than actual American troops stationed on the peninsula is the potential U.S. involvement. North Korea cannot hope to win a war against the United States. Therefore, if the U.S. commitment to the South remains strong the likelihood of war on the peninsula is slight.

Nuclear weapons are political, not military, instruments. Their value is far greater unused than deployed and delivered. Particularly if North Korea has a tiny stockpile of weapons (one or two), they would do virtually nothing that conventional weapons cannot already do. North Korea already has the conventional capability to destroy Seoul. North Korea can already target the Japanese islands with their Scud missiles.

There is only one difference that would occur from using nuclear weapons:their deployment would remove any barriers on the part of the U.S. and South Korea for a limited war. "The gloves would come off," with no limit to the escalation the U.S. could bring. Virtually any domestic constraint in the United States against using nuclear weapons or overwhelming force would most likely vanish, and the result would undoubtedly be the destruction of the North Korean regime.

The main difference between North Korea and Osama bin Laden is that we know exactly where North Korea is. And, were they to launch a missile, we would know exactly who fired it from the minute it was fired, and know exactly where to aim our retaliatory strikes. This is a major difference, and a major deterrent to nation-states when they consider the use of force.[35]

Whether the goal was a bargaining chip or an effective deterrent, the pursuit of nuclear weapons by North Korea should come as no surprise. As Andrew Mack writes, "From the North Korean perspective, the reasons for not going nuclear may be outweighed by the perception of a growing strategic need for nuclear weapons."[36] Their allies have deserted them. North Korea has a stagnant and crumbling economic infrastructure. The U.S. is threatening to them.[37] In 1990, North Korea's Foreign Minister Kim Yong-Nam, said that détente between the Soviet Union and South Korea " . . . will leave us no other choice but to take measures to provide us for ourselves [sic] some weapons for which we have so far relied on the Soviet Union."[38]

In addition, there is heated debate in the United States over whether North Korea's missile program is actually as dangerous as some have suggested. The longest-range missile currently deployed by North Korea is the No Dong missile, which can carry a 1,500-pound payload approximately 800 miles. However, North Korea has reportedly tested the No Dong only once. The untested Taepo Dong 2 can potentially carry a several hundred–pound payload between 6,000 and 9,000 miles—far enough to reach the West Coast of the United States. But without adequate testing, such a nuclear missile would be highly unreliable. David Wright, a weapons expert at the Massachusetts Institute of Technology, said that a rocket like the one North Korea tested in 1998 "might be capable of reaching Alaska with a very small payload of no more than 100 kilograms (220 pounds)." Wright added that such a missile would be incapable of reaching either Hawaii or Alaska, let alone the continental United States, with a nuclear warhead weighing between 500 (1,100 pounds) and 1,000 kilos (2,200 pounds). "All the North Koreans have done is fire a few things into the air," said Zia Mian, of the Center for Energy and Environmental Studies at Princeton University. "That is a long way from developing an ICBM."[39] When criticized for their missile program, North Korean diplomats point out that "whether we testfire a satellite or a missile is a legitimate independent right to be exercised by a sovereign state because it in no way runs counter to the DPRK-U.S. Agreed Framework as well as to the recognized international convention."[40]

However, even if North Korea is deterred from using weapons of mass destruction, some may argue that it still might engage in terrorist activities. For two decades, from 1968–1987, North Korea pursued a policy of sporadic attempts to assassinate the authoritarian leaders of South Korea. After the South's democratic transition in 1987, those attempts ceased, because they would have been counterproductive. From the 1968 attack on the South Korean presidential mansion, to the attempted assassination of South Korean president Park Chung-hee in 1974, to the bombing of the Chun cabinet in Rangoon in 1983 to the destruction of a KAL airliner in 1987, for two decades North Korea consistently attempted to use terror as a means of foreign policy. For some, terrorism is proof that North Korea is both irrational and un-deterrable, a nation so bent on pursuing the overthrow of the South that it takes actions that are counterproductive to its own goals.

Terrorism in any form is morally repugnant, and the indiscriminate slaughter of civilians is abominable. I do not intend to defend North Korean actions, but rather to explain the causes and consequences of their actions. Even abhorrent tactics such as terrorism can have political causes, and my purpose in this section is only to delineate what those causes have been, and to explain why North Korea has not attempted any action since 1987, and why it is unlikely to do so in the future. North Korea's attempts at subversion disappeared by the late 1980s as South Korea's domestic political situation became both more stable and more legitimate, and it was clear the South was not going to collapse from internal contradictions.

In explaining North Korea's subversion attempts, we need to answer two questions: why terrorism instead of war? And why assassination—a certain type of terrorism? Precisely because the North did not wish to challenge deterrence on the peninsula, they attempted terrorism.[41] I am not arguing that North Korean assassination attempts were morally defensible; they were not. Rather, I am only making the point that North Korea was well aware of the risks of challenging the central balance of power.

North Korea attempted to assassinate the military leaders of an authoritarian South Korea. Their aim was to kill these dictators, and to hope that something good would come of it.[42] Given that the North desired not only the overthrow of the South Korean government, but also the support of the South Korean citizenry, North Korea explicitly avoided attacking the population of South Korea itself. North Korean terrorists could blow up bombs in Downtown Seoul on a daily basis if that was their goal. But the goal of the North Korean regime is not to turn the entire southern population against the north, but rather the opposite—to destabilize the South Korean regime in the hopes that there will be some coup or insurgency that will result in a government more favorable to the North.

What would have unified the South Korean populace against the North would have been terrorist attacks against the people themselves. And so, unsurprisingly, the North did not attack the population of the South. North Korea has generally not engaged in random killings of civilians, such as occurs between the Israelis and Palestinian *intifada*.

In addition, there is sufficient evidence that the South has been so unstable that the North could logically have hoped that a small shove might have toppled the South Korean regime. The record of unstable and repressive authoritarian regimes in the South was an inviting target to the North. With such obvious discontent among a large portion of the South Korean populace, the hopes that attacking the South Korean leadership might result in chaos or collapse.

North Korea will not use terrorism against the people of the South Korea. Because the South Korean government has become increasingly more legitimate through the use of both democratically elected officials and the redress of past crimes by its political leaders, the North has realized that the terrorism no longer has any chance of succeeding. Thus the more legitimate the South Korean government, the less likely North Korea will use terrorism.

There has been no war on the Korean peninsula for 50 years because deterrence has held. And as the North grows continually weaker relative to the South, the chances for war or unprovoked provocative acts becomes even slimmer.

WHY THE MADMAN HYPOTHESIS MAKES NO SENSE

If North Korea is so weak, and if deterrence has held for five decades, why did so many scholars and policymakers view the North as a threat? The answer is that scholars smuggled a number of ancillary or *ad hoc* assumptions into the theory. Because the scholarly literature has paid such scant attention to understanding the theoretical underpinnings of dissatisfied or revisionist states, this leaves ample room for poorly defined assumptions to be inserted into the argument. Evaluations of national capabilities and alliances are comfortably third-image and realist in nature, whereas evaluations of "satisfaction" and leadership rapidly probe into domestic politics and even psychology of individual leaders. Often this link is not directly stated, which both allows the scholar to make his case without clearly delineating the causal linkage and the evidence, and also plays on a generalized "assumption of guilt" that surrounds countries such as North Korea. When we don't know much about a country it is easy to expect the worst.

In the case of North Korea, these tended to be behavioral assumptions about the psychology of the North Korean leadership. Prominent among those assumptions was the notion that North Korean leaders had an intense preference for unifying the peninsula and that Kim Il-sung (and later, Kim Jong-il) were paranoid and irrational. North Korea has been described as a nation of "paranoid survivalists" and "a renegade state"[43] Typical of this approach is a statement by John Perry: "Rhetorical style and financial irresponsibility pale beside the impact on international public opinion of the inexplicable spasms of violence perpetuated by North Korea. Much can be said against the erratic ferocity of such behavior."[44]

In 1992, James Pierce of the U.S. Embassy in Seoul said "Why would North Korea attack? Because Kim Il-Sung is not rational."[45] The strong version of these psychological assumptions asserts that Kim Il-sung and Kim Jong-il were truly irrational or paranoid. The weaker version of this argument emphasizes that leaders of authoritarian and secretive regimes may have different preferences or pressures from those of more widely understood countries. In both cases, however, if variables such as leadership truly matter, then scholars must incorporate them explicitly and consistently into their theories. In arguing that North Korea was unpredictable or irrational, scholars relied on these assumptions—often without evidence—to do the bulk of the analytic lifting. Yet even a cursory glance shows how untenable these assumptions are.[46]

The strong version of this approach is fairly easy to dismiss. Discussions of irrationality do not get us very far. First, if a ruler truly is irrational or paranoid, it is impossible to make any causal link between that psychological state and expected outcomes. Second, such an approach is unfalsifiable and allows the scholar to post-dictively prove any argument that he makes. By resorting to an irrational demagogue as an explanatory variable, analysts appeal to a *deus ex machina* by which any North Korean action can be post-dictively explained, and by which any possible North Korean action can be possible.

Additionally, all the evidence about both Kim Il-sung and Kim Jong-il points to their ability to make sophisticated decisions and to manage palace, domestic, and international politics with extreme precision. Kim Jong-il has kept power for seven years despite the widespread belief that he would not be able to survive. There was speculation in the West that a coup or instability could follow after his father's death in 1994, but that has not occurred.[47] There has been no palace coup, no military coup, no extensive social unrest, no obvious chaos in the military, and no wholesale purge of various officials. Indeed, the transition from father to son was remarkably smooth. Kim Jong-il has remained in power through famine, flood, economic crisis, nuclear crisis, the loss of two major patrons in Russia and China, and U.S. pressure.[48] Military officials have become present at all levels of the government, but they have not vetoed the economic and diplomatic efforts made by the Pyongyang regime.[49] Either Kim Jong-il is an extremely adroit leader, or the social and political fabric of North Korea is more resilient than we might think, or both.

The record of Kim Il-sung is similar. During his 49-year rule (1945–1994), he kept power through tremendous change in North Korea and the world around it. As Nicholas Eberstadt wrote:

Because North Korea presents such an unattractive—even freakish—face to the outside world, it has often been misjudged. In important respects the regime has been underestimated. Fanatical or surreal as this "red dynasty" may appear, many of its policies have been practical and effective. Of all Asia's communist states (including the USSR), only North Korea avoided famine in the course of its collectivization of agriculture.[50]

The evidence used to argue that these leaders have been irrational or crazy is speculative, having to do with hair styles or propensities to like western movies. While it may be accurate to argue that western leaders do not like the preferences of the North Korean leadership, it is not possible to argue these were irrational leaders, unable to make means-ends calculations.

If the strong version of irrationality is fairly easy to dismiss, the weaker version is just as problematic.

Even if we grant that the two Kims' attitudes were important, the question becomes how much of their value systems and attitudes explain North Korean behavior? This question rests on a counterfactual: if their attitudes and rationality have been important in explaining North Korean foreign policy, we should be able to believe that a different North Korean leader would have produced a different set of outcomes. What a focus on personality ignores, of course, is that we cannot infer actions from attributes if the situation also matters. As Waltz writes, "Just as peacemakers may fail to make peace, so troublemakers may fail to make trouble. From attributes one cannot predict outcomes if outcomes depend on the situations of the actors as well as on their attributes."[51]

It is hard to imagine any North Korean ruler that would act substantially different toward the South or the United States. Any conceivable North Korean leader would be concerned with regime and state survival and deterring the U.S. and searching for security guarantees. Is it possible to imagine a North Korean leader who would NOT fear the United States? OR one who would pursue economic reforms any differently? Or who would surrender and disarm voluntarily?

The worldviews of leaders may be important to understand, especially when assessing a secretive and cautious nation's conception of its security. However, if preventive war and power transition theorists believe that variables such as leadership truly matter, then they must incorporate them consistently and explicitly into their theories. This is problematic: theories of war initiation are generally third-image and realist, yet evaluations of satisfaction with the status quo and characterizations of risk-acceptance are second or first-image. International relations scholars have not elucidated a theory of leadership that fits easily within the larger structure of preventive war or power transition theories, and the literature should be conscious of that fact. *Ad hoc* arguments are not convincing.

CONCLUSION: THEORETICAL AND POLICY IMPLICATIONS

This chapter has examined the pattern of North Korean foreign policy behavior over the past five decades, and concludes that North Korea does not threaten to take unprovoked military or terrorist actions. North Korea as a country fears the United States. Much of its behavior is designed to deter the U.S. from going after North Korea next, once the U.S. has finished with Iraq. Similarly, the U.S. deterrent restrains the North from becoming too adventurous. As a guide to explaining North Korean behavior and intentions, it makes sense to start with an examination of their geopolitical situation. Such a perspective allows us to avoid much of the emotion and ideological debate, and to ask how we would expect a country in North Korea's position to behave. By subsequently focusing more closely on the psychology of leaders and the political uses of terror, we are able to explain fairly easily North Korea's pattern of behavior.

Countries and leaders respond to the incentive and constraints that they face. In the case of North Korea, being told to disarm in the face of pressure creates the incentive not to disarm, for fear of the consequences. With the United States unwilling to discuss security assurances, the North has little incentive to trust it. Even paranoiacs have enemies. North Korea does not trust us any more than we trust them. Decades of animosity and mistrust on both sides makes negotiation and communication difficult. The U.S. *is* hostile to Pyongyang, and it is not accurate to pretend that the U.S. only wants to be friends and that North Koreans are merely paranoid. This is not to argue about which side holds the moral high ground, nor to argue that the North Koreans are innocent; clearly America has reason to mistrust the North. But North Korea also mistrusts the U.S.—they know very well that the ultimate U.S. goal is the transformation or even the obliteration of their way of life—and North Korea has reason to be wary. The image of North Korea and the reality are not always the same, especially given the ideologically charged perceptions that exist on both sides. Whatever our fears of North Korea, sound policymaking will occur only when we realize that North Koreans, despite having an odious regime, have legitimate national concerns as well.

One counterargument that often arises is the "you never know" critique. In several guises, this critique says that "you never know, North Korea may attack," and that therefore we should take steps to counter that possibility. This critique is theoretically and methodologically unfounded. Whether couched in terms of "accidents happen" or "mistakes get made" or "you never know, leaders under stress do irrational things," this argument is no more than an assertion that uncertainty exists in the world. Without a causal argument that links North Korean leaders to an unprovoked attack, using "uncertainty" as the prime reason to expect dangerous North Korean behavior is unconvincing. We have no reason to think that deterrence which has held for 50 years might suddenly dissolve like dew in the summer sun. Predictions of a missile attack or an invasion are especially susceptible to "you never know-ism." If in 1992 (or 1978, or 1961) scholars argued strongly that a window of opportunity was closing for North Korea, and yet by now there has still been no invasion, it is spurious to argue "you never know," and that North Korea may still launch a preventive war next year.

If North Korea is not the threat that most scholarship believes that it is, U.S. policy may be inadvertently raising tensions in the region, and the U.S. may also be wasting resources designed to counter a threat that does not exist. The implicit U.S. sentiment—if not policy—of expecting unilateral disarmament by the North is ineffectual; as the nuclear crisis has shown, North Korean leaders will not back down to pressure. Such a U.S. approach might be good for domestic politics and for rhetoric about standing tough to bullies, but it will neither further U.S. foreign policy nor will it contribute to stability in the Asian region. There is a significant segment of U.S. policymakers who see no point in compromising our ideals. This is an entirely justified perspective. However, such a perspective also has clear consequences: North Korea has made very clear they will not surrender. North Korea has also made very clear that they intend to be treated with respect. This, no matter who is morally right, is the reality of the situation. And thus the United States needs to realize that a policy that expects North Korean capitulation has fairly predictable—and negative—consequences.

The United States faces a historic opportunity in the coming years to resolve an acute conflict that has survived for five decades. Managed properly, and with patience, North Korea can be brought into the community of nations. Even if Pyongyang wants to go in the same direction that the West wishes it to go, that process will be cautious and halting, and North Korea will not quickly let down its guard. Slow change is not bad—rapid change on the peninsula will be dangerous. The stakes are high—war or even chaos in North Korea could end up involving four major powers and costing billions of dollars and millions of lives, many of them American. Because the stakes are so high, it is all the more imperative that the United States remain patient, take the long-term view, avoid outdated cold war caricatures, and deal with North Korea as it is.

VICTOR CHA

WHY WE MUST PURSUE
"HAWK ENGAGEMENT"

3

While David Kang and I have shown our different views of the threat posed by the DPRK, we also have significant areas of agreement. First, we agree that deterrence works. Second, we agree that engagement is the right policy. Where our disagreements are most substantial are on the question of whether the North truly seeks reform and integration into the international system. I believe we also differ with regard to the rationales that generate a U.S.-ROK-Japan engagement strategy with the reclusive DPRK regime, and therefore support such a strategy with disparate degrees of optimism.

DETERRENCE WORKS

David Kang and I concur that deterrence has prevented a second DPRK invasion. Under the auspices of the U.S.-ROK alliance, robust defense capabilities and credible commitments to repel any attempt by the North to replay June 1950 have been the primary cause of peace and stability on the peninsula. Kang argues that this basic fact flies in the face of threat-inflaters and other analysts who argue that Pyongyang is aggressively-intended and on the brink of another attack. As he argues, the onus is on analysts to explain the theoretical reasons that lead to the prediction that North Korea—having waited 50 years—would finally attack now.

My primary disagreement with this view is that there is more than one way to define "peace and stability" on the peninsula. That is, I agree with Kang that the United States and ROK have deterred the DPRK from all-out invasion. If one defines the threat largely in these terms, then as Kang argues, the chances for war are remote as the North has not, and will not, challenge the central balance of power. But just because Pyongyang has been discouraged from invasion, this does not rule out the possibility of other forms of violence and aggression by the North. In social science terms, Kang has defined the dependent variable too narrowly. Threats to "peace and stability" on the Korean peninsula should not be equated simply with a second massive invasion, but also with *other acts of violence short of war that the North might undertake even if there is no objective chance of military victory.*

Under what conditions might the North threaten peninsular "peace and stability" with acts of violence short of war? What is the rationale for such actions if there is no chance of military victory? As explained in my initial statement, the permissive conditions for this type of calculation exist when the status quo is deemed unfeasible. This is defined as a situation in which a country and its people become so dysfunctional that the current state of affairs becomes unbearable. When things get this bad, one's frame of reference changes, so that action is motivated less by seeking new gains, and more by avoiding further losses.

To elaborate: If one remains inactive when faced with a losing status quo, this effectively means incurring constant and unbearable losses. Therefore the operative rationale becomes doing anything, even if it is high-risk, to arrest such losses. Imagine a medical patient suffering from an ailment but with some chance of recovery. She is offered the prospect of undergoing a radical high-risk medical procedure that offers a remote chance of recovery and significant possibility for failure and death. Weighing the probability of recovery versus the risk, the patient is not likely to opt for the procedure. If, however, her condition begins to steadily degenerate while her chances of recovery remain slim, then the status quo is truly unbearable. Now, the same high-risk medical procedure becomes more appealing despite the low chance of success, because the patient's frame of reference has shifted from seeking recovery (i.e., gains-motivation), to avoiding further loss (i.e., arresting the daily and eventually fatal degeneration of her condition). In sum, one becomes much more risk-acceptant when the current situation is a losing one.

COERCIVE BARGAINING

It is my belief that North Korea, given the dire circumstances that befell the country in the early 1990s, became susceptible to this sort of "double-or-nothing" mentality. Moreover, this situation generated a de facto coercive bargaining game that Pyongyang has become adept at playing. Pyongyang has followed a strategy of undertaking limited acts of violence against the United States, ROK and Japan. These provocations are deliberate pinpricks— i.e., they fall short of all-out war but are serious enough to rattle the allies and raise concerns about escalation. Washington, Seoul, and Tokyo are thus manipulated into the awkward position of wanting to respond punitively to DPRK misbehavior, but are constrained by fears of provoking an unnecessary and costly larger conflict. As a result, the allies usually issue a denouncement of the DPRK act, but still come to the negotiating table to reduce tensions. From Pyongyang's perspective, the purpose of these provocations is not to win some military advantage but to create a crisis, disrupting the status quo and initiating a coercive bargaining process that eventuates in a new status quo on current or new negotiations more favorable to the North.

The ROK-DPRK naval altercation on the west coast of the peninsula in June 1999 offers an ominous precedent. Several North Korean patrol boats violated South Korean waters, prompting the ROK navy to ram the trespassers and initiate a firefight that left 20 to 30 North Koreans dead. This constituted one of the largest losses of life in an altercation since the 1953 armistice and was a clear demonstration of the ROK's superior naval combat capabilities and training. What grabbed the headlines were the military clash itself and loss of life. But few really stopped to ask *why* the North undertook such an action. Why provoke a naval clash that it had no chance of winning? Many observers just assumed the DPRK underestimated the ROK's naval capabilities and resolve. Others argued this as another example of DPRK irrationality and unpredictability. Yet this otherwise puzzling behavior is fully consonant with the logic of coercive bargaining. Dissatisfied with the status quo, Pyongyang undertook an isolated act of violence to disrupt the state of affairs, with the hopes of renegotiating a new status quo more favorable to it. In the West Sea incident, the DPRK provocation was designed to extort concessions from a fearful ROK and its foreign patrons on the validity of the Northern Limitation Line, the maritime boundary between South and North Korea.[1] In effect, the calculation was to initiate a military act—albeit an unwinnable one— the ultimate purpose of which was to make the NLL an issue for negotiation, which had not previously been the case.

It is worth noting that this coercive bargaining strategy by the DPRK explained here and in my other studies of the topic,[2] is not merely a post–cold war phenomenon for North Korea. Pyongyang was adept at this strategy during the cold war, often in bizarrely convoluted ways. For example, in February 1973 the United Nations Command gave prior notification to DPRK authorities of its intention to replace military demarcation line markers as part of a maintenance detail in the central sector of the DMZ. Yet in March, North Korean forces fired on the UNC work detail killing two and wounding one. This was extremely puzzling behavior given the prior notification, a general relaxation in tensions in the aftermath of the July 1972 North-South joint communiqué, and an upcoming meeting in Panmunjom of the North-South Coordinating Committee (the oversight body set up to reduce tensions between the two Koreas mandated by the 1972 communiqué). According to Chuck Downs, the primary motivation behind this bizarrely provocative act was a coercive bargaining rationale. The North wanted to negotiate a reduction in heightened tensions (created by their actions) in exchange for forcing onto the agenda of the upcoming NSCC meetings a discussion about the formal political recognition of the underground communist movement in South Korea.[3]

North Korea historically also used provocations against the United States and South Korea as opportunities to gain leverage on the *Soviet Union*. A quintessential example of this were the series of provocations by Kim Il-sung in 1968 including a failed commando raid on the South Korean presidential compound, shootings in the DMZ, and the seizure of the USS *Pueblo* in January 1968. These extremely provocative actions ratcheted up tensions on the peninsula immeasurably and raised real concerns in the Soviet Union that Kim might entrap Moscow into another war on the peninsula. Recently released archives from East Germany and Hungary document how Soviet embassy officials met with Kim Il-sung in January and May 1968 and urged him to reduce tensions as "the socialist countries had already made use of the incident as much as possible, and now it was time to put an end to the crisis in order to prevent a dangerous confrontation."[4] The North Korean leader responded with a list of requests regarding aluminum shipments, special air route privileges, and accelerated construction of ongoing infrastructure and energy projects.[5] Pyongyang therefore shows no bias in either coercing allies or adversaries to the negotiating table.

Two observations about this DPRK strategy are relevant with regard to David Kang's argument. First, the coercive bargaining strategy is undoubtedly an extremely provocative and dangerous one which raises the risks of escalation; however, it is also a *rational* one if one views the status quo as unacceptable. Second, basic deterrence is a necessary but insufficient condition for maintaining peace on the peninsula. Deterrence is effective at preventing a second DPRK invasion, but it cannot prevent coercive bargaining behavior. Thus, for Kang to define the DPRK threat as largely invasion and to argue that such a threat has been neutralized by simple deterrence is an incomplete assessment of the problem. There are threats posed by the North short of military invasion; moreover, there are very rational reasons for the DPRK to instigate violence even if the central balance of power on the peninsula inclines against a realistic chance of DPRK military victory.

THE STATUS QUO AFTER SEPTEMBER 11

The likelihood that the North might instigate violent acts, I would argue, has probably increased in 2003.[6] The terrorist attacks of September 11, 2001 do not bode well for the North's situation. The reason for this assessment is not, as conventionally speculated, that the United States might focus on North Korea as "Phase III" of the war against terrorism after Central Asia and Iraq.[7] On the contrary, the corrosive effect of September 11 on the DPRK's situation is the relative *lack* of attention paid by the United States to the problem. In spite of President George Bush's designation of North Korea as part of an "axis of evil" regimes threatening the United States with weapons of mass destruction, the war against terrorism in Central Asia, homeland defense, and the war against Iraq have greatly obscured the previous preoccupation of American post–cold war security strategy with such states (formerly termed "rogue regimes"). This new priority ensures that the DPRK will encounter a period of stasis in relations with the United States. At worst, the terrorism priority might make the United States more openly hostile, but more likely, it will mean American ambivalence and reluctance to invest any time or resources into dealing with North Korea when there are bigger fish to fry.

At the same time that September 11 has taken the DPRK off the front-burner with Washington, Pyongyang's relations with Japan are going nowhere fast. Since the DPRK scoffed at earnest Japanese proposals for reconciling relations during failed normalization talks at the end of 2000, there has been no public support and even less impetus from the foreign policy establishment in Tokyo for new initiatives with the North.[8] Prime Minister Koizumi's summit in Pyongyang in 2002 with Kim Jong-il constituted an attempt to break out of the deadlock, but this was cut short by the groundswell of negative public sentiment following Kim's "confession" at the summit that some of the Japanese nationals abducted to North Korea had died, followed by the revelations of North Korea's secret uranium-enrichment nuclear weapons program (discussed in chapter 5). Moreover, at this point, any political capital the Japanese leadership might need to expend for new or unpopular policy proposals to improve relations with the DPRK is better spent on initiatives related to the war in Afghanistan, domestic economic reform, or Iraq, not North Korea. Prospects for an improvement in relations remain dim. A Japanese police raid of the pro-DPRK residents association (Chosen Soren) headquarters in 2001 for alleged illicit financial activities related to a local credit union collapse was a strong affront to DPRK sovereignty (the association serves as the de facto embassy for North Korea given the absence of diplomatic relations between Tokyo and Pyongyang).[9] Relations spiraled down even further in 2002 with a sea altercation involving a Japanese coast guard vessel sinking a North Korean spy ship that had been operating in Japan's 200-nautical mile exclusive economic zone. Most significant was the total support of the Japanese public and government for both actions, attesting to the absence of any palpable support for engaging North Korea in spite of Koizumi's diplomatic efforts.

The North's best hope remains the South Korean "sunshine" policy. President Roh Moo-hyun has steadfastly committed to continuing his predecessor's policy. But even here, the combination of a weak ROK economy, graft charges against Kim Daejung for "paying off" the North Koreans for the June 2000 summit, and Kim Jong-il's nuclear brinkmanship have undercut the strategy's credibility and made it very difficult for the ROK government to offer new carrots to the North (especially if these are perceived to be financed off the backs of South Korean taxpayers). To compound matters, poor harvests and a harsh winter ensure more severe food shortages in the North precisely when "donor fatigue" has set in vis-à-vis the DPRK after several consecutive years of World Food Program appeals and countries see more pressing cases for donation in Afghanistan.

Thus, a concatenation of forces after September 11 lead to a collective "neglect" of North Korea in 2002 after a prior period of two-to-three years when the North enjoyed the fruits of U.S. and ROK engagement (and coincidentally was noticeably more complacent). This results in a deterioration of the status quo for the DPRK and potentially a "losing" situation—precisely the conditions conducive to coercive acts of violence. Indeed, unexplained provocations by the DPRK in the aftermath of September 11 accord with this line of reasoning. The North engaged in a series of low-level provocations with DPRK patrol boats again violating the NLL with South Korea; DPRK troops firing unprovoked shots at ROK guard posts in the DMZ; a DPRK vessel provoking an exchange of fire with Japanese coast guard vessels; DPRK MiG fighters intercepting a U.S. intelligence plan in the Sea of Japan; sales of SCUD missiles to Yemen; and the importing of secondary materials for making nerve agents (October 2002 nuclear revelations are dealt with in chapter 5).[10] Why? This behavior appears puzzling only if one views the North—being rationally deterred from another invasion—as also being deterred from other violent acts short of all-out war. However, it is not at all puzzling if viewed as a symptom of a status quo perceived increasingly unfavorably by Pyongyang and one in which acts of violence are meant to coerce negotiations more to the North's favor.

THE DECLINE OF THE DPRK MILITARY

The second trend that contributes to the DPRK's propensity for violent acts is, ironically, the deterioration of its military capabilities in the 1990s. I agree with David Kang that the Korean People's Army (KPA) poses a less credible threat of conventional invasion, however, this does not rule out the possibility of coercive acts of violence. Indeed, it increases the likelihood of such acts given the North's current portfolio of military capabilities. Let me explain. Any who follow the security balance on the peninsula are familiar with the current profile of the KPA military threat: 1.1 million man army, 3,500 tanks, 2,500 armored personnel carriers, 10,600 artillery guns, 2,600 multiple rocket launchers, and 500+ combat aircraft all forward-deployed near the DMZ. But interesting insights can be drawn from a longitudinal analysis of the evolution (and devolution) of these forces. From the end of the Korean war until about the mid-1970s, the KPA threat was largely infantry and artillery-based. Heavy fixed artillery was the mainstay of the force (a lesson of the Korean war when artillery dominated the terms of battle) and KPA forces, while larger than in June 1950, were still only a fraction (400,000) of the 1.1 million benchmark associated with the threat today. While DPRK intentions were aggressive and desirous of unification by force (*songong t'ongil*), they did not have the capability to invade. They had neither the logistic requirements[11] nor the right composition of forces. Large amounts of artillery (protected from enemy ground assault by infantry) are good for defense but moving large amounts of artillery for deep offensive strikes is not easy. Thus, this period in the KPA's evolution potentially fits with Kang's argument about the illusory nature of the DPRK invasion threat.

During the 1980s, however, the story was quite different. Changes in DPRK military equipment, structure, and organization of the KPA signaled a more credible threat of offensive invasion. There were three aspects to this change. First, there was greater mechanization of the infantry, armored, and artillery forces. In addition, the KPA amassed significant amounts of self-propelled artillery to supplement the heavy artillery already held. These forces were then reorganized from divisions to corps-level formations.[12] Taken discretely or in combination, these measures suggested deliberate efforts at implementing an offensive doctrine. Mechanization, and in particular, the shift to corps-level formations under a single commander was necessary to sustain deep invasive attacks (separate divisions cannot sustain deep attacks because of attrition). Self-propelled artillery alone is not necessarily indicative of an offensive doctrine, but in combination with large amounts of heavy artillery bunkered down in defensive positions, these same forces become a tool of offensive maneuver. Finally, these new forces were all forward-deployed in the 1980s behind the first echelon of conventional deployments, posing a new mechanized, armored, and artillery dimension of the threat.[13]

The credible threat of invasion posed by the DPRK military in the 1980s slowly diminished in the 1990s. As a Defense Intelligence Agency study on DPRK conventional warfighting capabilities observed, "North Korea's capability to successfully conduct complex, multiechelon, large-scale operations to reunify the Korean Peninsula declined in the 1990s. This was, in large measure, the result of severe resource constraints, including widespread food and energy shortages."[14] Acute material constraints imposed by a sclerotic economy moved military modernization away from purchases of offensive equipment to three alternate areas: special operations forces; hardening forward deployed artillery positions; and asymmetric capabilities, in particular weapons of mass destruction.[15] The absence of paved roadways, limited east-west routes, a deteriorated railway system, and other infrastructural deficiencies also detracted from the threat.[16]

The deterioration of DPRK military capabilities in the 1990s has led many, including David Kang, to argue that the North no longer poses a threat. They do not have the capabilities now to carry out a successful invasion, Kang argues, and they are rationally deterred from contemplating such an act. I do not deny that the "default" position for the DPRK military today, given the unfavorable balance of military capabilities on the peninsula, may be some form of deterrence. Evidence in this vein is the North's hardening of forward artillery positions which could be interpreted as a strategy to hold Seoul hostage to deter any U.S.-ROK

action. Though plausible, this interpretation, however, completely overlooks another equally plausible interpretation. In other
words, everyone assumes simply that because the DPRK military
can no longer wage a successful invasion, it must therefore have
shifted to a deterrence and defense-oriented doctrine and away
from the offense orientation of the 1980s. This is an inference
based on very little concrete evidence (e.g., we see no moth-
balling of deteriorated equipment from the 1980s usable for an
offensive action).

Moreover, there has been no explicit change in military doctrine or in the basic principle that doing harm to the South is defined in DPRK interests (elaborated below). Military analysts
who study the balance of forces on the peninsula see a DPRK
military currently incapable of carrying out a replay of 1950-
type ground invasion, but still harboring significant capabilities
based on the boom years of the 1980s to inflict considerable
damage on Seoul. Given the current portfolio of capabilities
(and absent explicit evidence of a shift to a non-offensive doctrine), there exists a high propensity for the North's undertaking violent acts short of all-out war because it is the *only* effective military action the KPA could conceivably undertake. As
one analyst noted "North Korea could conceivably attempt . . .
a broad front attack, with only limited objectives, . . . what purpose it might have is not known, but the idea is possible."[17] Such
a scenario fits well with DPRK coercive bargaining behavior.
Pyongyang undertakes limited acts of violence whenever the status quo is deemed to be a losing situation. In this vein, a limited
but forceful frontal assault into the South aimed not at all-out
invasion, but at negotiating down from the crisis to the North's
advantage (would be the ultimate in DPRK coercive bargaining
behavior). Again such an act would not be based on winning militarily, but on arresting further losses. My point is not that this
is the only interpretation of the KPA's decrepit state since the
1990s, but it is one that is neglected and often overshadowed by
the popularized "new look deterrence" argument about the KPA
espoused by Kang.

THE HEART OF THE MATTER: INTENTIONS

At the heart of David Kang's and my debate on the wisdom of understanding North Korea is a fundamentally disparate interpretation of how much DPRK intentions have changed. Kang argues that these intentions have shifted in the direction of reform and away from revisionism (foreshadowing his arguments in chapter 4). At a minimum, he argues that the North's dire material condition in the post–cold war era, and its nonbelligerent behavior force nonbelievers to admit that such a change cannot be ruled out. I am more skeptical of the true degree of change in North Korean intentions. What Kang might point to as evidentiary DPRK efforts at interacting with the world community, I see as largely tactical actions aimed at improving the short-term situation, and not representative of a deeper, more fundamental change in intentions. I am not ideological about my skepticism. I am willing to be proved wrong about DPRK intentions, but as yet such evidence is not apparent in DPRK actions or statements.

These different views naturally inform the way we view, for example, the economic situation in North Korea and the prospects for engagement. Kang and others sympathetic to the North cite the baby steps made by Pyongyang in the economic arena (e.g., sending a delegation to the U.S. to study international contract law; or not cracking down on the black markets that have sprouted up on the Sino–North Korean border) as evidence of an inexorable push toward economic reform.[18] They argue that those obsessed with the military situation miss out on these important and real changes. These proponents therefore argue that economic engagement with the North is the answer. Economic carrots will "pacify" the reform-oriented regime by giving them what they want. The problem with this argument is again the distinction between tactics and intentions. Kang and his like are assuming that tactical actions represent true change in the North's intentions. Upon what basis is this assumption that economic carrots should be associated with reduced DPRK belligerence? Contrary to what engagers posit, if one looks at the history of North–South Korean

interaction, Pyongyang has been the most belligerent in its security behavior when it has been economically *strong*. In the 1960s
and 1970s, for example, DPRK provocations against the South
were at their highest (both in number and severity), and this was
when the North was equal to or superior to the South on economic terms (measured in terms of per capita GNP).

The counter-argument to my skepticism would be that history
for the North fundamentally changed after June 2000. That is,
the inter-Korean summit showed the genuine desire for engagement behind Kim Dae-jung's sunshine policy, and in particular
the South's move toward a policy of peaceful coexistence.[19] As a
result, Pyongyang's intentions in turn shifted away from belligerence and toward reform and regime stabilization. For this reason,
the consequences of encouraging economic growth in the North
are not nearly as dire as the skeptics posit.

At the risk of sounding like a broken record, the problem with
this counter-argument is again the lack of evidence. I would be
happy to agree with Kang on this interpretation if he could point
to real signs of a change in Pyongyang's intentions after the summit. In theory, what should one look for in terms of such evidence? Short of an outright statement by Kim Jong-il of his new
intentions (which is highly unlikely), there are ways of doing this.
Behavioral theories of social science tell us that a change in an actor's intentions generally requires an underlying change in the
principles and values that give rise to those intentions. If changes
in an actor's behavior do not correspond with a prior change in
values and principles, then this is merely a change of tactics, not a
deeper change in intentions. What is so interesting in this respect
is how distinguished scholars of North Korea (who presumably
know much more about the North's intentions than either Kang
or myself) argue that the basic principles and values by which the
North has lived since the establishment of the regime in 1948
have *not* changed. These are: 1) the DPRK is the true representative of the Korean people and the puppet regime in the South (a
military colony of the United States) is the ultimate threat to the
Korean people; 2) the people of South Korea (not the govern-

ment) would welcome unity with the North if not for the Americans and their puppets; therefore the DPRK should pursue united front tactics for revolution with sympathetic elements in South and divide the people from the government; and 3) ultimately, the North's position will win because it is the morally correct one and will gain the support of Koreans on both sides of the DMZ Hence, the regime is justified in dealing directly with the ROK leadership as a feasible tactic for unification.

Charles Armstrong, for example, argues that these principles established since 1948 have not changed. He sees them as the "theology" of the DPRK.[20] But if these continue to be the fundamental principles for the DPRK, even if they do not influence policy today (a point that North Korea scholars also assert), it is difficult to see how this theology is not relevant to unchanged intentions. Armstrong and others argue that such principles are recessed because of the economic hardships faced by the regime today. However, if the DPRK adheres to the same revolutionary "theology," but does not openly live by them today for material reasons, then: 1) once the material factors that cause the repression of principles are gone (i.e., attaining economic stabilization), then DPRK behavior can be dictated again by these revolutionary principles; moreover, 2) any apparent accommodating behavior we see today from North Korea is a function of tactics rather than intentions (i.e. principle #3—tactical opening to the ROK is acceptable). Put another way, my beliefs and values as a Christian may not influence my behavior in every situation, but in the end these values are critical to how I view the world and the fundamental choices I make in it. To argue that a deeply held set of revolutionary beliefs and values in North Korea may temporarily fail to inform current behavior is also to argue that the basic intentions of the DPRK have not changed.

Unfortunately the history of North Korean peace initiatives provides little evidence of more than purely tactical motivations. In what Nicholas Eberstadt has described as the height of DPRK "strategic deception" on the eve of the Korean war in 1950, Pyongyang put forth a major peace initiative largely to distract the

South. Recently released GDR archives of letters and memoranda of conversation between East German and North Korean officials show with bitter clarity that North Korea's motivation in the historic July 4, 1972 North-South joint communiqué aimed at reducing tensions on the peninsula was purely tactical and not linked to a deeper desire to seek a peaceful solution to the division. The archives show that the DPRK ambassador to East Berlin, Lee Chang-su, explained the peace initiative as designed to increase pressure on U.S. military forces to leave the peninsula, as well as reduce Japanese influence. This was a decision decided at a November 1971 meeting of the Korean Workers' Party.[21] The breakthrough summit between Kim Jong-il and Japanese Prime Minister Koizumi in September 2002 is often pointed to by David Kang and others as strong evidence of a shift in North Korea's fundamental views on the world, seeking a new relationship with a historically demonized state in North Korean history and propaganda. Maybe so. Unfortunately, there is also a proximate tactical explanation for Kim's actions: Food. The summit came at a time when WFP appeals for international donations to North Korea had fallen off from the previous year. Which country had been one of the largest donors in 2001 that then zeroed out their donations in 2002? You guessed it: Japan.

Kang's other argument is that North Korea, although seeking reform and integration, still engages in belligerent behavior because of basic insecurity. They fear the growing disparity in the balance of forces on the peninsula in favor of the United States and the ROK. They fear a "Yugoslavian-type aggression" against their homeland and that they may be next on the U.S. unipolar "hit list" after Iraq. As Kang argues in chapter 2, "Even paranoiacs have enemies. . . . The U.S. *is* hostile to Pyongyang . . . [the North Koreans] know very well that the ultimate U.S. goal is the transformation or even obliteration of their way of life . . . "

There is no denying that for a small country like North Korea, the presence of U.S. power on its border must seem awesomely threatening. At the same time though, the North still holds a very credible conventional deterrent with its artillery and ballistic missile threat. The warning time for a North Korean artillery shell to hit Seoul is 57 seconds, and for a ballistic missile on Japan is 10 minutes. At present, there is no entirely effective means of defending against either of these threats. The cost in lives could be in the range of one million. The cost in damages in the range of one trillion dollars. This is the reality of North Korea's deterrent. It seems credible enough, assuming the United States still values the lives of its troops, expatriate community, and allies.

The best argument that David Kang and North Korean apologists can offer is the "waiting and reform" thesis. This view argues that the North is currently in a muddle-through mode—it is basically living day by day, doing what it can to survive and to maintain stability. It is benefiting from the strategic calculations made in China, the United States, South Korea, and Japan that a regime collapse carries too many uncertainties and costs. Hence Pyongyang survives from the food aid, fuel, and other goods provided by these powers.[22] In this view, there is no longer-term objective for the North aside from waiting and reform; indeed, this view remains agnostic on the question of whether or not DPRK accommodating behavior reflects a shift away from traditional revisionist intentions. In short, behavior is less aggressive largely because the regime has neither the time nor the resources to contemplate such fantasies in the face of real material hardships.

This explanation of DPRK behavior is more reasonable than others offered by the apologists in the sense that it avoids heroic (yet unproven) claims that underlying DPRK intentions have changed fundamentally for the better. But the implications of this view are no less troubling. If Pyongyang has indeed chosen the "wait and reform" path, one is hard pressed to understand where this path ultimately leads. As has been the case with all other closed regimes that tried to open up in the post–cold war era, North Korea faces a fundamental reform dilemma—it needs to reform in order to survive, but in the process of opening up, it unleashes the forces that ultimately lead to the regime's demise.[23] So it is incumbent upon David Kang and others who advocate the "wait and reform" thesis to explain how Pyongyang sees itself circumventing this dilemma. I believe history works against the North in this regard, and that the "wait and reform" thesis actually validates my own view about what is dangerous about North Korea. If Kim Jong-il is muddling through and seeking some short-term reform, but in the end realizes that the reform dilemma faced by Romania, East Germany, and others is inescapable, this leaves him and his country in a situation where the status quo truly is unacceptable. And if the present situation is so unbearable and inescapable, this raises the incentive to lash out in a limited, crisis-inducing fashion with the hope of negotiating a new and better situation. The notion that the North may be in "wait and reform" mode does not make me comfortable at all.

"HAWK ENGAGEMENT"

My assessment of the North Korean threat and Kim Jong-il's unchanged intentions adheres to a more hawkish line of reasoning than David Kang's. Despite what readers might expect, this does NOT mean that I advocate a policy of hardline isolation and containment to deal with the North. On the contrary, I believe that engagement still remains the most advisable policy (the extent to which the 2003 nuclear crisis changes my policy recommendations and commanding rationales of the model follow in chapter 5). The reasoning is simple: 1) the primary threat posed by North Korea is no longer invasion (as they are rationally deterred), but other forms of violence short of all-out war; 2) the likelihood of the North provoking such violence is highest when Kim Jong-il deems the status quo a losing situation (in the hopes of negotiating down from the induced crisis to a more favorable position); THEN 3) coercion or isolation strategies that focus on threats and intimidation only exacerbate the North's incentive to lash out by expanding the North's window of vulnerability, pushing the leadership further into framing the status quo in the domain of losses, and raising the costs of peace. On the other hand, engagement (i.e., containment-plus-engagement) ameliorates North Korean desperation. While maintaining necessary deterrent measures, it lengthens time horizons, reduces the threat of imminent attack, reduce the costs of the status quo, and can help change Pyongyang's frame of reference.

What is so deceiving and at the same time ironic about this policy conclusion is that it runs contrary to the lessons of the cold war. Containment and isolation were very effective throughout the cold war at deterring a second North Korean invasion (not to mention defeating the Soviet Union!). For this reason, people reflexively assume that continuing along these same lines is the antidote for the North Korean threat today. After all, if it worked with the Soviet behemoth, it should work with a puny country like North Korea. Although this strategy is correct when dealing with the threat of invasion, it overlooks, as I have argued, the additional threat posed by a regime that increasingly sees itself in a box with no good options and could lash out as a result of this. The irony is that what worked so well during the cold war to prevent violence and loss of lives on the peninsula may now have the reverse effect. Containment-plus-isolation or containment-plus-coercion only increases North Korea's rational incentives for hostility without victory. Conditional engagement, on the other hand, will carry its own risks and moral hazard in terms of unrequited cooperation by Pyongyang, but these are far less than the costs that would be incurred by a coercion/isolation strategy that backfired and led to war.

BUSH'S POLICY TOWARD NORTH KOREA

I believe elements of this hawk engagement rationale lay behind the first two years of the Bush administration's seemingly innocuous policy on North Korea. Prior to the administration's shift to a harder line following the October 2002 revelations of North Korea's violations of the Agreed Framework (chapter 5), the one major policy review on North Korea, in June 2001, concluded that engagement was the appropriate policy to undertake. The tremendous attention given to Bush's "axis of evil" statement, his personal "loathing" of Kim Jong-il, and his skepticism of the sunshine policy overshadowed a string of consistent statements and assurances at lower levels of policy implementation that the United States would pursue some form of engagement with North Korea; that it was willing to undertake a "bold" initiative on the peninsula to address both Washington and Pyongyang's concerns; and that it was willing to meet with the North Koreans without precondition. Compared with the effusive advances to North Korea by the Clinton administration, media mistook Bush's tough posturing as a dramatic shift in policy, but the policy predisposition for engagement remained. How was this possible when the group in power had so little faith in North Korea's true intentions to reform? In the words of Deputy Secretary of State Richard Armitage, engagement seizes the initiative in negotiations with the DPRK rather than "responding as Pyongyang acts as demandeur."[24]

The added motive for taking the initiative through engagement was to counteract the DPRK's coercive bargaining behavior. As noted earlier, Pyongyang's provocations were very effective at manipulating past administrations in Washington, Seoul, and Tokyo into the awkward position of wanting to respond punitively to DPRK misbehavior, but being forced into negotiations to minimize the risks of a costly larger conflict. From Pyongyang's perspective, a new status quo more favorable to the North eventuated from this coercive bargaining process. In this context, the ulterior purpose of hawk engagement is to counteract this dangerous and destabilizing behavior. If Pyongyang's bad behavior is motivated by a status quo deemed unacceptable, then engagement's purpose is to give the regime a stake in the status quo. In short, the North becomes less likely to leverage the current situation if they have something to lose.

WHY HAWK ENGAGEMENT

In the end, the normative arguments against engagement are most compelling. The North Korean regime and its practices are anathema to nearly every civilized value. The starving of children; the relative deprivation that forces farmers to sell their daughters for Chinese cattle; the physical handicaps that a generation of youth will bear due to a basic lack of nutrition and medicine all occur while the political regime and military survive in relative splendor.[25] Eberstadt's demographic studies have shown that the average North Korean seven-year-old is eight inches shorter and 22 pounds lighter than her South Korean counterpart.[26] Moreover, engagement creates the worst combination of moral hazard and demonstration effects—sending the wrong message to North Korean hardliners' that the West is weak, and giving incentives to others to try similar things. As critics argue engagement, rather than transforming rogue regimes, only reinforces their convictions to remain "rogue."

Undoubtedly, seeking accommodation with rogue regimes is morally unappealing. In a sense, the choices were more clear and less difficult during the cold war when the fight for Western values intersected with the fight against the adversary. But the cold war is over. Regimes such as North Korea's should be regarded not as moral deviants to be reprimanded, but as security problems that need to be solved.[27] There are many who cannot accept this and would be even willing to risk war as the price of a more "moral" foreign policy. However, if the objective is achieving peaceful change, and solving (rather than fighting) the security problem, then the issue becomes one of explaining how engagement can be an acceptable alternative even to hawks in favor of isolation or coercion. Fortunately there are at least five reasons in support of such a stance.

First, engagement should be the desired strategy for hawks because this is the best practical way to build a coalition for punishment tomorrow. A necessary precondition for coercing North Korea is the formation of a regional consensus that every opportunity to resolve the problem in a nonconfrontational manner has been exhausted. Without this consensus, implementing any form of coercion that actually puts pressure on the regime is unworkable. In 1994, there was resistance not only from China (who could veto a resolution for sanctions in the Security Council), but also from the U.S. allies (i.e., Japan, which was reluctant to curb remittances to the North from resident North Korean organizations) about proceeding prematurely to a sanctions policy.

Similarly, prior to the North's 2002 violation of the Agreed Framework, the Bush administration's contemplation of unilaterally revising or abandoning the Framework would have elicited little consensus for punitive action. On the other hand, pursuing engagement—the endgame of which would be to put the onus for taking any last chance for cooperation on North Korea—is the most effective way to build a coalition for punishment. In this sense, many of the criticisms of the Agreed Framework at the outset of the Bush administration's policy review on North Korea were misplaced. Among other cited problems, critics argued that the Framework was an open-ended appeasement policy that rewarded bad behavior, assumed (rather than verified) cooperative DPRK intentions, and lacked any clear "exit" strategy. In fact, U.S.-ROK-Japan good-faith efforts at implementing the Agreed Framework were building the coalition for punishment if the North did not hold up its end of the agreement.[28] Such reasoning was reflected in a 1999 North Korea policy review led by now-Deputy Secretary of State Richard Armitage: "Diplomacy strengthens the ability to build and sustain a coalition if North Korea does not cooperate. . . . The failure of enhanced diplomacy should be demonstrably attributable to Pyongyang."[29] Indeed, when the North was found in 2002–3 to be developing secret uranium-enrichment facilities in violation of the Framework, the United States was in a very strong position to call for the suspension of the Framework's heavy fuel oil deliveries to which even sunshine policy-advocate Kim Dae-jung had to agree. Rather than being devoid of an exit strategy, engagement and the Agreed Framework, in effect, *are* part of the exit strategy.

Second, today's carrots are tomorrow's most effective sticks. Sticks only work if North Korea has a stake in the status quo. When the North is in the domain of losses, then brandishing more sticks becomes futile. For example, continuing to impose

TABLE 3.1 Principal U.S. Sanctions Policy on North Korea

TYPE	TERMS	COMMENTS
Trading with the Enemy Act	Total embargo on US trade and financial relations with the DPRK	Imposed in 1950 Can be removed or modified by legislation or by executive action.
Trade Act of 1974	Denial of most-favored-nation status to the DPRK	Jackson-Vanik amendment requires compliance with freedom-of-emigration
GSP and OPIC Denials	DPRK denied status as a beneficiary developing country (BDC)	BDC status would allow DPRK exports duty-free Investors not allowed to use Overseas Private Investment Corporation for insuring investments in DPRK
Terrorism	Denies Export-Import Bank credit facilities to states designated as terrorist supporters	DPRK designated as state in 1988 President can waive after consultations with Congress

Source: Zachary Davis, "Korea: Procedural and Jurisdictional Questions Regarding Possible Normalization of Relations with North Korea," *Congressional Research Service*, Library of Congress, November 29, 1994; and Morton Abramowitz and James Laney, *Managing Change on the Korean Peninsula* New York: Council on Foreign Relations, 1998), pp. 25–26.

Clinton relaxed sanctions making exceptions for telecommunications, humanitarian trade of minerals, and financial transactions related to implementation of the Agreed Framework.

June 2000. US relaxed sanctions on a wide range of trade in commercial and consumer goods, eased restrictions on investment, and eliminated prohibition on direct personal and commercial financial transactions.

June 2001. Bush imposed sanctions on the DPRK under the Iran Nonproliferation Act 2000 for DPRK secondary transfers of missile components to Iran.

the half-century of sanctions listed in table 3.1 is unlikely to elicit a positive change in behavior.

However, lifting sanctions, letting the North gain what little it can from new opportunities thus made available, and then using the possibility of reinstating sanctions as a potential stick later, is more likely to elicit changes in behavior. The idea would be to push Pyongyang into the domain of gains first for sticks to work. If they have a stake in the status quo—something they cannot lose—threats of punishment become effective.

This dynamic could explain DPRK behavior on the detainment of an ROK tourist in June 1999 on alleged spy charges. The ROK retaliated by suspending further Kumgang mountain tours. The tours conducted by Hyundai represented a new and substantial source of hard currency for the North which was hardly worth losing over the propaganda value of capturing a South Korean "spy." The DPRK promptly released the tourist almost sheepishly after coercing a written confession. In this sense, the Hyundai tour, formerly the "carrot," was also an effective "stick" in influencing North Korean behavior.

Third, conditional engagement is probably better than coercion at creating fissures among the DPRK regime elites. American policies of containment and outright hostility give the regime in Pyongyang and its people—despite their reliance on outside aid givers including the United States—an unambiguous symbol around which to muster full support. Conditional engagement is more ambiguous. It confuses the target state's elite by challenging preconceived notions about the "evil" Americans, and raises internal debates as to whether the engager's intentions are genuine or duplicitous. These debates in turn can create or exacerbate traditionalist/reformist, party/military, or generational leadership divisions, contributing to possible elite clashes or coup attempts that might precipitate the regime's crumbling from the top.

Fourth, rather than prolonging the rogue regime's existence (as commonly argued by the critic), engagement can hasten its demise. As noted above, North Korea faces the same reform dilemma of other illiberal regimes in the post–cold war era: They need to open up to survive, but the process of opening up unleashes forces that ultimately lead to their demise. In this sense, engagement mechanisms like the Agreed Framework, inter-Korean trade, tourism and investment bring into play the institutional and nongovernmental influences that nudge the North down the slippery slope of political reform. Anathema to the hawk, this strategy results in an interim improvement in the North's economic situation, but very much in line with the hawk's preferences, it also spawns the conditions for upheaval from below. As history has shown, revolutions and regime instability in downtrodden states are most likely to occur not when conditions are at their worst, but when they begin to improve.

Fifth, should the hawk seek destruction of the North, engagement strategies offer better preparation for such an event. Proponents of cold war-era containment-plus-isolation would fixate on discouraging and, if necessary, repelling a northern invasion, but they never really considered what to do after the North was defeated. Containment-plus-isolation was therefore a status quo policy that maintained the opaqueness of the DPRK regime and applied a simple but intimidating logic to tame it. Engagement on the other hand compels more proactive thinking about unification. It does not just black-box the North Korean state as isolation strategies do; rather it promotes dialogue and information exchanges to increase transparency and reduce the eventual start-up costs of unification. The institutional ties between the two governments and economic development that grow out of engagement also help ease the costs of any future absorption process.

WHITHER THE CRITICS? HUMAN RIGHTS AND MISSILE DEFENSE

Many of the rationales for hawk engagement are plainly intuitive and factored into the Bush policy review's conclusion in June 2001 to resume a process of engagement with the DPRK. Yet hawk engagement might face criticism on two counts. From the hard left, many human rights activists would criticize engagement because it does not address the true victim—the North Korean people.[30] From the hard right, critics would dismiss engagement as neither credible nor feasible because of the Bush administration's emphasis on missile defense and the need to maintain the DPRK as the "poster child" for missile defense systems.

Many on the left see the DPRK problem in elegant and simple terms: end the regime, save the people. Non-dialogue and hostility might therefore be preferred by this group as the most direct route to absorbing the North, but this overlooks the most important factor in the success of an absorption exercise—the North Korean population. The conventional wisdom is that after the evil DPRK regime is gone, northerners will view southerners as their saviors and elder brethren. This overly optimistic view underestimates the degree of enmity, non-contact, distrust, and bloodshed between the two regimes, a situation that does not augur well for social integration. If this is at all hard to fathom as a reaction by northerners, just imagine how confident a southerner would feel about being absorbed under the "good graces" of a united North Korean government.[31] A policy of hardline coercion and isolation that drove the Pyongyang leadership into the ground, would also have the effect of alienating and frightening the northern populace, reinforcing decades of DPRK demonization of the United States and ROK. Engagement, by contrast, might convey a more compassionate image of Americans and South Koreans to northerners. As President Bush stated during his summit trip to Seoul in February 2002, though he considered Kim Jong-il evil and despicable, "Our nation provides more food to the North Korean people than any nation in the world. We are averaging nearly 300,000 tons of food a year. . . . And so, obviously, my comments about [North Korea as] evil was toward a regime, toward a government—not toward the North Korean people. We have great sympathy and empathy for the North Korean people. We want them to have food. And at the same time, we want them to have freedom."[32] Engagement in the form of food aid, for example, would mean empty sacks of food scattered around North Korea imprinted with "USA,"

"ROK," and "GOJ" (Government of Japan) would start the process of unraveling half a century of negative indoctrination in the North, and would lay the foundation for the Southern polity and people to emerge as a credible patron of popular northern loyalty after the DPRK state collapses. Coercion may be more attractive to the hawk's dream of northern capitulation, but engagement better equips the hawk for her desired objective.

The Bush administration's unswerving enthusiasm for pressing forward with national and theater missile defense systems (MD), conservative critics argue, are wholly at odds with an engagement policy with North Korea. MD proponents have held out Pyongyang's rogue ballistic missile threat as one of the primary rationales for the system. How can an administration therefore coherently pursue engagement and missile defense simultaneously?

MD advocates respond by proclaiming that their enthusiasm would be unchanged by the disappearance of the DPRK missile threat. Ther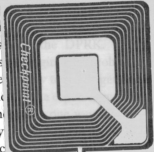le defense can actually strengthen th r success of engagement strategies vis ment is most effective when it (1) is nse capabilities and (2) communicate gagement is a choice of the strong and eak. Supporting missile defense is, th an enhanced engagement strategy ch a strategy would remain firmly c gagement pushing Pyongyang further into the domain of gains, but it would also neutralize the one most likely avenue of coercive bargaining by the DPRK, i.e., the missile threat.

There are numerous subissues here related to the type of system that might best handle the DPRK missile threat with the least negative consequences (e.g., midcourse interceptor versus boost phase interceptor systems versus anti-missile barges in the Sea of Japan). But the point is that the conversations on missile defense and engagement strategies on North Korea should be linked. Deploying MD systems alone as a stopgap measure against the North at best deals imperfectly with the missile threat but does little else to resolve the peninsula's tensions. Utilizing engagement to get at the deeper problem of transforming DPRK preferences and intentions is always subject to future acts of brinkmanship. The dilemma is apparent in the DPRK's moratorium on missile tests. Negotiated in 1999 in exchange for an additional lifting of some U.S. economic sanctions, one could see the outcome as the fruit of a successful engagement strategy. But what is to prevent the North from trying to coerce in the future using the threat of rescinding its moratorium? Very little.

Linking the MD and engagement conversations is, perhaps, the answer. Missile defense can make for an enhanced engagement strategy by the Bush administration. In combination with transparent and proactive engagement efforts by the United States, Japan, and the ROK, missile defense (at least lower-tier systems supported by the ROK on the peninsula) at once can give strength, credibility, and insurance to engagement. It distinguishes engagement as a policy of the strong—one that cannot possibly be interpreted as appeasement or capitulation by Pyongyang or domestic critics in Washington and Seoul. At the same time, it avoids the potential pitfalls of non-dialogue strategies which do little to solve proliferation problems presented by the regime. The success of engagement is not premised solely on conciliation but on a mix of conciliation and strength. Missile defense enhances engagement rather than undercutting or contradicting it.

WHITHER COERCION?

The argument laid out in this chapter has clear implications for future policy. First, if engagement is not an open-ended policy that places blind faith in the DPRK's ability to reform but instead constitutes an exit strategy that builds a coalition for punishment, then one can anticipate U.S. efforts at speeding up the engagement process. It is often forgotten that before the 2003 nuclear crisis, Pyongyang was rejecting U.S. offers to resume talks on the grounds that it was unilaterally setting the agenda; however, if a to open up to survive, but the process of opening up unleashes forces that ultimately lead to their demise. In this sense, engagement mechanisms like the Agreed Framework, inter-Korean trade, tourism and investment bring into play the institutional and nongovernmental influences that nudge the North down the slippery slope of political reform. Anathema to the hawk, this strategy results in an interim improvement in the North's economic situation, but very much in line with the hawk's preferences, it also spawns the conditions for upheaval from below. As history has shown, revolutions and regime instability in downtrodden states are most likely to occur not when conditions are at their worst, but when they begin to improve.

Fifth, should the hawk seek destruction of the North, engagement strategies offer better preparation for such an event. Proponents of cold war-era containment-plus-isolation would fixate on discouraging and, if necessary, repelling a northern invasion, but they never really considered what to do after the North was defeated. Containment-plus-isolation was therefore a status quo policy that maintained the opaqueness of the DPRK regime and applied a simple but intimidating logic to tame it. Engagement on the other hand compels more proactive thinking about unification. It does not just black-box the North Korean state as isolation strategies do; rather it promotes dialogue and information exchanges to increase transparency and reduce the eventual start-up costs of unification. The institutional ties between the two governments and economic development that grow out of engagement also help ease the costs of any future absorption process.

WHITHER THE CRITICS? HUMAN RIGHTS AND MISSILE DEFENSE

Many of the rationales for hawk engagement are plainly intuitive and factored into the Bush policy review's conclusion in June 2001 to resume a process of engagement with the DPRK. Yet hawk engagement might face criticism on two counts. From the hard left, many human rights activists would criticize engagement because it does not address the true victim—the North Korean people.[30] From the hard right, critics would dismiss engagement as neither credible nor feasible because of the Bush administration's emphasis on missile defense and the need to maintain the DPRK as the "poster child" for missile defense systems.

Many on the left see the DPRK problem in elegant and simple terms: end the regime, save the people. Non-dialogue and hostility might therefore be preferred by this group as the most direct route to absorbing the North, but this overlooks the most important factor in the success of an absorption exercise—the North Korean population. The conventional wisdom is that after the evil DPRK regime is gone, northerners will view southerners as their saviors and elder brethren. This overly optimistic view underestimates the degree of enmity, non-contact, distrust, and bloodshed between the two regimes, a situation that does not augur well for social integration. If this is at all hard to fathom as a reaction by northerners, just imagine how confident a southerner would feel about being absorbed under the "good graces" of a united North Korean government.[31] A policy of hardline coercion and isolation that drove the Pyongyang leadership into the ground, would also have the effect of alienating and frightening the northern populace, reinforcing decades of DPRK demonization of the United States and ROK. Engagement, by contrast, might convey a more compassionate image of Americans and South Koreans to northerners. As President Bush stated during his summit trip to Seoul in February 2002, though he considered Kim Jong-il evil and despicable, "Our nation provides more food to the North Korean people than any nation in the world. We are averaging nearly 300,000 tons of food a year.... And so, obviously, my comments about [North Korea as] evil was toward a regime, toward a government—not toward the North Korean people. We have great sympathy and empathy for the North Korean people. We want them to have food. And at the same time, we want them to have freedom."[32] Engagement in the form of food aid, for example, would mean empty sacks of food scattered around North Korea imprinted with "USA,"

"ROK," and "GOJ" (Government of Japan) would start the process of unraveling half a century of negative indoctrination in the North, and would lay the foundation for the Southern polity and people to emerge as a credible patron of popular northern loyalty after the DPRK state collapses. Coercion may be more attractive to the hawk's dream of northern capitulation, but engagement better equips the hawk for her desired objective.

The Bush administration's unswerving enthusiasm for pressing forward with national and theater missile defense systems (MD), conservative critics argue, are wholly at odds with an engagement policy with North Korea. MD proponents have held out Pyongyang's rogue ballistic missile threat as one of the primary rationales for the system. How can an administration therefore coherently pursue engagement and missile defense simultaneously?

MD advocates respond by proclaiming that their enthusiasm would be unchanged by the disappearance of the DPRK missile threat. There is a better answer. Missile defense can actually strengthen the credibility and potential for success of engagement strategies vis-à-vis the DPRK. Engagement is most effective when it (1) is undergirded by robust defense capabilities and (2) communicates clearly to the target that engagement is a choice of the strong and not the expediency of the weak. Supporting missile defense is, therefore, one way of effecting an enhanced engagement strategy on the Korean peninsula. Such a strategy would remain firmly committed to the path of engagement pushing Pyongyang further into the domain of gains, but it would also neutralize the one most likely avenue of coercive bargaining by the DPRK, i.e., the missile threat.

There are numerous subissues here related to the type of system that might best handle the DPRK missile threat with the least negative consequences (e.g., midcourse interceptor versus boost phase interceptor systems versus anti-missile barges in the Sea of Japan). But the point is that the conversations on missile defense and engagement strategies on North Korea should be linked. Deploying MD systems alone as a stopgap measure against the North at best deals imperfectly with the missile threat but does little else to resolve the peninsula's tensions. Utilizing engagement to get at the deeper problem of transforming DPRK preferences and intentions is always subject to future acts of brinkmanship. The dilemma is apparent in the DPRK's moratorium on missile tests. Negotiated in 1999 in exchange for an additional lifting of some U.S. economic sanctions, one could see the outcome as the fruit of a successful engagement strategy. But what is to prevent the North from trying to coerce in the future using the threat of rescinding its moratorium? Very little.

Linking the MD and engagement conversations is, perhaps, the answer. Missile defense can make for an enhanced engagement strategy by the Bush administration. In combination with transparent and proactive engagement efforts by the United States, Japan, and the ROK, missile defense (at least lower-tier systems supported by the ROK on the peninsula) at once can give strength, credibility, and insurance to engagement. It distinguishes engagement as a policy of the strong—one that cannot possibly be interpreted as appeasement or capitulation by Pyongyang or domestic critics in Washington and Seoul. At the same time, it avoids the potential pitfalls of non-dialogue strategies which do little to solve proliferation problems presented by the regime. The success of engagement is not premised solely on conciliation but on a mix of conciliation and strength. Missile defense enhances engagement rather than undercutting or contradicting it.

WHITHER COERCION?

The argument laid out in this chapter has clear implications for future policy. First, if engagement is not an open-ended policy that places blind faith in the DPRK's ability to reform but instead constitutes an exit strategy that builds a coalition for punishment, then one can anticipate U.S. efforts at speeding up the engagement process. It is often forgotten that before the 2003 nuclear crisis, Pyongyang was rejecting U.S. offers to resume talks on the grounds that it was unilaterally setting the agenda; however, if a

U.S.-DPRK agenda is ever agreed upon and negotiations begin, then one can anticipate the U.S. side pushing for shorter (rather than longer) timelines. The reason has largely to do with the basic assumptions behind hawk engagement. If one believes, as South Korea's "sunshine" policy does, that the North will eventually turn benign as a result of food aid, economic transactions, and normalized relations offered to it by the rest of the world, then time is on our side. However, if one has less faith in this outcome and sees engagement as an instrument to reveal the DPRK's true, unchanged intentions, then "outing" the DPRK sooner rather than later is in U.S. nonproliferation interests. The premium on time was clearly expressed in President Bush's January 2002 State of the Union speech with regard to Iran, Iraq, and North Korea: "States like these, and their terrorist allies, constitute an axis of evil, arming to threaten the peace of the world. By seeking weapons of mass destruction, these regimes pose a grave and growing danger. . . . In any of these cases, the price of indifference would be catastrophic. . . . [T]ime is not on our side. I will not wait on events, while dangers gather. I will not stand by, as peril draws closer and closer."[33]

Second, if the DPRK reverts to brinkmanship tactics and bad "attention-inducing" behavior, then the likely American response will be a punitive one.[34] While the ROK sunshine policy emphasizes patience and allows for unrequited cooperation by the target state, the hawkish brand of engagement will be much less likely to tolerate bad DPRK behavior. If the Perry and Armitage Korea policy views each recommended an alternate coercive path to engagement, then hawks are less likely to give Pyongyang the benefit of the doubt on any questionable behavior and will shift with greater alacrity to the alternate path. Some may see this as finally giving U.S. policy some backbone. Others may see this as unnecessarily raising the risks of escalation. Yet this is the nature of hawk engagement.

Third, if engagement fails to elicit changes in North Korean behavior toward peaceful reform and nonproliferation, then one can posit a range of coercive options for the United States and its allies to pursue against the DPRK regime. None of these paths is desirable, but they comprise the endgame of hawk engagement. At the least desirable end of the spectrum is "true coercion": The policy imperative is to show the North's intention to proliferate despite the carrots offered to it; make clear to allies and regional powers that the U.S. exhausted all efforts at cooperation; and rally the coalition to coerce the regime through force and economic sanctions into nonproliferation compliance and/or regime collapse. Military responses might include preemptive action, massive retaliatory strikes (in response to a DPRK missile launch or artillery barrage), food distribution centers off DPRK shores and borders, and guarantees of safe havens for refugees. Implicit in this view is the conviction that early unification of the peninsula should be viewed as an investment in the future and not solely in terms of its daunting costs.

A more desirable albeit less likely option is to "stand down" the North Koreans: The imperative here is to utilize engagement to "out" the regime and then disarm them with a strong show of American and allied resolve. While the "coercion" option includes regime termination, this course of action does not rule out the DPRK state's continued decrepit existence minus the proliferation threat. Implicit in this view is the belief that war is not the likely outcome of engagement's failure because Pyongyang will concede before this point.[35] The stand-them-down option, although more desirable because it avoids war, is also unrealistic as the North is not likely to be passive if it has nothing to lose.

This leaves the third option of "malign neglect" to isolate and contain the regime: Once engagement has been proven a failure, this strategy rallies the United States and its allies to maintain vigilant containment of the regime's military threat and its WMD and missile proliferation. As will be discussed in chapter 5, this would mean an effective quarantine on arms and other transfers in and out of the North. Washington, Seoul, and Tokyo would guarantee safe haven for all DPRK refugees and would offer financial incentives to Russia and China to do the same. The United States and ROK might also undertake a reorientation of their military posture on the peninsula, focusing more on long-range, deep-strike capabilities to force the DPRK to scale back forward deployments in defense of Pyongyang.[36]

For the DPRK, if it is truly intent on improving relations with the United States and avoiding the scenarios above, then the burden of proof is on Pyongyang to provide quid pro quos in the future that prove hawk skeptics wrong. Pyongyang can ask for a lot in return, but the point is they must ante up real rather than potential quids. Hawks are not impressed with what sunshine policy advocates point to as the fruits of engagement because the North has thus far not conceded things they truly value. Arguably the U.S.-DPRK missile negotiations at the end of 2000 entailed "potential" rather than real North Korean quids for U.S. compensation (i.e., potential IRBM missile exports, production, and testing, but not existing deployments of No-dong missiles). In addition, Pyongyang's signing on to U.N. anti-terrorism conventions (one of which prohibits financing) in the aftermath of the September 11 terrorist attacks did not convince the skeptics. Hawks saw this as a costless gesture motivated more by situational imperatives rather than genuine dispositional desires. As quids, they mean little to the North and therefore provide no credible indicator of DPRK intentions to engage. Arguably this mindset explains the Bush administration's early inclusion of conventional military force reductions on the U.S.-DPRK agenda. Given relatively less attention in either the 1994 Agreed Framework or the 1999 Perry review, the DPRK's forward-deployed forces—artillery and other systems—are the heart of the North's military posture and therefore represent quids it truly values.

Japan and the ROK must make clear the imperative to the DPRK to move beyond smile summitry. Seoul can do so in the secret talks it conducts with Pyongyang. Tokyo can help expedite processes of engagement, the outcome of which would either validate or undercut hawkish skepticism about the North. Providing technical assistance in IAEA inspections in North Korea would be a step in this direction. Finally, it is incumbent on the trilateral coordination process among Seoul, Tokyo, and Washington to get a sense of what the American "red line" is on DPRK bad behavior. Agreement on this not only prepares a coalition for punitive action (if necessary), but also makes engagement more credible.

FIT POLICIES TO THREATS, NOT THREATS TO POLICIES

The policy imperative regarding North Korea is to be wary of cold war hangover. The Korean Peninsula is one of the last bastions of the bipolar conflict, but the internal and external circumstances surrounding the two regimes have changed dramatically since 1950. In spite of this, there is a stickiness inherent in decades of cold war thinking. Policymakers in Washington and Seoul fall into the trap of adhering to familiar policy templates and then, rather than reassessing the nature of the North Korean threat, they simply assume that the threat continues to fit with these templates. Fitting threats to policies rather than policies to threats in this manner is dangerous because the successful strategy that brought peace in one era could bring the opposite result in another.

In the case of Korea, the most prudent strategy is one that adheres to a preventive defense logic of engagement. That is, policy should be directed at preventing situations in which the DPRK perceives the status quo as unbearable and therefore sees belligerence and coercive bargaining as the rational option even if there is little hope of victory. Isolation or coercion only exacerbates the North's "double-or-nothing" motives for striking first. Engagement, on the other hand, reduces such incentives by giving Pyongyang a stake in the status quo and raising the benefits of peace (while maintaining robust deterrence capabilities). The preventive defense logic of engagement does not assume that DPRK preferences have changed toward peace. Engagement offers the DPRK opportunities to prove to the world that it seeks integration; but if this fails, the United States, the ROK, and Japan, through these failed entreaties are also tacitly building the coalition for punishment. In this sense, engagement does not operate without a net. It is the exit strategy.

DAVID KANG

WHY ARE WE AFRAID OF ENGAGEMENT?

4

North Korea is a repressive and brutal regime. Everyone would like to see it modify its behavior and join the community of nations. North Korean actions are at times mystifying to outside observers, and its anachronistic cold war rhetoric and bellicose behavior only serve to deepen mistrust of its intentions. The disagreement among U.S. policymakers is not over this goal, but rather over the means to that end.

The arguments set forth in the previous chapters reveal that it is possible to have a sensible discussion about North Korea that is neither vitriolic nor superficial in nature. Although both Victor Cha and myself come from very different perspectives of North Korea, we both arrive at the same conclusion that engagement is the best policy for the United States to pursue. Victor Cha has provided a compelling rationale for engagement, and also provided the most compelling argument in the literature that predicts a North Korean attack. According to him, even those who believe that North Korea has no intention of changing its behavior have an incentive to engage with North Korea, because the alternatives are far worse.

There is much that I find convincing in Victor Cha's thoughtful research, and much to admire in the sensible and reasoned manner with which he lays out his argument. Perhaps the key question that differentiates our two approaches is the issue of whether North Korea has any desire or capability to change. In contrast to the "hardline" approach, both Victor Cha and I have argued in the previous chapters that North Korea is threatened by the United States. The heart of our disagreement is over whether North Korea is truly trying to reach a *modus vivendi* with the rest of the world. In spite of Cha's worst-case scenario, I will show that there is still room for engagement. North Korea is opening up, and many of the changes are rapidly becoming irreversible. Any comprehensive view of North Korea must now include the economic sector; to focus only on the nuclear issue is to see only half the picture.

Victor Cha argues that countries falling to pieces have little to lose, so they may be tempted to launch a war even if the odds of success are very low, because the prospects for failure are certain with continued peace.[1] However, this theory has never been systematically tested, and is based on speculative assumptions about how the North Korean leadership perceives the world. There are good reasons to think that, from a North Korean perspective, any war would still be the worst conceivable outcome. With the examples of the U.S. determination for regime change in Iraq, U.S. military action in Kosovo in the late 1990s, and their own crumbling military, North Korea may very well perceive certain destruction from an angry United States if it initiates war, but see numerous examples of regimes—Cuba, for example—that have survived despite intense hardship and withering U.S. pressure. The flurry of North Korean diplomatic and economic initiatives in the past few years show that the North Korean leadership is actively pursuing a strategy they hope will ease their domestic problems. The collapse of the Agreed Framework in 2002 was disappointing because North Korea, unlike Iraq, has been actively seeking accommodation with the international community in a number of areas. We should encourage this trend, not hinder it. It makes no sense to criticize North Korea for being isolationist and then refuse to trade with them. The desperation thesis relies upon a number of heroic assumptions, and any discussion of the thesis should explicitly analyze North Korea's leadership perceptions and attitudes, rather than simply asserting them.

In this chapter I discuss the "hawk engagement" rationale adduced by Victor Cha, arguing that we have little evidence that North Korea is backed into a corner. In the first section I will make my case by showing that the engagement of the past nine years has been remarkably successful. North Korea has taken dynamic strides to open and reform its economy. This economic reform is just as important and central to explaining North Korean behavior as are its military and nuclear policies. While the North Korean regime has probably undertaken these reform measures unwillingly, they will nevertheless be difficult to control. The discussion of North Korea's economic situation in this chapter is not intended to be comprehensive. I am pointing out only that North Korea is taking steps to reform, and that the gains from reform could be substantial, if managed properly.[2]

In the second section I explore whether the North Korean regime can survive, and point out a number of overlooked diplomatic measures the regime has undertaken in the past decade. In the third section, I argue that engagement is the best and most viable way to promote regime change in North Korea. This book is focused primarily on making sense out of North Korea's foreign policy, but Northeast Asia has extraordinarily complex geopolitical relationships. The presence and different interests of South Korea, Japan, China, and Russia all have an impact on both North Korean and American foreign policy and so, in the fourth section, I briefly outline how these complex relations affect both countries. I conclude by discussing the future of U.S. foreign policy toward the Korean peninsula.

NORTH KOREA HAS ENGAGED IN ECONOMIC REFORM

Beginning in 1989, the North Korean economy underwent a series of severe shocks. The limits to a centrally planned economy had already begun to be reached during the 1980s, and to compound these problems, the Soviet Union and China abandoned North Korea and stopped providing aid and materials at "friendship prices." In 2003, industrial capacity was half what it was in 1989, and domestic savings was smaller than capital depreciation.[3] Combined with drought, flood, and famine of the mid-1990s, North Korea's economy is in a serious crisis that has affected everything from their military to the population as a whole. The current economic situation in North Korea is dismal. North Korea's gross national income in 2001 is estimated by the Bank of Korea to be $15.7 billion, with a per capita income of $706. The famine and floods of the past decade have decimated the agricultural sector, and reports of starvation and undernourishment are commonplace.[4] Under one unification scenario, Marcus Noland predicts that the North Korean economy would need $600 billion in order to raise living standards to 60 percent that of South Korea, while Williams, Hayes, and Von Hippel estimated the minimal cost of rehabilitation and infrastructure at between $20 and $50 billion.[5]

Given the horrible shape of the North Korean economy, it might seem surprising that I argue that North Korean leaders do not see imminent collapse of their regime. Yet there is evidence that the North Korean leadership—far from having lost all hope and going into a bunker mentality—has been actively pursuing a number of options through which it can survive into the future. The flurry of diplomatic initiatives in the past few years is *prima facie* evidence that North Korean leaders have not given up hope for survival. If the leadership truly saw no hope, they would not even bother to try such initiatives.

Up to and even after the nuclear revelations of October 2002, North Korea was still making a number of economic reforms. Thus, it is not unreasonable to ask, given the dire situation in which North Korea finds itself, whether the North Koreans are serious about their indicated desire to open normal relations with the rest of the world. In practical terms this means examining whether North Korea genuinely wishes to repair relations with the U.S., as well as with Japan and South Korea. The evidence points to a qualified "yes." While one might examine only the military and conclude that nothing has changed in North Korea, in fact the economic sector has changed dramatically. The proper comparison is not how closely North Korea has come to effecting a genuine capitalist transformation (very little), but rather how far they have come from the command economy of 1989 (very far).

There is growing evidence that North Korea is serious about opening to the West, and that it desires normal political and economic relations with the rest of the world. Former United States Ambassador to South Korea Donald Gregg notes that in April 2002, Kim Jong-il "realized that North Korea needed someone like Park" to stimulate its economy, and that Kim invited Park Geun-hye, daughter of Park Chung-hee, to visit him in Pyongyang. [6] Perhaps most significantly, in July 2002, the central government formally enacted a set of economic reforms, the most important of which was introducing of a pricing system whereby most prices are set by the market.[7] On August 1, 2002, North Korea's People's Assembly President Kim Yong-nam said that "we are directing our whole efforts to restructure our economic base to be in line with the information technology revolution . . . we are reforming the economic system on the principle of profitability."[8] Since the formal abrogation of a command economy in July 2002, most anecdotal reports indicate that the markets—although experiencing a significant surge in prices—have continued to function relatively normally.[9] There has been no widespread chaos, farmer's markets have moved to fill the void in rationing, and the population appears to have adjusted.

In 2000, the private sector was estimated to be less than 4 percent of the entire economy.[10] However, this has grown rapidly and some estimates suggest as much as one-quarter of North Korea's economy is now private.[11] The old public distribution system (PSD) had been largely abandoned in the mid-1990s as the economy went through severe shocks. Farmer's markets, long grudgingly accepted, became much more important to the entire economy. Much of what the central government decreed in 2002 was merely labelling what was already happening. Salaries increased 10 to 40 times, depending on occupation, and prices surged 40 to 80.[12]

In order to participate in the private sector, households keep foreign currency.[13] The Bank of Korea estimates that perhaps $964 million total foreign currency was held by North Korean households in 2000, with the average households holding $186.[14] This not only puts the North Korean households firmly in the marketplace, but it also takes money away from private savings. This affects the central government's ability to direct lending and construction projects. Of the foreign currency, more than 60 percent is U.S. dollars, with the remaining currency being Chinese *yuan* or Japanese *yen*. This is largely a result of the breakdown of rationing that occurred after 1995.

Perhaps as significant is the effect this will have on households. Given the amount of foreign currency in circulation, this must be accompanied by information about the state of the economy and also about the real quality of life. Although political control remains tight, as the economy changes, the average population will reorient its mindset. This will not have any immediate impact, but it will make it difficult for the regime to pull back from reform, and also further the creation of the informal economy that exists alongside the formal economy.

Another project that could have a large impact on North Korea's economy is the Kyongui railway. Even during the 2002 U.S.-North Korea standoff, North and South Korea continued to work toward reconnecting the railway line, which would run from South Korea through the DMZ into North Korea. The economic and political implications of the railway are potentially fairly large. Politically, its construction has required clearing a section of the DMZ of landmines. In order to actually clear the DMZ, military meetings were required, and the fact that both militaries were able to agree is a large step toward reducing tension along the peninsula. Work on the two corridors—eastern and western—continued throughout the crisis of 2002. The landmines were cleared by December 2002, and the laying of railway track has been almost completed. By January 2003, only 300 yards separated the tracks in the western corridor.[15] In addition, there are plans to put a four-lane highway next to the railroads in each corridor, and initial work has begun on the eastern corridor.

In economic terms, the planned railway will connect the Korean peninsula to the Trans-Siberian Railway, the Trans-Chinese Railway, and the Trans-Manchurian Railway. Such a reconnection has large potential economic benefits, because it would allow shipment of goods to go directly from Japan or South Korea to Europe. It could also be a conduit for further trade and investment in the region, as well as a significant lessening of tensions on the peninsula because of the throughway through the DMZ. The Korea Transport Institute estimates that earnings could be significant within three years of completion of the railway, up to $149 million in fees.[16] In mid-January 2003, North Korea proposed opening talks with South Korea to continue discussion about connecting cross-border railway and roads.[17]

Politically, North Korea has changed a number of its laws and the constitution itself in order to provide a legal framework for foreign investment. Although there has been foreign investment in North Korea since the 1970s, a major push for opening has occurred only in the past decade. There were 11 Constitutional amendments relating to foreign investment in 1998 alone. In 1999 the Joint Production and the Joint Venture laws were amended to allow for projects outside the Rajin-Sonbong area. Until that time pure foreign investment enterprises were allowed to invest only in the Rajin-Sonbong area.[18] The government continues to create the legal foundations that allow international investment. In 2001, the central government enacted the "Processing Trade law," the "Lock Gate law," and "Copyright law," in April 2001 to expand the scope of foreign trade.[19] These laws cover such areas as which sectors are open to foreign investment and in which sectors foreign firms can own 100 percent of the capital, as well as a guarantee against nationalization, the right to lease and use land for up to 50 years, and certain tax and tariff preferences.[20]

North Korea has also been attempting to join a number of international institutions. To date, North Korea attempted unsuccessfully to join the Asian Development Bank in 1997, and has recently indicated that it may apply to join the IMF. In addition, North Korea has also been actively courting middle powers around the region. Australia and Italy have recently normalized ties with the North, and Canada formally recognized North Korea. Australian National University has trained two groups of North Korean officials from the Ministry of Foreign Affairs in a yearlong economics course.[21] In July 2000, the Philippines became the last ASEAN country to normalize relations with North Korea. On May 3, 2000, the International Chamber of Commerce accredited the Pyongyang Chamber of Commerce.[22]

In economic relations, the North is increasingly open to a foreign presence on its soil. South Korea has led the way, with South Korean conglomerates rapidly expanding their activities in the North with the blessing of both South and North Korean governments. Hyundai continues to be the most ambitious South Korean company, most recently announcing plans to restore an inter-Korean railroad and create a trade zone near Haeju on the west coast of Korea that could produce $20 billion of exports, and the Haeju project will add to its existing Kumgang tours and other construction projects already underway.[23] Samsung is currently negotiating with the North Korean government in an attempt to place its logo in Pyongyang, and has recently begun exporting consumer electronics from its electronic industrial complex of over 1.65 million square meters in factories in the north.[24] LG has been manufacturing televisions in North Korea since 1996. There are more than 700 South Koreans currently living and working in North Korea, and Nampo port houses 180 South Korean companies. In 2002, 39 firms were granted permission to establish cooperation partnership arrangements with North Korea. Before 2001, companies from other nations had begun to cautiously explore the possibility of investing in the North.[25] In June 2000, for example, more than 80 U.S. companies attended a briefing by the Commerce Department regarding the recent lifting of U.S. sanc-

TABLE 4.1. Inter-Korean Trade, 1989–2000 (US$ mn)

YEAR	NORTH TO SOUTH	SOUTH TO NORTH	TOTAL
1989	18.9	0.1	18.7
1990	12.3	1.2	13.5
1991	105.7	5.5	111.3
1992	162.9	10.6	173.4
1993	178.2	8.4	186.6
1994	176.3	18.2	194.5
1995	222.9	64.4	287.3
1996	182.4	69.6	252.0
1997	193.1	115.3	308.3
1998	92.3	129.7	221.9
1999	121.6	211.8	333.4
2000	152.4	272.8	425.1

Source: Inter-Korean interchange and cooperation bureau, Ministry of Unification, December 2000.

tions to North Korea. The companies included IBM, Hewlett Packard, Oracle, Caterpillar, Dupont, and Phillip Morris.

Trade has also picked up. There was a huge dip in the mid-1990s as the economy came crashing to a halt. So overall levels of trade are still lower than in 1990, although the trend is upward (table 4.1). In November 2002, inter-Korean trade totaled $126.55 million, a 29.3% increase from October, and a 284% increase YoY. Total foreign trade for 2001 was $2.27 billion, or 14.4% of GDP (table 4.2).[26]

The Rajin-Sonbong free trade zone continues to show slow and halting progress. This zone has a mixed history: by the end of 1999 total foreign investment was estimated at $125 million, of which almost half came from the Emperor Group of Hong Kong for its construction of a hotel and casino.[27] However, with help from the UNDP, in late 1998 North Korea opened its own

TABLE 4.2 North Korea's Total Foreign Trade, 1995-2001 (US$ billion)

YEAR	1995	1996	1997	1998	1999	2000	2001
Total trade	2.05	1.98	2.18	1.44	1.48	1.97	2.27
Rate of growth	-2.7	-3.7	10.1	-33.7	2.6	33.1	15.1

Source: Ministry of Unification, "Data on North Korea," (www.unikorea.go.kr)

business school in the SEZ, the Rajin Business Institute (RBI) along with a Business Information Center (BIC). In addition, in September 2002, the North Korean government announced the creation of a second, larger, SEZ—the "Sinuiju Special Adminis- trative Region"—which would be 50 square miles and be located on the border with China. A Chinese businessman, Yang Bin, was originally put in charge of the zone, although complications with the Chinese government sidetracked his appointment. Sinuiju itself would allow foreign currencies to be used, and was designed to take advantage of the reconnected railway between North and South Korea.[28]

Table 4.3 shows a sample of North Korean government steps in the past three years.

The North has also begun—tentatively—to learn about capital- ism: both the Australian National University and Portland State University have concluded agreements to teach bureaucrats about modern economics, and law professors have lectured in North Ko- rea on topics such as bankruptcy law. In 2001 alone, more than 480 North Koreans visited China, Australia, Italy, and Sweden for training programs in finance, trade, and accounting.[29] In 2001, seemingly following a Chinese practice, former military officers have been assigned as directors of factories and enterprises, in an apparent attempt to turn them from military elites into economic

TABLE 4.3. A Sample of North Korean Economic Outreach Steps

COUNTRY	FIELD	PROGRESS
Russia	Link Trans-Siberian Railway with the Trans-Korean Railway Energy cooperation	Meeting of railway ministers (3-2001) NK Railway delegation to Moscow (7-2001) North Korea–Russia common declaration (8-2001) Russian railway delegation to NK (9-2001)
Germany	Electricity, railway transportation, communication	Delegation of Bavaria to NK, establishment of Common Economic Community (9-2001) NK delegation to Bavaria (9-2001)
Australia	Exploitation of mines Agriculture ANU economic training program for NK bureaucrats	NK delegation for trade in Australia (2-2001) Australian delegation for mining in NK (5-2001) Australian delegation for agriculture in NK (5-2001) Australian delegation for agriculture in NK (12-2001) NK bureaucrats (3 groups, the first group in 1999 of 6 bureaucrats, increased to 12 in 2001)

TABLE 4.3. (continued)

COUNTRY	FIELD	PROGRESS
Netherlands	Cooperation for electricity generation, import of mineral products	Netherlands delegation for economy in NK (7-2000; three visits total)
Italy	Import of machinery (footwear, textiles)	Investment guarantee, economic cooperation, cultural cooperation agreements (7-2000) NK delegation to Italy (2-2001) Italian delegation to NK (6-2001)

Source: Adapted from Yoon Deok-ryong, "Economic Development in North Korea: a possible time line for North Korean transformation," *Korea's Economy 2002* (Washington, D.C.: Korea Economic Institute, 2002), p. 74.

elites. Park Kyung-ae notes that nongovernmental contacts increased significantly in the latter part of the 1990s. Medical and energy delegations visited the United States in 1999, and other visits included an economic delegation in 1998, as well as poultry, academic, and other energy delegations. Groups studied in Mexico, Canada, Thailand, the Philippines, and Singapore. By far the most delegations traveled to China, although industrial management training occurred in India and Malaysia. In Europe, North Koreans studied medical techniques in Switzerland, with agricultural and cultural groups visiting Sweden, Great Britain (language training), Austria, Denmark, the Netherlands, Italy, and Hungary.[30]

Finally, and perhaps as significant as these large changes in North Korean foreign policy, are the "quiet changes" that have taken place. International agreements and government negotiations tell one story, but the changing actions of the average North

Korean is just as important. In 1995 English replaced Russian as the required foreign language in high school. At the Northeast Asian Economic Forum in 1999, which included Russia, China, Mongolia, Japan, and the two Koreas, all other representatives spoke in their own language, while the North Koreans spoke English.[31] Interpreters get daily articles from the *Wall Street Journal* and other western newspapers. UN personnel have now visited almost every county in the North, and Chinese investors have begun to locate in the North. The World Food Program has foreigners living in every North Korean province, a previously unthinkable situation. CNN and BBC are available in Pyongyang. When Ken Quinones, director of the Mercy foundation, made plans to visit Pyongyang in 1999, the North Koreans asked him to bring videos of *Titanic* and *The Little Mermaid*.[32]

Some of these changes are very small. North Korea is in no sense an "open society." But the relevant point is the comparison to how different North Korea is today than where it was even five years ago. The changes are obvious and consequential. Most importantly, these changes could not have occurred without the explicit consent of the top leadership. Even the North Korean military has been reported to be supportive of these recent moves. South Korean newspaper *Jungang Ilbo* reported that Jo Myong-nok, the first deputy chairman of the DPRK National Defense Commission, said on June 15, 2000, that the DPRK National Defense Commission appreciates with satisfaction the construction of the unification begun with ROK President Kim Dae-jung's visit to Pyongyang. Jo said at the farewell luncheon hosted by DPRK leader Kim Jong-il, "Let's practice the joint declaration with all our heart and with loyalty."[33] Jo also traveled to Washington and met with President Clinton in autumn 2000, and for his official visit he wore his military garb. This was widely interpreted as a symbolic show that the military was supportive of the opening by the North.

These changes do not mean that North Korea will engage in wholesale economic reforms anytime soon. North Korea's opening is cautious and tentative—one not likely to foster the kind of wholesale rhetorical and ideological changes that the United States expects and wants. But the key point is that the North Korean leadership—both military and political—has been vigorous and active on the economic and diplomatic fronts for more than a decade. The desperation thesis may therefore be theoretically interesting, but, the evidence demonstrates that the North Korean leadership realizes not only that a war would be suicide, but alsothat some reform and opening may allow it to survive into the future.

A hardline policy of pressure and threats from the United States will not start a war, but it will jeopardize these gains. As I will discuss later in this chapter, South Korea has seen these gains over the past decade, and is the country that stands to lose the most from conflict on the peninsula. Engagement has worked. North Korea is slowly coming out of its shell. The process of reform and opening in the North will be fraught with suspicion and subject to backsliding. But patient engagement by South Korea and the United States has worked and may continue to do so.

HAWK ENGAGEMENT AND WHY IMMINENT COLLAPSE IS UNLIKELY

The hawk engagement strategy that Victor Cha adduces relies on the argument that a desperate nation may compare the certainty of collapse with the slim chance that they could win or at least improve their situation through a war, and that such a nation might rationally choose to initiate a fight they have little probability of winning. In the case of North Korea, it is argued that their economy has contracted by at least 25 percent over the past decade, and famine and stagnation are overtaking the land. In this situation, the argument goes, North Korean leaders may see a certain collapse awaiting them if they do nothing, and so may rationally decide that a quick invasion of the South may be their only hope for survival. Desperation theorists argue that a "cornered tiger" can be increasingly dangerous and risk-acceptant in the hopes of some miraculous event changing the situation.[34]

The biggest problem with the desperation thesis is that it is based on scarce—and largely speculative—data about North Korea. Neither optimists nor pessimists have good data on North Korean attitudes, perceptions, or intentions. Thus we must be aware that we are inferring attitudes from little data, and be as self-conscious as possible about not imputing preferences through wishful thinking. Often the desperation thesis is merely asserted, without evidence that explains the psychological or perceptual bases of the North Korean leadership. The lack of evidence can cut both ways, and this section is aimed primarily at showing an equally compelling alternative interpretation that arises from the little data that we do have.

Indeed, there is a compelling alternative hypothesis about the North Korean leadership's perceptions. North Korea, far from seeing its imminent demise and thus planning a desperate war against the South in hopes of survival, might well view its options in precisely the opposite manner from those who advocate the "desperation" thesis. The North might see a war against the U.S. as guaranteed suicide, but view economic survival as a distinct possibility.

The North has actually engaged in a number of steps that show good faith. Perhaps the most convincing was the missile moratorium that Kim Jong-il announced in September 1999.[35] At that time, after Washington announced that it would ease some of the economic sanctions it had with North Korea, Kim Jong-il reciprocated by declaring a voluntary moratorium on all missile testing until 2003. [36]

Another clumsy but seemingly positive step occurred in September 2002. In late September 2002, Kim Jong-il admitted that the North had kidnapped Japanese citizens in the 1970s, and vowed that "mistakes will not be repeated," an astonishing rebuke of his father's policy.[37] What makes this step so intriguing is that for three decades the North had denied having kidnapped the Japanese. Only by finally admitting it would the North and Japan be able to move forward. Kim Jong-il said that the time had come to "liquidate the past." Japan had to "apologize sincerely" and "the issue of compensation must be correctly resolved." An end to "abnormal relations," Kim said, "will also dissipate the security concerns of the Japanese people."[38] All of these actions point to an attempt by the North to began dealing with the past and resolving these issues—a necessary step if they are to continue moving into the community of nations.

The current political situation is stable. There has been no palace coup, no military coup, no fighting in the streets, no obvious chaos in the military, no wholesale purge of various officials. Military officials have become present at all levels of the government, but they have not vetoed the economic and diplomatic efforts made by the Pyongyang regime. The older generation is passing, and younger leaders are rising. Personalities remain more important than institutions, and the military is still very influential. The leadership, although firmly in power, is apprehensive that economic change will lead to political change.

Countries falling to pieces do not engage in long-term planning, nor do they undertake orderly reforms. Although the flow of refugees from the North has increased, and estimates are that perhaps 300,000 North Koreans have fled over the border to China, these numbers are still lower than from East Germany before its collapse. North Korea's economy is clearly in a desperate situation, but the signs of imminent collapse are absent. Victor Cha focuses on the worse-case scenario, and although that scenario is an extremely dangerous scenario, it is not likely to occur.

WHY ARE WE AFRAID OF ENGAGEMENT?

Why are we afraid of dealing with the North? If we really want capitalism and American values to influence the North, let's start exporting them as soon as possible. If we really have no intention of starting a war in northeast Asia, let's put it in writing, conclude a peace treaty, and finally end the cold war. There is considerable skepticism in the U.S. that North Korea is anything other than a dangerous menace. However, North Korea is serious about opening to the outside world, but they are also cautious and fearful about what those changes might mean. Decades of animosity and mistrust on both sides make negotiation and communication difficult. The United States *is* hostile to Pyongyang, and it is not accurate to pretend that it wants only to be friends and that only the North Koreans are paranoid. This is not to argue which side, if either, holds the moral high ground, nor to argue that the North Koreans are innocent lambs; clearly America has reason to mistrust the North. But North Korea also mistrusts the United States—they know very well that the ultimate U.S. goal is the transformation or even the obliteration of their way of life—and North Korea has reason to be wary. Looking for an "original sin" may make one momentarily feel self-righteous but is unlikely to lead to any resolution to the crisis.

As Marcus Noland wrote, "Pyongyang already holds Seoul hostage with its forward-deployed artillery. The marginal increase in effective threat associated with revitalization of the North Korean economy is minimal. Ergo, it is worth engaging with the North and hoping that through a policy of engagement either Pyongyang will evolve toward a less threatening regime, or engagement will undermine the ideological basis of the Kim Jong-il regime and eventually cause its collapse."[39] Although Noland argues that the calculus for the United States is different because it does not face the same threat from the North, his general point is still valid—engagement increases the dangers slightly but has potentially large payoffs.

North Korea is a nation in uncharted territory. The country is under tremendous stresses, internationally, politically, and economically. It faces many enemies, and almost all its traditional allies have drastically curtailed their economic and military support. In the past decade North Korea has experienced famine, flood, economic crisis, a nuclear crisis that almost resulted in war, and withering pressure from the outside world. Pyongyang wants to open up to the wider world, but this is very dangerous. The leaders in Pyongyang have seen the chaos that can occur when such a transition is not handled adroitly; and nobody wants a Romania or a Yugoslavia to occur in North Korea. Under these circumstances, no nation in such a situation is going to be confident and calm; any country would be touchy, sensitive, and wary. North Korea is opening its doors after spending thirty years in the dark. It will take time to adjust to the bright light of the outside world, and if we pound on the door too hastily, the leadership may just pull back.

What makes the new policy of pressure even more discouraging is that engagement has been shown to work on the Korean peninsula. This may be an odd statement to make, considering that North Korea admitted in 2002 to have been pursuing a secret nuclear weapons program. However, only the most naïve of observers expected steady progress by both sides. As I will show in chapter 6, both sides abrogated the Agreed Framework. Taken on its own terms, the past years of engagement toward the North have seen genuine progress.

North Korea does not want war but it does not trust the United States or South Korea very much, either. Mutual deterrence makes both sides vulnerable—but it also makes the use of force highly unlikely. History has shown that continued pressure and antagonism will lead to a similar response from North Korea. Such hardline policies are counterproductive. The U.S. can either facilitate or retard North Korea's progress: attempting to force open the door too quickly will likely be unsuccessful, while slow rapprochement will likely be more successful.

Engagement also makes the most sense as a careful policy that allows the United States to have some sense of control over the process. Many of the possible outcomes in North Korea are very volatile and could lead in the worst-case to disastrous results. As I noted in chapter 2, any war has unintended consequences, and on the peninsula war could bring four great powers into confrontation with each other. Attempting to promote internal collapse also amounts to essentially no policy in the region and likewise could have unintended consequences. Refugees, a military split in

North Korea, and other problems with uncontrolled collapse are not palatable and could be deleterious to stability in the region. What engagement does is allow the United States to proceed cautiously and also to slowly transform the regime.

THE KEY ELEMENTS OF MY ARGUMENT

The heart of my argument is that North Korea has genuine security concerns. If the United States fails to address these concerns, its only options are either to wait for the regime's collapse or to add pressure in hopes that eventually the North will buckle under. Both policies are unlikely to succeed, and both policies also contain an element of real risk, because such policies could easily lead to situations that end up hurting U.S. interests in the region. In addition, I have argued that North Korea realizes which way the wind is blowing, and is cautiously—and admittedly very tentatively—taking steps to modify its economic system. External geopolitical conditions have combined with internal economic collapse to force North Korea into a situation where it must undergo economic reform and pursue a policy of accommodation with the United States.

Our two contrasting arguments can be pushed further: what evidence would allow us to discern between two approaches? Is it possible to set up a test that would allow us to more deeply understand North Korean behavior, or to probe more deeply into the questions raised in this book? To use the language of social science, what would falsify my argument? One of the difficulties about studying North Korea is that information has been somewhat harder to obtain than would be the case in another country. In this case both our pieces would benefit from greater information about the various perspectives that might exist within the military and government of the DPRK.

However, my argument is not built on unobservable guesses as to the thoughts of the North Korean regime. The key to my approach rests on the premise that the North Koreans realize their objective weakness. As such, there are three situations that would be especially troubling for my argument, and would force me to rethink my position.

1. The U.S. commits to a genuine nonaggression pact (or something even more concrete, such as a peace treaty or even normalization of ties), and then North Korea does not fully disarm its nuclear program. This is the key test of my argument. Note, however, that if the United States does not give the North security guarantees, it is not possible to determine whether North Korea's behavior arises because of its fear of the U.S. or because of other causes. This is another way of saying that the essence of my argument is North Korean fear. If North Korea feels threatened, more threats are unlikely to make them feel less threatened.

2. The North actually undertakes an unprovoked terrorist act, whether it be firing a missile at South Korea or Japan, or having its operatives attempt to assassinate South Korea's leaders, as they did in the past. This does not include the test-firing of a missile, but the actual firing of a missile or blowing up of a bomb in order to kill civilians. Were the North to engage in such behavior, the case for their changed behavior would also be falsified.

3. The North actually starts a war on the peninsula. Were war to break out without the U.S. starting it, my analysis would also be shown to be terribly wrong. My argument is built on the threat that North Korea perceives from the United States. Such a threat deters the North from engaging in a military attempt to unify the peninsula. Were the North to start an unprovoked war, this would show me wrong.

Note, however, that if the U.S. initiates war itself, through either a preemptive strike at Yongbyon or through other measures, this actually confirms my argument about North Korean perceptions of a U.S. threat. However, what is not convincing evidence is the recent spate of provocative actions that both sides have taken, which include incidents between North Korean and U.S. jets over the sea of Japan, the deployment of 24 U.S. B-52 bombers to the region, and the test-firing of a short-range (60 mile range) missile. In the current situation, both sides are engaging in provocative acts.

Why are we afraid of engaging the North? As a basis for policy, both Victor Cha's analysis and my own result in the same policy prescription: engage North Korea from a position of strength. Victor Cha provides a rationale for engagement even to those who might be skeptical of North Korea's willingness to change. Second, U.S. policy can significantly quicken North Korea's opening to the outside world.

KEY FACTORS THAT WILL INFLUENCE U.S. POLICY

September 11 only reinforced the Bush administration's increasingly confrontational stance toward the North. Since coming to office, the Bush presidency has taken a harder line and has emphasized pressure and threats toward North Korea. If past history is any guide, this will be unsuccessful in forcing Pyongyang to submit. Especially because Northeast Asia is one of the most complex geopolitical regions in the world, finding a resolution to the standoff is difficult. American foreign policy to North Korea is not conducted in a vacuum, considering that South Korea, China, Japan, and even Russia have vital interests on the Korean peninsula, and have the potential to play an important role in either resolving or sustaining the situation.

The current situation is complicated by the presence of three of the world's strongest countries—China, Japan, and Russia—that surround the Korean peninsula. In addition, South Korea is perhaps the most important country in the region. Long a staunch U.S. ally, any military operation would need South Korean approval to go forward. After discussing the critical role of South Korea, I will briefly review China's interests on the peninsula.

THE ROLE OF SOUTH KOREA AND CHINA

South Korea has seen the success of the past decade, and will also have the costs of failure fall upon it, not the United States. There has long been anti-Americanism on the Korean Peninsula, and the extent of it has often been exaggerated. Roh Moohyun, who favors greater autonomy from the United States, was elected president of South Korea in December 2002. The election of Mr. Roh was not simply an outbreak of emotional anti-Americanism. Both North and South Korea have deep concerns about United States policy toward the peninsula. It would be a mistake to dismiss South Korea's increasingly tense relations with the United States as ephemeral, or the North's recent belligerence as irrational. Koreans in both the North and South are concerned about an erratic United States policy that veers between neglect and overattention—and that for the last two years has lacked an overarching vision.

The Bush administration has done well to avoid overreaction to the North's renewed nuclear threat. But after two years the administration has yet to articulate a coherent policy toward the peninsula—North or South. This has led to a situation in which both North and South Korea worry about American policy.

Viewed in this context, the outcome of the South Korean election is understandable. South Korea has historically been one of the strongest allies of the United States. It is naive to dismiss its concerns as emotional. Certainly American troops stationed in South Korea can cause tension, and there was a strain of anti-Americanism in the recent protest of some 300,000 South Koreans over the acquittal (in an American court martial) of two soldiers accused of accidentally crushing two Korean girls to death while on an armored patrol.

But South Korea's concerns are rooted in a much deeper apprehensions. In large part, the South Korean election came down to a referendum on South Korea's stance toward North Korea and the United States. Voters resoundingly chose the moderate Roh, who favors continued engagement with the North, over Lee

Hoi-chang, whose stance toward North Korea—suspending assistance until it cooperates on issues like arms control—more closely reflected America's. In electing Roh, voters voiced their displeasure with the Bush administration's inflexible stance.

Thus, both North and South Korea's share frustration with the United States, which may have the effect of driving them closer together. These concerns are likely to grow, especially as democratic politics in South Korea matures. As voters increasingly demand more openness with the North, South Korea's elected officials are likely to show relatively less deference to American policy.

For America the implications of these changes in Korean attitudes are clear. Washington must create a comprehensive strategy for resolving the nuclear issue with the North in such a way that responds to North Korea's desire for security guarantees and full normalization with the United States. The United States cannot just hope that North Korea goes away—nor should it risk escalating tensions and creating a geopolitical crisis, like the recent controversy over North Korea's missile shipments to Yemen. To have any hope of resolving the tensions on the Korean Peninsula, the United States must pay more attention to the needs and goals of both countries. In recent years South Korea has made major strides in economic and diplomatic relations with the North, only to see those gains jeopardized in the last year by clumsy American diplomacy toward North Korea. United States troops have been in Korea for more than 50 years, and most Koreans have complicated feelings about America. Some of them are anti-American, to be sure, but many are grateful. Right now, however, the prevailing mood is anxiety—not about North Korea starting a war, but about American policies eroding the slow gains both Koreas have made in the last decade in their relations with each other. A more carefully engaged America would help alleviate tensions in Northeast Asia rather than contribute to them. As one advisor noted, "They're [the U.S.] locked in a cold war mindset when this region is experiencing capitalist growth."[40]

China is also in a position to play a critical role in the resolution of the crisis. First, it should be noted that the United States and China have not yet come to a stable relationship. The U.S. is wary of China's growing power, and has veered in the past decade from "Strategic competitor" to "strategic partner."[41] China, for its part, also views the U.S. as potentially helpful and potentially harmful. Given these conditions, the role of China can be a big step in either resolving the crisis or limiting U.S. policy options. If only because of the potential for the United States to end up unwittingly drawing China into a confrontation, the military option is unlikely to be used without Chinese consent. Alternatively, Chinese pressure on the North can be a significant influence. However, China has no inherent reason to abandon North Korea just because the United States would like it to. Without a clear policy toward the region, Chinese help will be minimal at best.

In January 2003, the Chinese government was reluctant to discuss sanctions or military action on the peninsula. Chinese Foreign Ministry spokeswoman said that "Dialogue is vital to maintaining peace and stability on the peninsula and China is willing to work with all parties toward an early, peaceful solution to the issue."[42] Without Chinese support, sanctions or other hardline policies are unlikely to become effective. One key question is the extent of Chinese influence on North Korea. Although there is little knowledge of the extent of influence, it is widely agreed that China is likely to have more influence than any other country.

The presence of China, Japan, Russia, and South Korea—all with different interests toward North Korea—complicates U.S. attempts to formulate a policy toward North Korea. If these nations agree on a policy, it can be much more effective. If these nations disagree on policy, the U.S. will be constrained in its ability to impose a solution on the peninsula.[43]

U.S. POLICY TOWARD THE KOREAN PENINSULA

North Korea, though wary and mistrustful, is actively seeking better and more open relations with the West. North Koreans can be proud and stubborn, but they are also pragmatic. North Korea wants from the U.S. a slowly developing relationship where both sides can learn to trust each other. The implicit U.S. sentiment—if not policy—of expecting significant unilateral concessions is likely to be ineffectual; as the nuclear crisis has shown, North Korean leaders will not back down to pressure. Such an approach might be good for domestic politics and for rhetoric about standing tough to bullies, but it will neither further U.S. foreign policy nor will it contribute to stability in the Asian region. A significant segment of U.S. policymakers see no point in compromising our ideals—and this is an entirely justified perspective. However, such a perspective also has clear consequences: North Korea has made very clear it will not surrender. North Korea has also made very clear its determination to be treated with respect. And the United States needs to realize that a policy that expects North Korean capitulation has fairly predictable—and negative—consequences.

Nevertheless, North Korea may not be able to deal "on their terms." The outside world—and in particular the United States—will have problems with that. The U.S. is clearly the most powerful nation on the earth, and this provides us both an incentive and a responsibility to help order affairs around the world. If the picture I have painted is accurate, what are the implications for how the United States might best take advantage of this situation? How might we facilitate North Korea's moves toward normalcy?

The United States should not overreact to saber-rattling, making it very clear it will walk away from the table if the North Koreans don't behave; but it should also facilitate economic opening by allowing U.S. companies to trade and invest with the North. This is not "rewarding bad behavior." Rather, if North Korea wants to join the international community—something the U.S. has been urging it to do for decades—the United States should facilitate that entry, not retard it. As James Cotton notes, "In Australian policymaking circles, the view has emerged that the time has passed when quarantine was an effective instrument in dealing with the suspicious and embattled regime in Pyongyang. Keeping North Korea isolated has done little to improve its behavior."[44] It makes no sense to call the North Koreans isolationist and then not allow them to trade. North Koreans need economic education: knowledge of how market economies work, commercial habits, and contracts. The U.S. can address a knowledge gap and a perception gap that exists in North Korea. Handling this economic transition will be critically important for domestic and regional stability.

First, we take a long view toward North Korea. Their opening will come at a measured pace and over time, and it is unlikely that there will be any quick resolution, whether through a summit or dramatic breakthrough. The North-South summit is very important, but for symbolic reasons that show North Korea desiring better relations. Indeed, rapid change can be quite destabilizing, and all interested parties want to avoid collapse or chaos in the North.

Second, it makes no sense to call the North Koreans isolationist and then not allow them to trade. The partial lifting of the U.S. embargo in 2000 was a start, but the U.S. economic and trade policies could be changed even more. With exposure to U.S. companies and goods, North Korean mindset can change, and the exposure will help to promote a capitalist system. The more we trade with the North, and the more exposed North Korean citizens become to capitalism and western ideas, the harder it will be for the North Korean leadership to reverse the reforms. Regime change through economic integration may be slow, but it ultimately can be just as transformative.

Third, the U.S. can address a knowledge gap and a perception gap that exists in North Korea. Handling this economic transition will be critically important for domestic and regional stability. North Koreans need economic education: knowledge of how market economies work, commercial habits, and contracts. This has already begun with private agreements made by U.S. academic institutions and other entities; official government policy could help further this line of approach. More than this, however, is a deeper point: economic reform is difficult. A good point of comparison is China two decades ago—from the announced change in economic policy in 1978, China has taken decades to move to genuine reform and to open its economy to the outside world.

Even compared to China in 1978, North Korea has an almost complete lack of personnel trained in a capitalist system. The most basic tasks of reform will be difficult. Bureaucrats do not know how to privatize an economy. Cadres and factory managers have no idea how to conduct a business. It is not possible to declare capitalism by fiat. Ministries have to change their plans, mindsets, and skill-sets. This will be enormously difficult, and the most helpful and genuine way to change the North Koreans will be to teach them about capitalism and the outside world. This has already begun, but it must occur on a much larger scale.

Finally, the United States could also remember that rhetoric matters immensely. In dealing with a nation that is attempting to reform, the form matters as much as the content. You can't *tell* a Korean anything, but suggestions of a solution might be met by receptive ears. Lecturing or condescension is counterproductive in any society, even the United States.

Because the stakes are so high, it is all the more imperative that we remain patient, take the long-term view, and avoid outdated cold war caricatures and understand North Korea as it is. North Korea is an odious and authoritarian regime. We would all like it to disappear as soon as possible. But only by understanding it can we make the proper policy responses.

VICTOR D. CHA | DAVID C. KANG

HYPERBOLE DOMINATES: THE 2003 NUCLEAR CRISIS

5

THE DEFAULT STRATEGY?

Hyperbole dominates the public discussion on North Korea. Extravagant stories about the idiosyncrasies of the opaque leader Kim Jong-il abound. Media reports from the Sino-Korean border of mass starvation evoke feelings of pity, disgust, and anger among the general public. Nongovernmental groups and international relief organizations scream for the world to help. Conservative ideologues reject this and want to end the regime, pure and simple.

Policy on North Korea has become a political football. In South Korea, the conservatives bash the liberal incumbent government over what they term an appeasement of North Korea. Kim Dae-jung's "sunshine policy" has become so politicized that one can no longer distinguish between criticisms of the policy, and character assassinations of the president. In the United States as well, engagement of North Korea and the Agreed Framework have become such a partisan issue that one cannot tell whether detractors object to merits of the policy or the policy's association with the Clinton administration.

This book has offered two differing paths to the same commanding rationales for dealing with North Korea. David Kang believes that the threat posed by North Korea has been unduly inflated. In spite of the forward deployments on the DMZ, Pyongyang has been rationally deterred from aggression for more than 50 years, so that there is no reason to believe they would change their minds today. He believes that if instead of fixating on military deployments one looks at the North's economic and political behavior in a broader historical context, there is a story to be told of slow, plodding reform. As a result, he argues that engagement works with the North. It sends the right signals to the insecure regime that the United States, ROK, and Japan are interested in trading the North's proliferation threat for a path of economic reform and integration. Kang argues that this has been validated already by the record of DPRK responses thus far.

Victor Cha believes the threat posed by North Korea still remains. Although Pyongyang has been rationally deterred from attempting a second invasion, there still exists a coercive bargaining rationale for violence. The North undertakes limited but serious crisis-inducing acts of violence with the hope of leveraging crises more to the North's advantage. This is extremely risky, but it is also extremely rational when a country has nothing to lose and nothing to negotiate with. Moreover, Cha is skeptical of how much Pyongyang's intentions have really changed. Yet in spite of this pessimistic assessment, he too believes engagement with the North is the most advisable path. Engagement deals with the threat; at the same time, it probes DPRK intentions and, if necessary, builds a coalition for punishment if engagement fails. Whether you are a hardliner or softliner, hawk or dove on North Korea, the default strategy on the Korean peninsula today remains engagement.

THE MAKINGS OF A CRISIS

The 2002–2003 revelations of a second secret North Korean - nuclear weapons program raise interesting "tests" for our two "models" of DPRK behavior. *And it is here that we potentially part company.*

130
David Kang and Victor Cha have disparate evaluations of the motivations as well as implications of these latest North Korean actions. Kang, while finding the nuclear revelations a disappointing setback in our evaluations of DPRK reform and opening efforts, nevertheless sees a consistency in Pyongyang's behavior as well as an opportunity for the United States to negotiate an end to the proliferation threat on the peninsula. Cha sees the implications of these revelations as fairly grave and as strong evidence validating hawkish skepticism of North Korean intentions. In light of these activities, his support of engagement is highly conditional (i.e., only if the North Koreans return to the status quo ante); otherwise, the United States and its allies would be forced to pursue some form of isolation and containment of the regime.

NORTH KOREA'S NUCLEAR "CONFESSION"

In October 2002 the Assistant Secretary of State for East Asian and Pacific Affairs, James Kelly, accompanied by a delegation of administration officials, set off for two days of talks in Pyongyang with their North Korean counterparts (October 3–5, 2002).[1] The first of their kind in well over one-and-a half years of non dialogue between the United States and the DPRK, the talks were preceded by protracted speculation about what policy the Bush administration would pursue with the regime. Following from the 2002 State of the Union Address in which President Bush included North Korea in the "axis of evil," and later offered other choice negative personal opinions about Kim Jong-il (referring to Kim as a "pygmy" and how he "loathed" him), many speculated a dark future for US-DPRK relations.[2] Other pundits, however, cited various statements by administration officials and a June 2001 internal policy review that indicated the administration would eventually pick up where the Clinton administration left off, negotiating some form of engagement with the North Koreans.[3]

The meeting between Kelly and his counterpart Kim Kye-gwan took place against a backdrop of recently thawed relations between

North Korea and U.S. regional allies. Following a deadly naval provocation by the DPRK against ROK vessels in June 2002, North-South relations appeared to cycle back to a more positive path with high-level meetings throughout the summer that resulted in ministerial talks, family reunions, resumption of infrastructural projects (road and railway corridors), and North Korean participation in the Asian Games in Pusan.[4] On July 31, Secretary Powell met briefly with DPRK foreign minister Paik Nam-sun on the sidelines of Asian multilateral meetings in Brunei. One week later Charles Pritchard, the U.S. State Department's chief representative to KEDO went to Kumho, North Korea for the first ceremonial pouring of concrete for construction of the light water reactor. Contemporaneous with these confidence-inducing events, the North announced a series of new economic reforms and projects, including a special economic zone on the Sino-Korean border and most significant, the lifting of price controls.[5] North Korean–Japanese relations appeared also to take a major step forward with the breakthrough meeting between Kim Jong-il and Japanese premier Koizumi in Pyongyang in September 2002.[6] The summit produced a North Korean admission and apology for the past abduction of Japanese nationals for the purpose of espionage training, and held out aspirations for diplomatic normalization. This course of positive events led many to conjecture that the stage finally had been set for a U.S. reengagement with North Korea.

On the contrary, Assistant Secretary Kelly's mission produced North Korea's bombshell assertion that it was secretly pursuing a second nuclear arms program through uranium enrichment technology. Kelly's initial demarche acknowledged that the United States was interested in pursuing a new relationship with North Korea in the political, economic, and security arenas, but before any such path could be taken, the North Koreans needed to come clean on their past and future proliferation activities. Kelly then informed the North Koreans that the United States knew about the North's pursuit of a secret nuclear weapons program. This was through a different method of production—highly enriched uranium (HEU) technology—and on a scale comparable to the plutonium-based bomb program frozen in 1994.[7] Suspicions of such a program's existence dated back to 1997 or even earlier, but intelligence was spotty. Confirming evidence took the form of intelligence tracing of North Korean purchases of high-strength aluminum (a critical secondary material associated with an HEU program) and Pakistani sales of centrifuge technology to the North Koreans in exchange for DPRK missiles.[8]

The North Koreans initially denied such accusations, claiming it was an American fabrication, and continued on with regularly scheduled meetings (a total of four over the two days). Kim reported Kelly's statements to superiors during the first break, which set off all-night consultations within the North Korean leadership (presumably including Kim Jong-il). The three-hour meeting on October 3 was followed by a dinner that evening, and a 2.5 hour meeting with Kim Kye-gwan the next morning. The North Koreans did not yet respond to Kelly's initial demarche at either of these meetings. A short ceremonial meeting (of about 35 minutes) with Supreme People's Assembly chairman Kim Yongnam at 3:00 PM on October 4 followed again with no apparent North Korean response. It was at the fourth scheduled meeting of the trip, between 4:15 and 5:10 PM on October 4, however, that the North Koreans returned with higher-level rerpresentation (Kang Sok-ju). In an extensive and scripted fashion that left little time for an exchange of views, Kang said he spoke on behalf of the Party and the Government of the DPRK in asserting that North Korea was justified to pursue such capabilities and that it considered the agreed framework nullified. Kang blamed Bush, for putting North Korea in the axis of evil, and declared the DPRK had even "stronger weapons" to wield against the United States if threatened (Kelly noted that the program in question indeed started before the axis of evil statement).

A 10-day news blackout of sorts ensued as administration officials revealed very little of the deliberations. (Press conferences in Seoul and Tokyo during Kelly's return from Pyongyang were either shortened to official statements without questions or canceled; Bush did not mention North Korea publicly for five days after Kelly's return.) The blackout raised speculations ranging from the very optimistic (a "grand bargain") to the pessimistic.[9] News became public on October 16, 2002 when the administration released a statement in order to preempt press leaks.[10]

The United States demanded that North Korea return to their existing nonproliferation agreements before any further talks could take place, and in conjunction with EU, Japanese, and South Korean representatives of the KEDO board, suspended further shipments of heavy fuel oil to North Korea under the original terms of the 1994 Agreed Framework. By December 2002, the makings of a crisis (despite Bush administration assertions to the contrary) were evident as United States officials boarded for inspection an intercepted North Korean ship in the Arabian Sea (which proved to be carrying missiles to Yemen).

The North Koreans responded to these events with a series of steps at the Yongbyon nuclear facilities frozen under the 1994 agreement in late-December 2002. Over a period of little more than one week, they removed the seals at all frozen facilities (experimental reactor, storage building, reprocessing laboratory), dismantled IAEA monitoring cameras, and the expelled the three IAEA international inspectors. In defiance of IAEA resolutions demanding the North Koreans come back into compliance, Pyongyang announced on January 10, 2003 their withdrawal from the Nonproliferation treaty. Subsequent North Korean actions, including evidence of tampering with stored fuel rods (source of weapons-grade plutonium), restarting of the experimental reactor, resumption of missile tests, declaration of their nuclear weapons status, and likely plutonium reprocessing suggest deliberate and purposeful moves in the direction of producing an extant mid-sized nuclear weapons arsenal.[11]

OUR (DIFFERING) ASSESSMENTS OF THE CRISIS

Debates raged inside the US government and among outside experts about how to respond to the 2002–2003 nuclear revelations.

Yet again, the public policy debates became quickly shaped by needlessly inflammatory invectives levied against all parties concerned. Mary McGrory's column in the *Washington Post* (February 9, 2003) named Kim "the little madman with the passion for plutonium."[12] Others blasted the Bush administration's North Korea policy as the source of the crisis, labeling it "amateur hour," and exemplary of what happens when "It talks before it thinks."[13] Still others resorted to blaming the Clinton administration as the root cause of the crisis, referring to Clinton's negotiation of the 1994 Agreed Framework as a "queer amalgamation of [postwar British Labour Prime Minister] Clement Atlee and Alfred E. Neuman."[14] As in the past, what is at issue substantively vis-à-vis North Korea gets lost in partisan politics, bureaucratic rivalries, sensationalist arguments, and a whiff of racism.[15]

DAVID KANG: GETTING BACK TO "START"

For David Kang, the nuclear revelations of October 2002 intensified an already acute dilemma for both the United States and North Korea. For the United States, their focus on Iraq was now potentially diverted by an unwanted crisis over an "Axis of Evil" country in Northeast Asia. For North Korea, their slowly intensifying economic and diplomatic moves of the past few years were also potentially thwarted. For both sides, their worst suspicions were confirmed in the worst of ways. North Korea concluded that the United States had never had any intention of normalizing ties or concluding a peace treaty. The United States concluded that North Korea never had any intention of abandoning its nuclear weapons program.

Many Western policymakers and analysts viewed the nuclear revelations with alarm and surprise. However, much of the Western hand-wringing has elements of Kabuki theater to it, and the accusations ring hollow. "Outrage and shock! at North Korean nuclear programs" is not so convincing when the Bush administration has been openly derisive of Kim Jong-il, been contemptuous of the Agreed Framework, and known about North Korea's nuclear program since June 2001.[16] An American intelligence official who attended White House meetings in 2002 said that "Bush and Cheney want this guy's head on a platter. Don't be distracted by all this talk about negotiations. . . . They have a plan, and they are going to get this guy after Iraq."[17] As was argued in chapter 2, a North Korea that feels threatened, and perceives a U.S. administration actively attempting to increase pressure on it, is unlikely to trust the United States.

Does North Korea have legitimate security concerns? If not, then their nuclear program is designed for blackmail or leverage. If so, then it is not that surprising that such a program exists, given the open hostility toward the regime that the Bush administration has evidenced. In any event, despite the furor over the revelation, not much has changed on the peninsula. Deterrence is still robust. North Korea's basic strategy remains the same: simultaneously deter the United States while finding a way to fix its economy. The United States, for its part, faces the same choices it did a decade ago: negotiate, or hope that the North collapses without doing too much damage to the region.

Without movement toward resolving the security fears of the North, progress in resolving the nuclear weapons issue will be limited. It is unsurprising that the 1994 Agreed Framework fell apart, because it was a process by which both sides set out to slowly build a sense of trust. Both sides began hedging their bets very early in that process. Because even during the Clinton administration neither the United States nor North Korea fulfilled many of the agreed steps, the framework was essentially dead long before the nuclear revelation of October 2002. Neither side acts in a vacuum; both the United States and North Korea react to each other's positions, and that has led to a spiral of mistrust and misunderstandings. Threats and rhetoric from one side have an impact on the other side's perceptions and actions, and this interaction can either be a mutually reinforcing positive or negative spiral.[18]

The accepted wisdom in the United States is that North Korea abrogated the framework by restarting its nuclear weapons program. The reality is more complicated . Both the Clinton and Bush administrations have violated the letter and the spirit of the agreement. Admitting that the U.S. is hostile toward North Korea does not make one an apologist—the United States *is* hostile, and it is unconvincing to pretend that we are not. The Bush administration made clear from the beginning that it had serious doubts about the Agreed Framework and engagement with the North. This began with the inception of the Bush administration—South Korean president Kim Dae-jung's visit to Washington D.C. in March 2001 was widely viewed as a rebuke to his own "Sunshine policy" that had engaged the North, with Bush voicing "skepticism" at the policy.[19] By the time of President Bush's now famous "axis of evil" speech, it had long been clear that the Bush administration did not trust the North. For the Framework to have had any hope of being even modestly successful, both sides needed to have worked more genuinely toward building confidence with each other.

THE 1994 AGREED FRAMEWORK The Agreed Framework of 1994 was not a formal treaty—rather, it was a set of guidelines designed to help two countries that are deeply mistrustful of each other find a way to cooperate. But both sides began backing out of the agreed framework well before the autumn of 2002. From its inception, the Bush administration made very clear how much they disdained the framework, and the North had begun its nuclear program as far back as 1998. The core of the framework was a series of steps that both sides would take that would ultimately lead to North Korea proving it had no nuclear weapons or nuclear weapons program, and to the United States normalizing ties with the North and providing it light water nuclear reactors that can make energy but not weapons. Table 5.1 shows the key elements of the framework.

Neither side fulfilled its obligations under the framework.[20] The key elements on the U.S. side were a formal statement of nonaggression (article 2.3.1), provision of the lightwater reactor

TABLE 5.1 Key Conditions of the Agreed Framework

AGREED FRAMEWORK CONDITION	IMPLEMENTATION AND DISCUSSION
The U.S. agrees to provide two light water reactor (LWR) power plants by the year 2003 (article 1.2).	Four years behind schedule. There has been no delay in South Korean or Japanese provision of funds. The delay has been U.S. implementation and construction
The U.S. agrees to provide formal assurances to the DPRK against the threat or use of nuclear weapons by the U.S. (article 2.3.1).	No. The U.S. maintains that military force is an option on the peninsula. The U.S. continues to target N.K. with nuclear weapons via the "Nuclear Posture Review"
The DPRK agrees to freeze its nuclear reactors and to dismantle them when the LWR project is completed (article 1.3).	Until December 2002
The DPRK agrees to allow the IAEA (International Atomic Energy Agency) to monitor the freeze with full cooperation (article 1.3).	Until December 2002
The U.S. and the DPRK agree to work toward full normalization of political and economic relations, reducing barriers of trade and investment etc. (article 2.1).	Limited lowering of U.S. restrictions on trade, No other progress toward normalization or peace treaty. U.S. continues to list N.K. as a terrorist state.
The U.S. and the DPRK will each open a liaison office in the each other's capital, aiming at upgrading bilateral relations to the ambassadorial level (articles 2.2, 2.3).	No

Source: Compiled from KEDO, "Agreed Framework Between the United States of America and the Democratic People's Republic of Korea," Geneva, Switzerland, October 21, 1994).

(article 1.2), and progress toward normalization of ties (article 2.1). The reactor is four years behind schedule.[21] The United States has also failed to open a liaison office in Pyongyang, nor has it provided formal written assurances against the use of nuclear weapons. As noted in chapter 2, the U.S. "Nuclear Posture Review" still targets North Korea with nuclear weapons. The North did freeze its reactors and allow IAEA monitoring, but in December 2002 it backed out of the agreement and expelled inspectors from North Korea.

It is possible to argue that the uranium enrichment plant is a "more serious" breach of the framework than not providing a formal nonaggression pact or not providing a reactor. But this will be compelling only to domestic constituencies. Given U.S. reluctance to fulfill its side of the framework, it was unlikely that the North would continue to honor its side of the agreement in hopes that at some point the Bush administration would begin to fulfill its side. This implicit U.S. policy has demanded that the North abandon its military programs, and only afterwards would the U.S. decide whether or not to be benevolent. As Wade Huntley and Timothy Savage write:

> The implicit signal sent to Pyongyang was that the Agreed Framework . . . was at its heart an effort to script the abdication of the DPRK regime. Immediate reticence by the United States to implement certain specific steps toward normalization called for in the agreement, such as lifting economic sanctions, reinforced this perception. . . . such an underlying attitude could never be the basis for real improvement in relations.[22]

The United States and North Korea are still technically at war—the 1953 armistice was never replaced with a peace treaty. The United States has been unwilling to discuss even a nonaggression pact, much less a peace treaty or normalization of ties. While the U.S. calls North Korea a terrorist nation and Defense Secretary Donald Rumsfeld discusses the possibility of war, it is not surprising that North Korea feels threatened. For the past two years, U.S. policy toward the North has been consistently derisive and confrontational. Table 5.2 shows a selection of statements by U.S. and North Korean officials.

The Bush administration began adding new conditions to the Agreed Framework early on in its tenure. On June 6, 2001, the White House included conventional forces in the requirements it wanted North Korea to fulfill, saying that "The U.S. seeks improved implementation [of the AF], prompt inspections of past reprocessing . . . [and] a less threatening conventional military posture." On June 11, 2001, North Korea replied that "Washington should implement the provisions of the D.P.R.K.-U.S. Agreed Framework and the D.P.R.K.-U.S. Joint Communiqué as agreed upon." The Bush administration continued its stance. On July 3, 2001, a senior Administration official said that "We need to see some progress in all areas. . . . we don't feel any urgency to provide goodies to them."[23]

In 2002, Secretary of State Colin Powell added the North's missile program to the list of conditions necessary for progress on the framework. Missiles had originally been excluded from the Agreed Framework, and the Clinton administration had begun working out a separate agreement with the North about them. On June 10, 2002, Colin Powell said that "First, the North must get out of the proliferation business and eliminate long-range missiles that threaten other countries. . . . the North needs to move toward a less threatening conventional military posture . . . and living up to its past pledges to implement basic confidence-building measures."[24]

The North consistently maintained that it wants the U.S. to lower the pressure. On October 20, 2002 Kim Yong-nam, Chair of the Supreme People's Assembly, said that "If the United States is willing to drop its hostile policy toward us, we are prepared to deal with various security concerns through dialogue."[25] On November 3, 2002, Han Song-ryol, DPRK ambassador to the UN, reiterated that "Everything will be negotiable, including inspections of the enrichment program. . . . our government will resolve all U.S. security concerns through the talks if your government has a will to end its hostile policy."[26] As the crisis intensified, Colin

TABLE 5.3 Selected U.S.–North Korean Rhetoric
Over the Agreed Framework

DATE	U.S. STATEMENTS	D.P.R.K. STATEMENTS
October 9, 2000	"Neither government will have hostile intent towards the other." (Joint communique)	
June 6, 2001	"The U.S. seeks improved implementation [of the AF], prompt inspections of past reprocessing . . . [and] a less threatening conventional military posture." (White House press release)	
June 11, 2001		"Washington should implement the provisions of the D.P.R.K.–U.S. Agreed Framework and the D.P.R.K.–U.S. Joint Communique as agreed upon." (D.P.R.K. Foreign Ministry spokesman)
July 3, 2001	"We need to see some progress in all areas . . . we don't feel any urgency to provide goodies to them . . . " (senior Administration official, on the broadened demands to North Korea)	
January 2002	"States like these . . . constitute an axis of evil, arming to threaten the peace of the world." (George Bush, State of the Union speech)	
February 2, 2002		"His [Bush's] remarks clearly show that the U.S.-proposed "resumption of dialogue" with the DPRK is intended not for the improvement of the bilateral relations but for

TABLE 5.3 (continued)

DATE	U.S. STATEMENTS	D.P.R.K. STATEMENTS
		the realization of the U.S. aggressive military strategy. It is the steadfast stand and transparent will of the DPRK to counter force with force and confrontation with confrontation." (Korean Central News Agency)
February 7, 2002		"As we always say, a nice word will be answered by a nice word," but setting conditions ahead of negotiations "is not acceptable at all . . . If Washington continues to make very, very hostile policy-making statements [and chooses] military options . . . then our armed forces and our people would have no other choice but to react on the same basis. It is entirely up to the United States." (Pak Kil-Yon, DPRK Ambassador to the U.N.)
June 1, 2002	"We must take the battle to the enemy . . . and confront the worst threats before they emerge." (GWB)	
June 10, 2002	"First, the North must get out of the proliferation business and eliminate long-range missiles that threaten other countries . . . the North needs to move toward a less threatening conventional military	

TABLE 5.3 (continued)

DATE	U.S. STATEMENTS	D.P.R.K. STATEMENTS
	posture . . . and living up to its past pledges to implement basic confidence-building measures." (Colin Powell)	
		Pyongyang accepts the agenda. Also sets up a military hotline
August 29, 2002	North Korea is "in stark violation of the Biological weapons convention . . . many doubt that North Korea ever intends to comply fully with its NPT obligations." (Undersecretary of State John Bolton)	
August 31, 2002		"The DPRK clarified more than once that if the U.S. has a willingness to drop its hostile policy toward the D.P.R.K., it will have dialogue with the U.S. to clear the U.S. of its worries over its security." (DPRK Spokesman)
October 20, 2002		"If the United States is willing to drop its hostile policy towards us, we are prepared to deal with various security concerns through dialogue." (Kim Yong-Nam, Chair of the Supreme People's Assembly)
October 25, 2002		"The D.P.R.K. is ready to seek a negotiated settlement of this issue on the following

TABLE 5.3 (continued)

DATE	U.S. STATEMENTS	D.P.R.K. STATEMENTS
		three conditions: firstly, if the United States recognizes the D.P.R.K.'s sovereignty; secondly, if it assures the D.P.R.K. of nonaggression; and thirdly, if the United States does not hinder the economic development of the D.P.R.K." (DPRK spokesman)
November 2002		"Everything will be negotiable, including inspections of the enrichment program . . . our government will resolve all U.S. security concerns through the talks if your government has a will to end its hostile policy." (Han Song-Ryol, D.P.R.K. ambassador to the U.N.)
December 29, 2002	"We cannot suddenly say 'Gee, we're so scared. Let's have a negotiation because we want to appease your misbehavior. This kind of action cannot be rewarded." (Secretary of State Colin Powell)	
January 5, 2003	"We have no intention of sitting down and bargaining again." (State Department spokesman Richard Boucher)	
January 9, 2003	"We think that they [Russia] could be putting the screws to the North Koreans a little	

TABLE 5.3 (continued)

DATE	U.S. STATEMENTS	D.P.R.K. STATEMENTS
	more firmly and at least beginning to raise the specter of economic sanctions." (Senior U.S. official)	
January 9, 2003		"... we have no intention to produce nuclear weapons ... After the appearance of the Bush Administration, the United States listed the DPRK as part of an 'axis of evil', adopting it as a national policy to oppose its system, and singled it out as a target of pre-emptive nuclear attack ... it also answered the DPRK's sincere proposal for conclusion of the DPRK-US non-aggression treaty with such threats as 'blockade' and 'military punishment ... ' (DPRK official announcement of withdrawal from the NPT)
January 23, 2003	"First is regime change. It need not necessarily be military, but it could lead to that." (Senior U.S. official)	

Sources: "North Asian Leaders Criticize Bush on North Korea," *Wall Street Journal* (January 6, 2003); "South Korea is Optimistic About End to Nuclear Crisis," *Wall Street Journal* (January 4, 2003); "Powell says U.S. is Willing to Talk with North Korea," *New York Times* (December 29, 2002); "N. Korea pulls out of nuclear pact," MSNBC News Services (January 10, 2003); Leon Sigal, "North Korea is No Iraq: Pyongyang's Negotiating Strategy," (Special Report, Nautilus Organization, December 23, 2002); Susan V. Lawrence, Murray Hiebert, Jay Solomon, and Kim Jung Min, "Time to Talk," *Far Eastern Economic Review*, January 23, 2003, pp. 12–16.

Powell refused to consider dialogue with the North, remarking that "We cannot suddenly say 'Gee, we're so scared. Let's have a negotiation because we want to appease your misbehavior. This kind of action cannot be rewarded."[27]

As one North Korean diplomat noted: "The Agreed Framework made American generals confident that the DPRK had become defenseless; the only way to correct this misperception is to develop a credible deterrent against the United States."[28] At the time of writing, the situation is a standoff. North Korean statements make clear their fear that the Bush administration will focus on pressuring North Korea once the situation in Iraq is stabilized. The January 28, 2003, statement of the Korean Anti-Nuke Peace Committee in Pyongyang concluded by saying that:

> If the U.S. legally commits itself to non-aggression including the non-use of nuclear weapons against the DPRK through the non-aggression pact, the DPRK will be able to rid the U.S. of its security concerns. . . . Although the DPRK has left the NPT, its nuclear activity at present is limited to the peaceful purpose of power generation. . . . If the U.S. gives up its hostile policy toward the DPRK and refrains from posing a nuclear threat to it, it may prove that it does not manufacture nuclear weapons through a special verification between the DPRK and the U.S. . . . It is the consistent stand of the DPRK government to settle the nuclear issue on the Korean peninsula peacefully through fair negotiations for removing the concerns of both sides on an equal footing between the DPRK and the U.S.[29]

CAUSES AND CONSEQUENCES OF THE OCTOBER REVELATION Thus, the Agreed Framework of 1994 is dead. Both North Korea and the United States are now in essentially the same position they were in 1994—threatening war, moving toward confrontation. Given the levels of mistrust on both sides, this comes as no surprise. If North Korea already feels threatened, it is unlikely to be assuaged by more such threats.. Gregory Clark pointed out that "Washington's excuse for ignoring the nonaggression treaty proposal has to be the ultimate in irrationality. It said it would not negotiate under duress. So duress consists of being asked to be nonaggressive?"[30]

The explanation for the collapse of the Agreed Framework follows from the argument elucidated in chapters 2 and 4. An intense security dilemma on the Korean peninsula is exacerbated by an almost complete lack of direct interaction between the two sides. Levels of mistrust are so high that both sides hedge their bets. The United States refused to provide formal written assurances of nonaggression to the North. The North thus retains its military and nuclear forces in order to deter the United States from acting too precipitously.

The consequences are fairly clear: the United States can continue a policy of pressure in hopes that the North will buckle and give in to U.S. pressure or collapse from internal weakness, or it can negotiate a bargain of normalization for nuclear weapons. Without resolving North Korea's security fears, the opportunity for any quick resolution of the confrontation on the peninsula will be limited. This is disappointing, because North Korea, unlike Iraq, is actively seeking accommodation with the international community. Even while the Bush administration was increasing its pressure on the North, the North continued its voluntary moratorium not to test its missiles until 2003. The North's tentative moves toward economic openness have also been stymied for the time being. As noted in chapter 4, in July 2002, North Korea introduced a free market system allowing prices to determine supply and demand for goods and services. In September 2002, it announced a special economic zone in Shinuiju. Even in the last six months of 2002, work began to clear off a section of the demilitarized zone to allow the reconnection of the railway between North and South Korea. To cap all of these developments, Kim Jong-il finally admitted this September after three decades of denials that the North kidnapped Japanese citizens in the 1970s.

If North Korea really wanted to develop nuclear weapons, it would have done so long ago. Even if North Korea develops and deploys nuclear weapons, it will not use them, because the U.S.

deterrent is clear and overwhelming. The North wants a guarantee of security from the United States, and a policy of isolating it will not work. Isolation is better than pressure, because pressure would only make it even more insecure. But even isolation is at best a holding measure. Nor would the imposition of economic sanctions or economic engagement be likely to get North Korea to abandon its weapons program.

Above all, the North Korean regime wants better ties with the United States. The policy that follows from this is clear: the United States should begin negotiating a nonaggression pact with the North. It should let other countries, such as South Korea and Japan, pursue economic diplomacy if they wish. If the North allows back UN nuclear inspectors and dismantles its reactors, the United States could then move forward to actual engagement. But to dismiss the country's security fears is to miss the cause of its actions.

The Bush administration's steadfast refusal to consider dialogue with the North is counterproductive. Even at the height of the cold war, Ronald Reagan, despite calling the Soviet Union "the Evil Empire," met with Soviet leaders and held dialogues with them. The United States had ambassadorial relations with the Soviets, engaged in trade with the Soviets, and interacted regularly—precisely in order to moderate the situation and keep information moving between the two adversaries and to keep the situation from inadvertently escalating out of control. The United States was in far greater contact with the Soviet Union during the cold war than it is with North Korea in 2003. By refusing to talk, the United States allows the situation to spiral out of control, and harms its own ability to deal with the reality of the situation.

Does the October nuclear revelation provide any insight as to North Korea's foreign policy strategy? Essentially, no: North Korea has always sought to deter the United States, and has viewed the United States as belligerent against it. Thus the nuclear program is consistent with its attempts to provide for its own security. It is also important to remember that a nuclear weapons program does not mean that North Korea is any more likely to engage in unprovoked military acts now than before. North Korea was deterred before the revelations, and it remains deterred. The way to resolve the crisis is by addressing the security concerns of North Korea. If the United States genuinely has no intention of attacking North Korea or pressuring it for regime change, the administration should conclude a nonaggression pact. It is not that surprising that North Korea does not believe the Bush administration's occasional assurances about having no intention of using force, when the administration refuses to formalize those assurances.

In terms of U.S. policy toward the North, the revelations are actually an opening. It is impossible to negotiate with a country over an issue they deny exists. In the case of the nuclear program, the U.S. has the opportunity to actually reach a conclusion to this problem. Handled adroitly, the Bush administration could possibly finally resolve an issue that has plagued Northeast Asia for far too long.

VICTOR CHA: PAST THE POINT OF NO RETURN?

Many moderates argued, as David Kang has done, that this new nuclear confession is revealing of Pyongyang's true intentions. They argue that these actions represent North Korean leader Kim Jong-il's perverse but typical way of creating a crisis to pull a reluctant Bush administration into serious dialogue. By "confessing" to the crime, in other words, Pyongyang is putting its chips on the table, ready to bargain away this clandestine program in exchange for aid and a U.S. pledge of nonaggression.[31] They would therefore advocate continued negotiations by the United States and its allies, providing incentives for the North to come clean on its uranium-enrichment activities as well as extend a more comprehensive nonproliferation arrangement to replace the Agreed Framework. In exchange for this, the allies would put forward a package of incentives including economic aid and normalization of political relations.

Before the world accepts this "cry for help" thesis, however, the North's confession must be seen for what it is: a serious violation of a standing agreement that could in effect be North Korea's last gambit at peaceful engagement with the United States and its allies. North Korea's actions constitute a blatant breakout from the 1994 US-DPRK Agreed Framework designed to ensure denuclearization of the North. Those who try to make a technical, legalistic argument to the contrary are patently wrong. Though the Agreed Framework dealt specifically with the plutonium reprocessing facilities at Yongbyon, this document was cross-referenced with the 1991–1992 North-South Korea denuclearization declaration, which banned either Korea from the uranium-enrichment facilities now found to be covertly held in the North. Moreover any legal gymnastics over this issue was rendered moot by North Korea's subsequent withdrawal from the nonproliferation treaty, the only country to have done so in the NPT's history.

Moreover, the implications of this act extend beyond a mere violation of legal conventions. Arguably all of the improvements in North-South relations including the June 2000 summit, breakthroughs in Japan-North Korea relations in 2001, and the wave of engagement with the reclusive regime that spread across Europe, Australia, and Canada in 2000–2001, were made possible by what was perceived to be the North's good-faith intentions to comply with a major nonproliferation commitment with the United States in 1994. The subtext of this commitment was that the North was willing to trade in its rogue proliferation threat for a path of reform and peaceful integration into the world community. The subsequent diplomatic achievements by Pyongyang, therefore, would not have been possible without the Agreed Framework. And now the North has shown it all to be a lie.

ALTERNATIVE EXPLANATIONS FOR NORTH KOREAN MISBEHAVIOR

Many of the justifications offered by either Pyongyang or mediating parties in Seoul (an irony itself) for the HEU program and restarting of its plutonium program at Yongbyon are, at best, suspect. North Korea claimed its actions were warranted as responses to American failure to keep to the timetable of the Agreed Framework, as well as Washington's reneging on promises to normalize relations with the North. Moreover, they argued that U.S. aggressive language and President Bush's "axis of evil" statements compelled the regime in Pyongyang to their misbehavior. Nevertheless, as assistant secretary Kelly noted in the meeting with Kang Sok-ju, the North Koreans had been pursuing the HEU program before the Bush administration assumed office, and were indeed doing so while they were enjoying the benefits of Kim Dae-jung's sunshine policy from 1999 to 2002.

There is no denying that the United States and KEDO fell behind in the implementation of the Agreed Framework in large part because the signing of the accord in October 1994 was followed by congressional elections that put in control Republicans with strong antipathy to Clinton (and by definition then, the Agreed Framework). The North Koreans were aware of this possibility and therefore sought a personal guarantee during the negotiations from President Clinton that the United States would do what it could to keep implementation on schedule: "I will use the full powers of my office to facilitate arrangements for the financing and construction of a light-water nuclear power reactor project within the DPRK, and the funding and implementation of interim energy alternatives for the DPRK, pending completion of the first reactor unit. . . . in the event that this reactor project is not completed for reasons beyond the control of the DPRK, I will use the full powers of my office to provide, to the extent necessary, such a project from the United States, subject to the approval of the U.S. Congress. . . . I will follow this course of action so long as the DPRK continues to implement the policies described in the Agreed Framework." (Text of President Clinton's Letter to Kim Jong-il.) In other words, as far back as October 1994, Pyongyang was cognizant of such potential problems in implementation. To argue otherwise as justification for their illicit nuclear activities is a stretch. Moreover, although the Agreed Framework was not a legally binding document, arguably there is a distinction between negligence in implementing a contract and completely reneging on one. Washington could certainly be guilty of the former, but that does not warrant the other party's actions to do the latter.

Kim Jong-il's justification that he needs to wield the nuclear threat as a backstop for regime survival and deterrence against U.S. preemption also does not hold water. This is not because anyone should expect Kim to believe Bush's public assurances that he has no intention to attack North Korea, but because any logical reasoning shows that the North already possesses these deterrent capabilities. Its 11,000 artillery tubes along the DMZ hold Seoul hostage, and its Nodong ballistic missile deployments effectively hold Japan hostage. As noted earlier, the warning time for a North Korean artillery shell landing in Seoul is measured in seconds (57), and for a ballistic missile fired on the Japanese archipelago, measured in minutes (10). There is no conceivable defense against these threats that does not result in hundreds of thousands, if not millions of casualties. As long as the United States values the welfare of these two key allies in Northeast Asia (as well as the 100,000-plus American service personnel and expatriate community), the North holds a credible deterrent against any hypothetical contemplation of American preemption.

Finally, the argument that North Korea is seeking direct negotiations with the United States rather than a bona fide nuclear weapons capability with the latest crisis is both disturbing and logically inconsistent. North Korea seeks a nonaggression pact, these advocates argue, and a new relationship by using the only leverage it can muster—i.e., its military threat. There are three glaring problems with this argument.

First, the notion that North Korean proliferation is solely for bargaining purposes runs contrary to the history of why states proliferate. Crossing the nuclear threshold is a national decision of immense consequence, and as numerous studies have shown, is a step rarely taken deliberately for the purpose of negotiating away these capabilities.[32]

Second, even if one were to accept as true these North Korean intentions, the moral hazard issues become obvious. Rather than moving Pyongyang in the direction of more compliant behavior, indulging the North's brinkmanship is likely only to validate their perceived success of the strategy. Such coercive bargaining strategies in the past by the North might have been met with engagement by the United States, but in the aftermath of the October 2002 nuclear revelations, such behavior is more difficult to countenance. The difference, will be explained below, largely stems from the gravity of North Korean misbehavior in 2002 and violation of the agreed framework.

Third, the "negotiation" thesis for North Korean proliferation, upon closer analysis, actually leads one to the *opposite* logical conclusion—in other words, a North Korean "breakout" strategy of amassing a mid-sized nuclear weapons arsenal. South Korean advocates of the negotiation thesis maintain that Pyongyang is aware of the antipathy felt by the Bush administration toward the Clinton-era agreements made with it. Therefore, Pyongyang seeks to leverage the proliferation threat to draw the Bush administration into bilateral negotiations, ostensibly to obtain a nonaggression pact, but in practice to obtain *any* agreement with this government. Ideally this agreement would offer more benefits than the 1994 agreement, but even if this were not the case, the key point, according to these officials, is that the agreement would have the Bush administration's imprimatur rather than that of Clinton, and therefore would be more credible in North Korean eyes.[33]

Such an argument, while plausible, leads to a compelling counterintuitive conclusion. If North Korea wants a new and improved agreement from that of 1994, and knows that this current administration is more "hardline" than the previous one, then the logical plan of action would not be to negotiate away its potential nuclear capabilities (the modus operandi in 1994) but to *acquire* nuclear weapons and *then* confront the United States from a stronger position than the one in 1994. Indeed, North Korean actions in December 2002 appear to be more than a bargaining ploy. If coercive bargaining were the primary objective, then the North Koreans arguably needed to undertake only one of several steps to denude the 1994 agreement. On the contrary, their un-sealing of buildings, disabling of monitoring cameras, expelling international inspectors, withdrawal from the NPT, restarting the reactor, and reprocessing represented a purposeful drive to develop weapons. As one U.S. government official observed, "we made a list of all the things the North Koreans might do to ratchet up a crisis for the purpose of negotiation. They went through that list pretty quickly."[34]

WHAT FOLLOWS HAWK ENGAGEMENT?

There is no denying that Bush's "axis of evil" statements exacerbated a downward trend in U.S.-DPRK relations. But actions matter more than semantics. The problem is not what the United States, South Korea, or Japan may have done wrong to irk the North. The problem is North Korea. What is most revealing about the North's actions is that hawkish skepticism vis-à-vis a real change in Kim Jong-il's underlying intentions, despite behavior and rhetoric to the contrary, remains justified.

This skepticism, as I have argued, is what informs the "hawk engagement" approach toward North Korea. Unlike South Korea's "sunshine policy" of unconditional engagement, this version of the strategy is laced with a great deal more pessimism, less trust, and a pragmatic calculation of the steps to follow in case the policy fails. The discussion in chapter 3 reminds us of the reasons why hawks might pursue engagement with North Korea: (1) Today's carrots can become tomorrow's sticks—particularly with a target state that has very little; (2) Economic and food aid can start the slow process of separating the North Korean people from its despotic regime; (3) Engagement is the most practical way to build a coalition for punishment by placing the onus of maintaining cooperation upon the North.

The 2002–2003 nuclear revelations confirm much of the skepticism that informs the hawk engagement approach. Remember, the premise of hawk engagement is to pursue engagement for the purpose of testing the North's intentions and genuine capacity to cooperate. If this diplomacy succeeds, then the sunshine policy advocates are correct about North Korea, and honest hawks (as opposed to ideological ones) would be compelled to continue on this path. But if engagement fails, then one has shown the North's true intentions, and built the consensus for an alternate course of action. The nuclear violations in this context have created more transparency about the extent to which the North's reform efforts represent mere tactical changes or a true shift in strategy and preferences. As hawk engagement believers had always expected, Kim Jong-il has now dropped the cooperation ball. What comes next? The first step is to rally a multilateral coalition for diplomatic pressure among the allies. The fall 2002 APEC meetings in Mexico, and the U.S.-Japan-Korea trilateral statement at these meetings took important first steps in this direction. Both Seoul and Tokyo decreed that any hopes Pyongyang might have for inter-Korean economic cooperation or a large normalization package of Japanese aid hinges on satisfactory resolution of the North's current violation (people also have wrongfully discounted the significance of a similar statement by APEC as a whole—the first of its kind explicitly on a security problem by the multilateral institution).

A second important step was taken in November 2002 when the three allies, through the Korea Energy Development Organization (KEDO) agreed to suspend further shipments of heavy fuel oil to North Korea promised under the 1994 agreement until Pyongyang come back into compliance. A third step effectively "multilateralizing" the problem occurred in February 2003 when North Korea's refusal to return to the NPT prompted the IAEA to refer the issue to the UN Security Council. Critical additional steps in this direction include a UN Security Council resolution formally demanding DPRK cooperation and return to the NPT, and other possible multilateral fora that involve the regional powers in Northeast Asia.

Pundits and critics have blasted the United States for its "no-talk, no-negotiation" position until North Korea rolls back its

HEU program. On the contrary, hawk engagement would posit that the Bush administration's relatively low-key response to North Korea's violation (especially when compared to that of Iraq), coupled with its withholding negotiations with Pyongyang until it first makes gestures to come back into compliance, is effectively an offer to the North for one last chance to extgract itself from its own mess. In this sense, as Harry Rowen at Stanford University has observed, this *is* the negotiating position. Kim Jong-il needs to unilaterally address international concerns to dismantle verifiably the HEU program and return to the status quo ante. If he were to do this, then the possibility of new U.S.-DPRK negotiations that involve quid pro quos of economic aid for nonproliferation would lie ahead.

WHY NOT HAWK ENGAGEMENT AGAIN?

Prominent figures in the United States like former President Carter, Ambassador Robert Gallucci and others have argued for turning back the engagement clock and entering into new negotiations to gain access to the HEU program and roll back the 1994 agreement violations.[35] In a related vein, other commentators and journalists have argued implicitly that the United States should pursue some form of hawk engagement in the aftermath of the HEU revelations to at least "test" whether North Korea is interested in giving up the program.[36] Others have explicitly invoked the hawk engagement argument to criticize the Bush administration's non-engagement with North Korea.[37]

I (V. C.) don't find engagement a feasible option after the HEU revelations for one very critical reason: *The initial rationale for hawk engagement was based on some degree of ambiguity with regard to the target regime's intentions.* As long as such ambiguity existed, as it did in 1994, and Pyongyang remained somewhat compliant with the standing agreements that were the fruits of engagement thereafter, it would be difficult for hawks to advocate otherwise. Hence when the North Koreans test-fired a ballistic missile over

Japan in 1998, conducted submarine incursions into the South, attacked South Korean naval vessels, and undertook other acts of malfeasance, I still believed that engagement even for hawks was the appropriate path. *The current violations by the North are, however, on a scale that removes any ambiguity about North Korean intentions.* As noted above, this behavior did not represent minor deviations from the landmark agreement, but a wholesale and secretive breakout from it. Negotiating under these conditions, for hawks, would be tantamount to appeasement.

If the current impasse is resolved diplomatically, however, by the DPRK taking unilateral steps toward dismantlement of the facilities, then regional diplomatic pressures, allied entreaties, and public opinion would again compel hawks to pursue some form of engagement. Such engagement would not be informed by any newfound "trust" in North Korea or its intentions. Indeed hawk engagement in such a scenario would be informed by infinitely more palpable skepticism and distrust than existed prior to the HEU revelations, and perhaps with an even shorter tolerance for additional misbehavior by the North before switching to an alternate more coercive path.

ISOLATION AND CONTAINMENT

If the North Koreans do not take the cooperative path out of the current crisis, then from a hawk engagement perspective there is no choice but isolation and containment. The strategy's general contours would be to rally interested regional powers to isolate and neglect the regime until it gave up its proliferation threat. Although this would be akin to a policy of benign neglect, it would not be benign. The United States and its allies would maintain vigilant containment of the regime's military threat and would intercept any vessels suspected of carrying nuclear- or missile-related materials in and out of the North. Secondary sanctions would also be levied against firms in Japan and other Asian countries involved in illicit North Korean drug trafficking in an effort to restrict the flow of remittances to the DPRK leadership. The United States and ROK might also undertake a reorientation of their military posture on the peninsula, focusing more on long-range, deep-strike capabilities, and betting that the DPRK will respond by scaling back forward deployments in defense of Pyongyang.[38]

This strategy of "malign neglect" would also entail more proactive humanitarian measures, including the continuation of food aid, designed to help and engage the North Korean people. The United States would urge China and other countries to allow the United Nations High Commissioner for Refugees to establish North Korean refugee processing camps in neighboring countries around the Peninsula enabling a regularized procedure for dealing with population outflows from the decaying country. Potentially a more significant watershed in this regard would be passage of a bill clearing the way for the United States to accept a limited number of North Koreans who meet the definition of refugee and desire safe haven in the U.S. In this regard, the United States would lead by example in preparing to facilitate passage out of the darkness that is North Korea to those people who have the courage to vote with their feet.

Two critical actors in pursuing such an unattractive course of action will be China and South Korea. China's stake in propping up its old ally on the peninsula is geostrategic and keyed to a competitive U.S.-China relationship. It has no desire to see a collapse of the regime and the specter of a U.S. military presence remaining on the peninsula. Chinese equities are undeniably shifting, however, as the North Koreans pursue a nuclear weapons capability. It is official Chinese policy to oppose nuclear weapons on the peninsula in large part because of the ripple effects that such weapons might have on Japanese and Taiwanese plans for such capabilities. Combining this worst-case contingency with frustration at the need to continue to pour food, fuel, and aid in large amounts (estimated around 70–90 percent of all North Korean external reliance) to a country that has shown virtually no progress toward reform might cause Chinese leaders to think differently. Although any major shifts in Chinese policy toward North Korea will await the Party Congress in March 2003, U.S. efforts at capitalizing on its more constructive post–September 11 relationship with Beijing, and helping China defray the negative externalities that might come from an isolation strategy toward North Korea might be the key variable in the strategy's feasibility and success.[39] If Beijing were to cooperate in diplomatically pressuring the North, moreover, this decision would not be seen as kowtowing to the United States, but rather as stepping up to a leadership role in the region. China's aspirations to great-power status in the region will be dependent on not only its economic capabilities but also the type of political leadership it will be seen as providing. A proactive role in reducing the North Korean nuclear threat would provide a security good to the region appreciated by all.

Where South Korea stands in a U.S. isolation policy undeniably will be a test of the alliance. Reduced perceptions of North Korean threat since the June 2000 summit particularly among the younger generation of South Koreans (despite little material change in the security situation on the ground), coupled with the upsurge of anti-Americanism during the December 2002 presidential elections (following the accidental USFK vehicular death of two South Korean teenage girls) resulted in an incredulous phenomenon in 2003. In the face of increasing DPRK nuclear threats, South Koreans demonstrated against the alliance with the United States, blaming it for provoking the crisis with North Korea.

If these two trends continue (i.e., anti-Americanism and no fear of North Korea), then an American isolation and containment policy toward North Korea would be unacceptable to South Koreans. If South Koreans, moreover, oppose such a U.S. policy at the expense of allowing a nuclear North Korea, then the alliance might be damaged beyond repair. Two critical variables in this mix will be the leadership of the Roh Moo-hyun government and the South Korean "silent majority." In spite of Roh's past political activities and his left-leaning ideology, many argue that pragmatism and some badly needed foreign policy experience will cause him to moderate his views to be more supportive of the alliance (such was the case with Kim Dae-jung).[40]

Even more important, if North Korean malfeasance grows more pronounced, the future of the alliance and a coordinated isolation strategy toward North Korea may rest in the hands of the South Korean electorate. Despite the media-hype of a younger Korean generation that purportedly fears George Bush more than a nuclear-armed Kim Jong-il, polls show that almost 50 percent of the electorate holds a more somber view of North Korea's nuclear weapons obsession, and this silent majority presumably would grow as the North moves close to such capabilities unchecked.[41] What deters many South Koreans are the costs that would come from an isolation strategy's precipitous collapse of the DPRK regime. This is understandable. South Koreans must also realize, however, that the costs of letting North Korea grow unfettered into a nuclear power are not free. Not only might these costs be measured in terms of lost alliance support from the United States, but also huge potential losses in investor confidence. Moody Investors downgraded South Korea's sovereign credit rating in 2003 because of the DPRK threat.[42] A nuclear North Korea places undeniable costs on South Korea that not even the younger generation should underestimate (more on this in chapter 6).

No doubt there are dangers associated with an isolation strategy, not least of which is North Korean retaliation. Pyongyang states clearly that they would consider isolation and sanctions by the United States as an act of war. To support isolation, however, is not to crave war on the peninsula. Indeed after engagement has been proven to fail (as it has for hawk engagers after the HEU revelations), then isolation is the *least* likely strategy to provoke war as the remaining options are all much more coercive (including preemptive military strikes).

There is no denying the gravity of the crisis in 2003. For hawk engagement, the offer to Kim Jong-il to resolve concerns about his dangerous uranium-enrichment and plutonium nuclear weapons programs if he wants to get back on the engagement path is, in effect, the last round of diplomacy. Not taking up this offer would mean a path of isolation and containment of the regime and an end to many positive gains Pyongyang accumulated since the June 2000 inter-Korean summit. Given the high stakes involved, one hopes that Kim Jong-il makes the correct calculation.

THE LAST WORD ON THE CRISIS

David Kang embraces the argument that the North's blatant HEU confession is a cleverly-disguised attempt to "retail" its new threat and thus draw a reluctant Bush administration into negotiations. Given these intentions as explained in chapters 2 and 4, he advocates negotiation by the United States and its allies to bring *both* the United States and the North Koreans back into compliance in exchange for a package of incentives including economic aid and normalization of political relations. As long as the United States threatens the North, Kang sees little hope that pressure will make the North disarm. But Kang sees great potential for reduced tensions and increased economic opening in North Korea if the U.S. makes a credible commitment to nonaggression.

The overall contours of such a package are not the point of disagreement for Cha. As explained in chapters 1 and 3, there are still good reasons for engaging such a dangerous regime. The primary point of departure for Cha would be the withholding of such a negotiation until the North Koreans first resolve international concerns about the HEU program and restore the status quo ante at Yongbyon. To engage with Pyongyang in the face of such a blatant breakout from the Agreed Framework would be tantamount to appeasement. However, maintaining a coalition of allies to impress upon Kim Jong-il in the strongest terms the need to first come clean in order to return to a path of engagement with the outside world appears to be the most prudent course of action. From a hawk engagement perspective, such a strategy also puts the cooperation ball clearly in the North's court, and in this sense, also contributes to a coalition for isolation and containment should Kim Jong-il fail to return serve.

VICTOR CHA AND DAVID KANG

BEYOND HYPERBOLE, TOWARD A STRATEGY

6

In this book, we reduce the signal-to-noise ratio on North Korea. We offer two systematic and scholarly assessments of the threat posed by North Korea, and the extent to which North Korean intentions are reform-oriented. We try to demonstrate that the dearth of evidence regarding this mysterious country does not require the debate on policy to take place only at a hyperbolic level. On the contrary, we show that one can have a serious and balanced discussion about what might be motivating Pyongyang's behavior, and what sort of dangers (or lack thereof) are inherent in this behavior. Neither of us are ideologues;. neither of us are politicos. But we clearly have our orientations. David Kang is less skeptical and more open-minded about the prospects for North Korea. He believes engagement is the best policy for dealing with the misunderstood regime. Victor Cha is more skeptical, particularly in the aftermath of the 2002–2003 North Korean nuclear revelations, but he too would advocate a "hawkish" form of engagement if North Korea came back into nonproliferation compliance.

BROAD CONTOURS OF THE POLICY

Our job is not to delineate all elements of such a policy. Rather, as scholars, our purpose is to debate and develop the commanding rationale for the policy. This is something that the policymaking world often cannot afford the time to do. Often, the current set of policymakers reacts to a policy from a previous administration. Or they try to extrapolate a more general foreign policy orientation without assessing the problem on its own merits. Moreover, it is only the pressures of a crisis that evokes either of these two less-than-thoughtful reactions from high-level White House principals after protracted periods of inattention. In this book, we tried to question the assumptions, arguments, and counter-arguments that inform the conventional wisdoms and rambunctious debates on North Korea. We claimed no more information on North Korea than others. We did, however, attempt to make the best use of what evidence exists by embedding it in conceptual and social scientific arguments and models. Once the commanding rationale for the policy choice becomes clear, it becomes the job of policymakers to assemble the elements of that policy.

Having said this, we can certainly enumerate what the broad contours of such an engagement strategy might entail. First, and critical to any engagement policy, is the maintenance of robust defense and deterrence capabilities on the peninsula against the threat of a second DPRK invasion or other forms of military adventurism. Such capabilities would require maintaining even as the U.S.-ROK alliance undergoes imminent change. The United States contemplates a change in the nature of its military presence on the peninsula, moving from a heavy, ground troops-based tripwire presence to one focused on more recessed forces and a larger air and naval component. If North Korea views this readjustment of forces within the alliance as a diminishing of the U.S. commitment rather than as a natural maturation of the alliance given domestic politics in South Korea and changing military technology, then not only deterrence, but also engagement would be undercut. Engagement only works when it is undergirded by such capabilities and communicates to the target state that engagement is a choice of the strong and not an expediency of the weak.

Second, a precondition for an effective engagement policy, whether one has dovish or hawkish orientations, is trilateral consultation and coordination among Seoul, Tokyo, and Washington. Such coordination is necessary not only to prevent North Korean attempts at wedge-driving, but also because any useful package of incentives that might elicit real and substantive concessions from the North requires the complementary carrots that can be offered by the three allies. The U.S. role would relate largely to security assurances and political normalization, while for Japan and South Korea the incentives would include more direct contributions to North Korea's food, energy, and infrastructure reform. A significant gap between the United States and South Korea, in particular, would not inhibit either party from pursuing engagement (or containment for that matter), but this would be at the expense of an effective policy that elicited real concessions from the North and, potentially, at the expense of the alliance. On the other hand, if all three allies are on the same page, then there is a convincing coalition for others in the region to follow.

Third, in more specific terms, we would encourage the Roh Moo-hyun government to continue with the basic tenets of the sunshine policy focused on family reunions, infrastructure restoration, and trade and investment, but ideally with greater conditionality and less outright side payments as was witnessed during Kim Dae-jung's administration. The South Korean public would only accept an economically rational engagement policy. In addition, we agree that the baseline of any comprehensive United States engagement strategy would include the lifting of economic sanctions against the North, a negative security assurance against unprovoked attack (i.e., some form of reaffirmation of the October 2001 U.S.-DPRK affirmation of no hostile intent), and a commitment not to seek the unilateral revision or abrogation of previous agreements. Again, our support derives from different rationales. Kang supports the first measure because they would further encourage the North down a path of reform they have already chosen. He supports the second one because doing otherwise would make the United States the provocateur absent any evidence of any DPRK misbehavior. Provided North Korea comes back into compliance with the NPT regime, Cha supports these engagement measures because they give the North a stake in the status quo, and provide carrots that could be employed as sticks later.

Fourth, we would agree that all three countries should continue to provide food aid to North Korea through the World Food Program, and insist on comprehensive monitoring and access to all regions. Despite the best efforts of all parties concerned not to leverage food as a political weapon, the 2003 nuclear crisis has resulted in reductions in contributions for North Korea. Japanese aid, in particular, went from $104 million in food aid in 2001 to no contributions in 2002. Although President Bush maintained that humanitarian aid to the North would continue in spite of its nuclear brinkmanship, U.S. donations also decreased from $185 million in 2000 to $63 million in 2002.[1] Food aid, ideally, should be separated from politics. Although many accuse Washington and Tokyo of using food aid as a weapon to coerce North Korea, we believe that Pyongyang's actions are equally responsible. North Korea's leveraging meetings with the South based on the provision of additional food, the distribution of food to the military rather than to children, and the transfer of internationally provided food stocks to third countries in exchange for military equipment are all examples of food aid for political purposes that cannot be blamed on the United States or Japan.

Fifth, we would agree that China should be consulted in the process of engagement and encouraged to offer their good offices to promote dialogue. Beijing played a quiet but critical role in inter-Korean dialogue leading up to the June 2000 summit. China has also been a seemingly important source of quiet influence on Kim Jong-il and his decision to tentatively reform the economy of North Korea. From the trip that Kim Jong-il took to Shanghai in 2002, to the decision in October 2002 to create a special economic zone in Sinuiju across the river from China, the Chinese provide a potentially important source of ballast to North Korea's journey of reform. Their inclusion creates opportunities that might not otherwise exist.

The flip side of China's critical role in a process of engagement with North Korea is the leverage they can bring to bear on the North if things go horribly wrong. Beijing foreign ministry officials' claims of the little influence they have in Pyongyang appear to fly in the face of the substantial amounts of unreported aid they provide. This is estimated in the range of 70 to 90 percent of the North's annual energy needs; one-third of its total outside assistance (thus making China's contribution nearly one-half billion dollars annually); and one-quarter of its total trade. These are not insignificant numbers and are testament to the capabilities Beijing can bring to bear on the North if the political will is there. There is no denying that the Chinese have traditional equities in not putting too much pressure on the isolated regime, most prominent of which is the desire to avoid a collapse of the regime and the flood of refugees across the border. But as noted in the previous chapter, Beijing's equities on the peninsula are shifting. Its throwing of food, fuel, and money down a rathole in North Korea with no prospect of reform contrasts with the burgeoning trade and investment that takes place with South Korea. A North Korea that continues with its bad behavior, moreover, can have countless negative externalities for China. A nuclear North Korea, for example, could lead to a higher level of armaments and nuclear proliferation in the region (including Japan and Taiwan) that would not sit well with Chinese interests. The best argument, however, for China to play a more active role in diplomacy with North Korea, is not to improve relations with the United States, but to fulfill Beijing's own aspirations to be a great power in the region. Through the North Korea problem, Beijing can take regional stability interests to heart and undertake a responsibility to provide a public good for the region. The relevant point here is not that China should yank all aid to North Korea, but that it must be willing to include the possibility as part of diplomacy with North Korea. This is the only way to make engagement more credible.

Sixth, engagement must make clear that retaliation against any bad behavior will be swift and decisive. The recently inaugurated ROK president Roh Moo-hyun declares that a nuclear North

Korea can never be condoned by Seoul. At the same time, Roh argues that the use of force is not an option in dealing with the North. Americans ask how one can rule out the use of force and hope to advance any policy with the nuclear ambitious regime beyond a toothless appeasement policy? The South Korean response is that coercive measures (i.e., surgical attack or sanctions) must be ruled out because they could precipitate a collapse of the North, the costs of which could be too crippling to the South.

This view, however, is based on the belief that the costs of unification are prohibitive for the South. More important, it implicitly assumes that there are relatively lower costs associated with North Korea going nuclear. Both are highly questionable propositions. Let's look at the first part of the equation. It has become a truism that the costs of unification are astronomical. South Koreans understand well that German unification was expensive, and all the macro socioeconomic indicators are that Korean unification would be more so. The population gaps between the Koreas are smaller, and the economic gaps are wider, engendering much higher absorption costs.

Beyond this superficial understanding, however, current research shows that the costs of unification may not be as high as the conventional wisdom argues. Marcus Noland at the Institute for International Economics in Washington DC shows, for example, that unification, while putting a drag on the economy, would not collapse the ROK economy, but would only slow absolute growth rates and increase the overall output of the peninsula relative to a no-collapse outcome. The right combination of fiscal and labor policy that took advantage of a younger North Korean work force (e.g., younger than that of East Germany); capitalized on efficiencies of DPRK marketization; and properly channeled labor and capital could turn the economic challenges of unification into opportunities for growth and profit.[2]

Perhaps more important, to fixate on avoiding the potential costs of unification, as the South Korean government and public do, implicitly assumes that the alternative outcome—a nuclear North Korea—is acceptable. Nothing could be further from the truth. A

North Korea with nuclear and ballistic missile capabilities would have untold costs both direct and indirect. These include capital flight, and a faltering stock market, not to mention the price of rolling back an extant North Korean nuclear weapons program and the costs associated with an arms race and nuclear proliferation ripple effect in a tension-filled region created by North Korea.

Skeptics might counter that such costs are negligible, if not impossible to calculate with accuracy. The recent record shows otherwise. In February 2003, Moodys downgraded South Korea's sovereign credit rating and country outlook for the first time after successive years of positive assessments since the financial crisis some five years ago. The following week, Standard and Poor's (S& did not increase Korea's foreign currency and local corporation credit rating, and cut back expected growth outlook from 5.7 percent to 5 percent. What makes this fairly innocuous judgment significant is that S&P had upgraded Korea's credit rating the year before (to A-) and its general country outlook to stable, leading many experts to bank on further upgrades given improvements in South Korean credit fundamentals in the public and private sectors, and progress in corporate restructuring.

The primary reason for these sober assessments? S&P Director Takahira Ogawa could not have been more direct, stating "There is a risk from the North, which constrains the sovereign rating of South Korea."[3] Those who think that an eternally optimistic South Korean government, committed to the peaceful status quo and engagement with North Korea will be able to muddle through are sorely mistaken. All it took was one short-range missile test by Pyongyang into the Sea of Japan for the KOSPI (Korean Composite Stock Market Price Index) to tumble almost 4 percent (24 points) in one day despite a litany of parallel confidence-inducing events including Roh Moo-hyun's inauguration, the U.S. announcement of the resumption of food aid to the North, and Secretary Powell's statements in Seoul that the U.S. would eventually seek to dialogue with North Korea.[4]

The anticipated costs of unification are lower than we think. And the costs of a nuclear North Korea are much higher than we think. The argument here is not to advocate the use of force, but that the Roh government may want to rethink the basic cost calculation that causes them to take it off the table completely as an option. Such a policy undercuts the credibility of engagement and makes it indistinguishable from appeasement. Keeping a military option on the table (e.g., the threat of sanctions, ship interdiction, or different military force postures on the peninsula), however, does not mean fixating only on the explicit threat of preemptive attack against North Korea. This does not enhance the engagement process.

Some might desire more specifics with regard to policy than we have provided. But such proposals are delimited by the areas on which we disagree. For example, in retaining robust defense and deterrence capabilities as the backbone of engagement, Cha might include a reorientation and expansion of conventional defense capabilities focusing on deeper strike capabilities and smart weapons targeted at Pyongyang (rather than on a holding action at the DMZ), which Kang would see as unnecessarily provocative. Other areas on which we differ include time limits on engagement, the degree of reciprocity expected, missile defense, and providing safe haven to North Korean refugees. Alternatively, Kang would press much more directly for opening and expanding economic relations with the North, whether U.S., Japanese, or South Korean.

KOREA POLICY FOR THE LONG-TERM

The analysis and debates contained in this book constitute an implicit plea for deeper and longer-term thinking on how the U.S. forms its policies on the Korean peninsula. Few would disagree that historically, American policy decisions on Korea have been ad hoc, reactive, and short-term. Included in this group are U.S. decisions no less important than the ceding of the peninsula to Japan's sphere of influence in the Taft-Katsura agreement; the occupation of the southern half of the peninsula in 1945; the decision to divide the peninsula at the 38th parallel; and the entrance into the Korean War.

The need for a thoughtful and long-term U.S. policy in the region runs deeper than just the Korean peninsula. Korea is geographically situated at the crossroads of Northeast Asia, and the interests of four major powers intersect on the peninsula. China, Japan, Russia, and the United States all have a stake in the situation on the peninsula, and each of these countries is affected by what happens there. The logic of Korea's importance to US interests in indisputable. As Nicholas Eberstadt argued, Korea is to Northeast Asia what Belgium was to Europe, the cockpit from which regional dynamics will flow.[5] And Northeast Asia, will remain an important part of the U.S. policy agenda well into the future, for both economic and strategic reasons.

The broader question in this vein is whether it is conceivable for the United States to think in the longer-term about its position on the peninsula beyond the problem of North Korea. We believe that such a discussion should not be limited to how and whether the U.S.-South Korea alliance should be continued, instead it is intimately tied with what the future of Northeast Asia will look like with Korean unification. It is at this macro level that a discussion about long-term U.S. policy on the peninsula must take place. And at this level, frankly, things do not look good. American strategists must squarely accept the fact that Korean unification may set off geostrategic currents in the region that do *not* favor American interests. We offer a perspective that may have seemed unlikely even a year ago, building on larger geopolitical changes occurring in the region and South Korea's domestic political situation. Both scenarios reveal that the United States needs to pay more attention to this corner of the globe.

What is often lost on the West is the observation that the post World War II and cold war formation of geopolitics in East Asia is aberrant in the larger historical context. Asian international relations historically emphasized formal hierarchy among nations while allowing considerable informal equality. With China as the dominant state and surrounding countries as peripheral or secondary states, as long as hierarchy was observed there was little need for interstate war. This contrasts sharply with the Westphalian tradition of international relations that consisted of formal equality between nation-states, informal hierarchy, and almost constant interstate conflict.[6] Thus when China was strong and stable, order was preserved. Chinese weakness, on the other hand, led to chaos in Asia.

With the intrusion of the western powers in the late-nineteenth century, the old Asian order was demolished as both western and Asian powers scrambled to establish influence, leading to the Sino-Japanese war (1894–95) and the Russo-Japanese war (1904–5). This led to a century of tumult until the late 1990s, with the reemergenceof a strong and confident China, the increasing stabilization of Vietnam, and soon, perhaps, a unified Korea. Many international relations and security experts at this time predicted that modern, post–cold war Asia will be potentially unstable.[7] If the system is reverting to its historical pattern, however, the result may be increased stability. China in 2003 is reemerging as the natural gravitational center of Asia. From a historical perspective, a rich and strong China would potentially stabilize the Asian region once again.[8]

While the most optimistic estimates about China's economic potential are probably unrealistic, it is also increasingly clear that China is emerging as the economic center of Asia. Japan, Hong Kong, and South Korea are three of the five largest trading partners with China. In 2002, China surpassed the United States as the largest recipient of foreign direct investment in the world. As China continues its economic growth and military modernization, the key question will be whether China will resume its place at the top of the Asian regional hierarchy.[9] From a western perspective, the answer to this question may seem obvious: Asian nations will balance against a rising China. But in a historical context this is a highly uncertain proposition. Korea was forced to adjust to China even while it attempted to retain autonomy, and this will most likely be the case in the future as well. Koreans are known for their stubborn nationalism, gritty pride, and proud history as a country independent from China, but Korea must also deal with a China that looms large over it. From this perspective, it would be more surprising if Korea attempted to balance China by relying on a U.S. commitment than it would be if they found a means of accommodating China. South Korea rushed to normalize relations with China (and Russia) in the early post–cold war. And even after China normalized ties with South Korea in 1992, North Korea and China have managed to have a close relationship. South Korea has shown considerable deference to China, especially in its reluctance to fully support U.S. plans for theater missile defense.[10] In economic terms, China's share of trade with Korea and the region is outpacing that of the United States. Finally, South Korean military planning—even the distant planning for post-unification defense—has been focused on water-borne threats, not the potential threat of a Chinese land invasion.[11] South Korea has not begun to envision China as a potential threat or competitor to national security.

History also teaches us that the domestic politics of Korea as it existed during the cold war again may be more an aberration than the rule. The cold war created a right-of-center, obedient, and authoritarian South Korean society that acted as a dutiful ally of the United States. American heavy handedness was tolerated, and management of the alliance accorded to American rules and preferences given the asymmetrical dependence of the two partners. Coinciding with the election of South Korean president Roh Moo-hyun, however, there has been a groundswell of nativist pride in South Korea. The causes for this are many. They are linked to a reduced threat perception of North Korea precipitated by the images of the June 2000 inter-Korean summit (despite no substantial reduction of forces on the North Korean side since the summit). Democracy, development, and generational change have given rise to a younger, affluent, and educated generation in their 20s and 30s who see the United States not as a savior in the Korean war, but as an overbearing ally with a burdensome military footprint in the center of the capital city and a past supporter of military-authoritarian regimes in Korea. The reduced adversarial attitudes toward North Korea among this youth coincide with the search for a modern, 21st-century Korean identity beyond the anti-communism identity of their parents. And in this sense, South Korea's hosting of, and the national team's success in, the 2002 World Cup soccer tournament had a cathartic effect on Korean identity and nationalism.

This confluence of forces resulted in a seemingly anomalous phenomenon emerging in 2003—at a time when the North Korean threat appears to grow, South Koreans were protesting against the alliance's inequities, questioning whether North Korean nuclear brinkmanship is the fault of US overzealous policies, burning American flags, and accosting U.S. servicemen on the streets of Seoul. This, in turn, has led to an emotional reaction from U.S. policymakers, who are insulted at how ungrateful the South Koreans are, and calling for the pullout of U.S. troops. The result is a train wreck in slow motion. Americans grow incensed and saddened at the disrespectful acts committed by South Koreans during their anti-American demonstrations. South Koreans discount the flag burnings as acts by the radical few, and complain that Americans are missing the broader message of these demonstrations: they are about peace and the expressions of a new generation, rather than that of anti-Americanism. Neither hears the other. Left unchecked, these passions could spin out of control, destroying the alliance. Given these two basic observations, one could easily imagine trends in Asia where for reasons of geography, history, culture, power, economics, and demography:

- The domestic politics of Korean unification push the United States military off the peninsula;
- The new Korean entity seeks a continental accommodation with China;
- Korea joins China in heightened tensions against Japan as a combination of resurgent Korean nationalism and new military capabilities incite security dilemmas with its historical enemy;
- A demographically old Japan is isolated from the rest of Asia but at the same time is uncomfortable as the last remaining U.S. outpost in the region.

A variety of other nonlinear dynamics might flow from Korean unification, but given current and past geostrategic trends this is a best estimate of how events might play out.[12] What is striking about this picture is how heavily it weighs against U.S. interests. If the United States has the will to remain an Asia-Pacific power after Korean unification, then it has no interest in being pushed out. This picture is not in the region's interests, moreover, because of its secondary and tertiary consequences. For example, a older, weaker and isolated Japan that does not want the label as the last American military colony in Asia might finally choose greater self-reliance in security. This would set off balancing reactions in China and Korea such that the net assessment for the region's security could be substantially worse with higher levels of tension, a higher level of armaments, and almost certain nuclear proliferation.

For American grand strategy, if this is the "natural" geostrategic current in Asia after Korean unification, then the imperative for American, Japanese, and Korean grand strategy in Asia is to shape a direction away from this trend. In short, what "stones" can be laid in the "stream" today to divert the future geostrategic current in a more positive direction? We believe that the most important way this longer-term imperative informs current U.S. policy to Korea is to promote stronger relations between its two main Asian allies Japan and South Korea, and to consolidate the trilateral U.S.-Japan-ROK relationship. There are four elements to such an American strategy.

An important element of this strategy is, first, to continue to encourage greater security cooperation between Japan and South Korea. In the most immediate and pragmatic terms, the DPRK contingency continues to provide a vehicle for building Japan–South Korea security cooperation. Throughout the 1990s, the threat of North Korean implosion or aggression drove the unprecedented security cooperation involving defense-minister-level bilateral talks, search and rescue exercises, port calls, noncombatant evacuation operations, and academic military exchanges despite the deep historical mistrust between Seoul and Tokyo. It was only within one generation's lifetime that the notion of Korean security cooperation with the Japanese military provoked such gut-wrenching reactions that any bilateral exchanges—even during the security-scarce conditions of the cold war era—were ceremonial, occasional, and unpublicized. These formerly taboo activities have now built confidence and created an entirely new dimension to Seoul-Tokyo relations beyond the political and economic relationship. Due to the high volume of interaction in the 1990s, security cooperation has moved beyond merely pragmatic and transitory exchanges and joint exercises to a more deeply rooted and pre-planned security relationship.

A second critical ingredient in the medium-term strategy for consolidation is to infuse the U.S.-Japan and U.S.-ROK alliances with a meaning and identity beyond the cold war. History shows that the most resilient alliances are those that share a common ideational grounding that runs deeper than the initial adversarial threats that brought the alliance into existence. Alliances in pre-20th-century Europe, for example, were almost without exception short-lived because their existence was a function of mutually convenient, utilitarian, and transient needs rather than being a relationship grounded in a deeper, more permanent affirmation of common values, ways of life, or international institutions. In the 20th century, precisely because NATO's identity evolved to stand for something more than merely a collective defense organization against the Soviet threat, the alliance was able to thrive once the initial raison d'être disappeared. In Asia, the Anglo-Japanese alliance that terminated at the beginning of the 20th century never possessed a rationale that went beyond the exigencies of balance of power politics. By contrast, the American-Australian relationship, embedded in a common language, new-world tradition, and history of fighting together in wars boasts a timeless quality that has extended the alliance well beyond the end of the cold war.

For the U.S.-Japan-Korea relationship, this means deliberate efforts at maturing the alliance beyond its narrow anti-DPRK rationale to encompass a broader definition. Currently, this process has gotten to "maintaining regional stability" as the alliance's future purpose, but there is room for further deepening. Beyond regional stability, there are a host of extra-regional issues that define the relationship. For example, the trilateral relationship represents the success of liberal-democratic values, the common belief in open markets, rule of law, civilian control of the military, the right to free association and speech in a region of the world that has not yet readily accepted these as universal. In addition, the allies share a host of concerns broader than the region: proliferation, human rights violations, constitutional injustices, terrorism, and failed nations. And together, the three allies help form the backbone of the global and regional regimes that deal with these problems. The ideal vision is U.S.-Korea and U.S.-Japan alliances that stand *for* something rather than simply against a threat—that is, alliances that are extra-regional and timeless rather than parochial and timely. This common ideational grounding not only gives the relationships a permanency, but also becomes the glue that prevents these alignments from being washed away by the region's geostrategic currents.

Third, this American strategy for Korea should have a "straddle" component. The United States should seek consolidation of the trilateral U.S.-Japan-ROK axis as a way to reaffirm the U.S. presence in the region, but should do so without an unconditional security guarantee to its allies. This is a lesson of history. The United States has always been the strongest advocate of better Japan-Korea relations (no country has been more keen on this, not even the Koreans and Japanese), but the likelihood of Seoul and Tokyo responding positively to these American burden-sharing entreaties has been highest (counterintuitively) when Washington has been perceived as less interested in underwriting the region's security. During the cold war, for example, Seoul and Tokyo set aside historical problems and took their first baby steps toward defining their bilateral security relationship as the United States declared its uninterest in carrying the primary burden of defense in the region.[13]

The American position in Asia should therefore be recessed enough in this new arrangement to impart responsibilities on the allies to consolidate their relationship, but not so recessed that Japan and South Korea choose "self-help" solutions outside the alliance framework (e.g. rearmament, balancing with other powers in the region). On the Korean peninsula, this reduced commitment would mean, in notional terms, a revised force structure meeting three basic criteria. First, the new force would be downsized but still remain lethal and *deployable*, offering with American forces in Japan the full range of mobility, strike, and maneuver. Second, it would take the character of an over-the-horizon presence, without the traditional tripwire forces and large facilities in the center of Seoul, but this force structure would still need to be a *credible* sign of the American traditional defense commitment to Korea. Third, the force structure, while being large enough to convey a credible commitment, must also not be seen as *obtrusive* in terms of its military footprint in the eyes of the host nation. Notionally on the ground, elements of this strategy on the peninsula would include a greatly reduced American ground troop presence, the likely removal of the Yongsan base complex in central Seoul, upsized basing at Osan airbase, a larger naval presence (perhaps with the addition of a port in the southern part of the peninsula), and maintenance of the nuclear umbrella.

The fourth and final element of such a strategy would be to advocate consolidation of the U.S.-Japan-ROK trilateral axis with nonprovocative forms of cooperation. This element is directed at China. Efforts at trilateral cooperation should be low-profile and transparent to Beijing to the extent possible. Promotion of Seoul-Tokyo bilateral security cooperation for example should not focus on military assets but transport platforms (for pre-planned disaster relief, or joint use of transport craft for out-of-area PKO). This type of cooperation was already being realized in 2002 in Japanese and South Korean participation in PKO missions in East Timor. The ideational and straddle elements of the strategy listed above already have a nonprovocative element to them. Regarding the former, transforming the "language" of the alliances from their cold war identity to, for example, permanent unions among U.S.-Asian market-democracies addresses Beijing's incessant complaints about the anachronistic nature of the U.S. alliances in Asia. The straddle element is also nonprovocative in the sense that this trilateral consolidation takes place absent the traditionally dominant ground troop presence, which the Chinese have always found disconcerting. More anathema to the Chinese than the continuation of the U.S.-ROK alliance after unification is the existence or upgrading of a U.S. ground troop presence on a unified Korea. Two full brigades, prepositioned equipment in Korea and Guam; an infantry division in Hawaii all set up to flow forces back onto the peninsular at a moment's notice would be seen as directed against China. However, a shift to more air and navy presence directed toward regional stability, less prepositioning, and a smaller army presence (10,000) south of the 38th parallel (and south of Seoul) would send a different signal to China. Beijing may not like this new configuration, but it's better than the alternative.[14]

WHY IDENTITY MATTERS

A pragmatic and material rationale therefore exists for U.S.-Japan-Korea alliance resiliency. As Ashton Carter and William Perry have argued, this is a "preventive defense" rationale where strategy is aimed at "dangers [that] are not yet threats to be defeated or deterred; they are dangers that can be prevented."[15] Surveying the elements of this strategy, the most distinctive and difficult task is creating a new "identity" for the alliances beyond the cold war. In other words, investigating the extent to which one can remake the image of the Japan and Korea alliances to stand for something more than merely deterrence against the DPRK threat. There are three reasons why this is important (and when history and political science are actually helpful to practitioners!).

First, although threats give rise to alliances, history has shown that every alliance, once formed, has an identity. In most alliances, this is a "realist" one where there is little in common between the parties except the issue at-hand; hence, once this issue is resolved, the alliance breaks up. What matters in terms of resiliency, therefore, is what forms and identities evolve within the alliance after inception. The U.S.-ROK and U.S.-Japan alliances, for example, both started in the early 1950s as quintessential utilitarian, threat-based security pacts. Very little was known about either country when U.S. occupation forces received the Japanese surrender at the end of World War II. The alliance convened with Japan was wholly a function of the emerging cold war in Asia and had little to do with any intrinsic appreciation of the relationship. And the U.S.-ROK alliance was arguably a "bribe" to get then South Korean president Syngman Rhee to stop sabotaging the armistice talks and sign the 1953 agreement. However, the nature of both relationships evolved considerably from these humble origins. No one would have imagined the three countries interacting as OECD partners in a dense multidimensional relationship that spans security, economics, politics, culture, technology, and society. Indeed, across the spectrum of indicators that define a successful alliance,[16] these two alliances arguably have been among America's most successful—rivaling even NATO. In sum, identity helps differentiate the short-term, narrow, threat-based alliance from the more deeply rooted and permanent union. It gives rise to a longevity and acceptability of the alliance that goes beyond the initial pressures that created it, and at the extreme it can create a consensus for permanency such that abrogation is not even considered.

Second, identity matters because it reflects on American evaluations of the reliability, durability, and indispensability of its relationships. During the cold war, the focus of the United States narrowed to the strategic utility of each alliance at the expense of all other factors. It was "us" against "them" and if allies were "different" in their values and domestic institutions, this hardly mattered given the bigger fight. The end of this overarching security imperative now draws greater attention to the qualitative differences among these alliances. These differences are both puzzling and important. They are puzzling because they do not correlate with the strategic rationales of each alliance. In other words, alliances that serve critical U.S. security interests are not necessarily the most deeply rooted, and ones that are grounded in a history of friendship and mutual trust are not strategically the most valuable. For example, the U.S.–Saudi Arabia alliance protects a key strategic asset and by most military criteria meets the definition of well-functioning alliance; however, one would hardly consider the language used to describe this alliance as "warm and fuzzy." Similarly, few would contemplate any future to the U.S.-Pakistan coalition against terrorism that outlived the end of the Al Qaeda threat. Conversely, the positive light in which discussions of the U.S.-Australia alliance are cast seems disproportionate to its strategic utility. There is more at work here than power and strategic purpose.

Third, identity matters because it helps explain why we make choices with regard to the fate of certain alliances and why we do not consider other alternatives. For example, in pure power politics terms, security competition in Asia could be resolved through a U.S.–China condominium; however, in practice, it is difficult to imagine that the United States would abandon the time-honored alliance with Japan in favor of an alliance with China. On the other hand, strategists have little trouble imagining or discussing the prospects of a future "ABCA" alliance of America, Britain, Canada, and Australia. With certain alliances, faith in the ally's commitment does not extend beyond a very specific contingency; moreover, little thought would be given to finding alternative partners if current relationships came apart. However, in other cases, certain allies are considered dependable and irreplaceable (e.g., U.S.–U.K.). And in some instances, alliances have come apart amiably (e.g. U.S.-New Zealand), but in others they have not (Anglo-Japan). While many would look for the immediate material factors to explain these cases (e.g., no power competition in the New Zealand case but competition in the U.K.–Japan case), qualitative differences among alliances are relevant to all these issues. In particular, they help to explain the *absence* of things—why certain choices regarding alliances are not made; why certain alternatives are not even considered; and why certain outcomes do not happen.

THE VISION

So what then is the vision of alliance identity for the U.S.–Japan-Korea relationship? It is one in which the meaning and rationale for the alliances evolve beyond the anti-DPRK basis:

---

1. Anti-DPRK → 2. "Regional stability" → 3. Extra-regional → 4. Identity

---

As alluded to above, the discussion on alliance resiliency has not moved beyond stage 2 where the post-DPRK rationale is equated with regional stability. But much more can be done. Beyond the general notion of stability, the U.S.-Korea and U.S.-Japan alliances could stand for a host of other values and institutions that resonate globally. Most prominent of these is their representation as three shining models of the success of liberal democratic values and open market economics (in an Asia that still remains somewhat skeptical of these values). When the dominant "identity" of the alliance assumes these traits and other common extraregional concerns—e.g., when the image of these alliances is not anti-DPRK, but as supporters of global nonproliferation, universal human rights, peacekeeping, and anti-terrorism—then the alliances will have made a major step toward resiliency (stage 3). As institutions, they will stand *for* something rather than simply against something. Looking even further into the future, the alliances, once they take on this extraregional quality, could evolve into permanent unions (stage 4). At this stage, the alliances take on a normative attachment and become a good in themselves. All parties see support of alliance resiliency as unquestioned and cannot imagine life without these relationships.

One could argue that verbal assertions that the alliances have moved on to stages 3 and 4 are not enough. In other words, to say an alliance has deeper meaning and an identity is one thing. For this actually to be the case is a totally different thing. This begs the question of how one would distinguish whether the discourse on U.S.-Japan-Korea alliance resiliency reflects reality, or is simply "talk."

There are at least four ways of testing or measuring whether the alliance has taken on this quality of resilience or permanence beyond the threat. First, allies have grown so confident of their mutual convergence of interests and nonadversarial nature that they no longer experience security dilemmas. In almost any alliance, a relative improvement in the capabilities of one partner is welcomed by the other as this augments the alliance's capacity to deter a threat; at the same time, however, a partner that grows stronger also can be a worrying proposition as there is no guarantee that this partner will be friendly tomorrow in the realist world of international relations. In alliances where a degree of resiliency has been attained, such insecurity spirals do not occur. If Australia or Canada were to develop greater force projection capabilities, this would hardly be perceived as threatening by the United States. On the other hand, if Japan were to do the same, this might be welcomed in the context of the alliance, but there also would exist some trepidation about how this might empower a future Japan outside the alliance. The more permanent the U.S.-Japan alliance becomes, the less relevant the latter insecurity becomes.

Second, alliance resiliency can be measured by the absence of abandonment and entrapment fears. History has shown that a key dynamic in alliances is the fear of being left out in the cold by an ally when it comes to one's security (abandonment); or being dragged by an ally into a conflict that does not accord with one's security interests (entrapment). As Glenn Snyder, an alliance theorist, has explained these anxieties of abandonment and entrapment persistently plague alliance commitments, create mutual mistrust, and in some instances can cause preemptive abrogation.[17] In cases of alliance resiliency, such fears do not motivate alliance behavior. This is largely because interests and identity within the alliance have become so tightly intertwined that commitments are perceived as common; moreover, the alliance is perceived as a good in itself.

Third, resilient alliances are substantively distinct in the amount of "sharing" that takes place between the parties. This refers to the nature of information and intelligence exchange that occurs in the relationship. A clear correlation exists between American alliances commonly perceived as having some qualities of alliance permanence (e.g., Canada, Britain, Australia) and the level of intelligence sharing in the relationships.

Fourth, discrete interests and discourse within the alliance look different from what we have grown accustomed to seeing. In the former case, we start on the path to alliance resiliency when national interests are not delinked vis-à-vis immediate threats. For example, when the artillery threat faced by the ROK becomes a security concern for Japan and when the missile threat from the DPRK is an integral security concern for Seoul. Similarly, civil-military problems in Okinawa become as great a concern for Seoul and it is for Tokyo. And historical problems between Japan and Korea become an integral concern for the United States. In the latter case, a true precedent was set at the summit between Kim Dae-jung and Obuchi in 1998. The two leaders changed the terms of dialogue and identity in the relationship by speaking about each other's countries in a wholly new light. Rather than resurrecting colonial images, Kim talked about how petty it was to destroy a relationship over a brief period in a much broader historical relationship. He went on to praise Japan's peace constitution, overseas development assistance, and nonproliferation policy. Similarly Obuchi talked about how Korea was a shining model of the success of democracy and development to be followed by others in Asia. The two leaders were changing the terms of the relationship for the better.

SKEPTICAL?

Skeptics might respond in the following ways: 1) This ivory-tower vision lacks reality; how can security alliances be based on such intangibles as values and ideals?; 2) Historical antagonism continues

to plague the alliances (particularly the Japan-Korea leg) and therefore mucks up any efforts at consolidation; 3) There is nothing in
current U.S.-Japan-Korea relations that resembles this vision; 4) finally (and perhaps most cynically), the vision of alliance resiliency
based on "identity" is really a function of common race and language which neither the Korea or Japan relationship possess.

A new vision that steps away from the mainstream is bound to
encounter these and other skeptical questions. However, we believe there are reasonable answers. The vision of future U.S.-
Japan-Korea alliance resiliency is certainly couched in the fuzzy
language of identity and a common values and like-mindedness
on extraregional issues, but at its base, it is still grounded in a
very clear strategic rationale. As noted earlier, this is the creation of a geostrategic current in East Asia after unification that
favors rather than undermines American, Japanese, and Korean
national interests (and at the same time minimizes downside risk
for China).

Historical animosity will continue to plague Seoul-Tokyo relations, but we do not see this as a significant impediment. History
will always be a problem in relations between these two peoples.
The problem will never be resolved as it is fundamentally a problem of historiography which inherently remains contentious. The
correct barometer of Seoul-Tokyo relations therefore is not historical enmity (which remains a constant), but how well the bilateral relationship advances in the economic, political, and security
arenas in spite of this history. And here, the record of success
since the mid-1980s is indisputable. Japan-ROK relations have
sprouted a host of bilateral institutions, ranging from presidential
summits to director-general-level dialogues that were previously
nonexistent in the relationship. These institutions have created
not only familiarity and bureaucratic inclinations toward cooperation, but also a maturing relationship between two democracies.

Skeptics might find the argument for alliance identity incredi-
ble because there is nothing in the present relationship to indicate
this. But that is exactly the point! The absence of such a discussion belies the need for it. Policy experts, foreign policy opinion-

184

makers, scholars, and practitioners need to start creating the new language and identity of this relationship today. It is only by undertaking this effort that the identity of the U.S.-Japan-Korea alliance can start to change. Among other things, this means American government officials talking about the meaning of these alliances in foreign policy audiences that extend beyond Asia. Former U.S. Ambassador to South Korea Stephen Bosworth's statements offer exemplary attempts at reconstructing the alliance in ideational terms:

> The third element of our relationship is philosophical—our shared commitment to democratic values and democratic practice. As Korean democracy has developed strongly in recent years, democracy has become in a real sense the cement of the overall relationship.[18]

Summits among Bill Clinton and Kim Dae-jung and Miyazawa in 1998, while framing the relationships in their traditional anti–North Korean context, also put forth images of alliances grounded in shared values of liberal democracy and free markets.[19] Similarly, President Bush during his Asia trip in 2002 spoke of the alliances' strength in deterring North Korea, but also in terms of the deepening and comprehensive partnerships that range out to extra-regional issues beyond the peninsula. For any who are skeptical about how this "positive spin" can matter substantively, one need only look at the June 2000 summit between the two Koreas. A single image of the two Korean leaders embracing (for better or worse) changed virtually overnight how South Koreans viewed their hated rival and the chance of peace on the peninsula. Words and images matter profoundly in how we view the world.

Finally, the argument for creating a new identity for the alliances is not an argument implicitly about race and culture. Clearly, the U.S.–Japan and U.S.–Korea alliances are not like the U.S.–Canada or the U.S.–UK relationships based on a common race, heritage, and language. The challenge instead is to imagine a common alliance identity emerging among *unlike* countries.

The bonds that reinforce alliance resiliency are not based in such primordial civilizational variables as race but in common liberal-democratic values, norms, and institutions that have emerged as predominant in the 21st century and transcend race. In this sense, the future resiliency of U.S.–Japan–Korea relations is a function of modernity, not tradition.

FINAL THOUGHTS

This strategy of trilateral consolidation is not the final solution for American geostrategic interests in Asia. If anything, it is just the beginning. The point to be made is that if the United States holds true to form and continues to react to events in the region and on the Korean peninsula, rather than getting out in front of them, we are likely to witness geostrategic currents flowing in a future direction inimical to U.S. interests as well as that of the region. Some might welcome such an outcome as the opportunity for the United States to disengage itself finally from Asia. American economic, political and security interests, we believe, are too intimately tied with the growth, democratization, and dynamism of the region to allow us to simply write these interests off. If one accepts the latter argument, then the imperative for the United States, we believe, is to shape the future environment by instituting policies and building relationships today that lay the proverbial stones in the stream that ensure a geostrategic current favorable to both America and its Asian allies in the future.

NOTES

NOTES TO INTRODUCTION

1. Victor Gilinsky, "North Korea as the Ninth Nuclear Power?" Nautilus Institute Policy Forum Online, PFO 02–10A, October 22, 2002 http://nautilus.org/fora/security/0210A_Victor.html; "Answering North Korea," *Washington Post* October 18, 2002; and "North Korea and the End of the Agreed Framework," *Heritage Foundation Backgrounder* No. 1605 October 18, 2002.

2. Jimmy Carter, "Engaging North Korea," *New York Times* October 27, 2002; Leon Sigal, "A Bombshell that's Actually an Olive Branch," *Los Angeles Times* October 18, 2002; and Jekuk Chang, "Pyongyang's New Strategy of 'Frank Admission,'" Nautilus Institute Policy Forum Online PFO02–11A, October 24, 2002 http://nautilus.org/fora/security/0211A_Chang.html

3. The Secretariat for the President, *The 1980s , Meeting A New Challenge: Selected Speeches of President Chun Doo Hwan* (Seoul: Korea Textbook Co, 1984), p. 181.

4. Margaret Thatcher, "Advice to a Superpower," *New York Times* February 11, 2002; and Statement by Dana Rohrbacher, "U.S. Policy Toward North Korea," Hearings of the U.S. House International Relations Committee, March 24, 1999. Available from: Lexis Nexis Congressional (online service). Bethesda, MD: Congressional Information Service.

5. "Worldwide Threats to U.S. National Security," Testimony of George J. Tenet, Director, Central Intelligence Agency, Senate Armed Services Committee, February 2, 1999; and Donald Rumsfeld, *Report of the Commission to Assess the Ballistic Missile Threat to the United States, Executive Summary Pursuant to Public Law 201 104th*

Congress July 15, 1998 (available at http://www.fas.org/irp/threat/missile/rumsfeld/index.html).

6. *Newsweek*, July 1994. Cited in Bruce Cumings, "The Structural Basis of Anti-Americanism in the Republic of Korea," paper presented at Georgetown University, January 30, 2003, p. 26.

7. *Washington Post* (op-ed), December 29, 2002 (Mary McGrory, "Bush's Moonshine Policy"), B7.

8. Fox News, January 15, 2003, 10:08 PM, cited in Cumings, "The Structural Basis of Anti-Americanism," p. 25.

9. *Washington Post* (op-ed), February 9, 2003 (Mary McGrory, "Fuzzy-Headed on North Korea"), B7.

10. Press release by Benjamin A. Gilman, Sept 17, 1999, U.S. House of Representatives International Relations Committee. Accessed at http://www.nautilus.org/napsned/dir/9909/Sept. 17.html; and Statement by Christopher Cox, Hearing of the U.S. House International Relations Committee, "U.S. Policy Toward North Korea," October 13, 1999. Available from: Lexis Nexis Congressional (online service). Bethesda, MD: Congressional Information Service.

11. Lee Hamilton, "Our Stake in Asia's Nuclear Future," *Washington Times*, May 13, 1998.

12. Statement by Dana Rohrbacher, "U.S. Policy Toward North Korea," Hearings of the U.S. House International Relations Committee, March 24, 1999. Available from: Lexis Nexis Congressional (online service). Bethesda, MD: Congressional Information Service.

13. Statement by John McCain, "The Crisis in Korea" (140 Cong. Rec. S7497; Date: 6/23/94). Text from Congressional Record. Available from: Lexis Nexis Congressional (online service). Bethesda, MD: Congressional Information Service.

14. Statement by Dana Rohrbacher, "U.S. Policy Toward North Korea," Hearings of the U.S. House International Relations Committee, March 24, 1999 and October 13, 1999. Available from: Lexis Nexis Congressional (online service). Bethesda, MD: Congressional Information Service.

15. Patrick J. Buchanan, "The Great Equalizer, *The American Conservative*, February 10, 2003, p. 7.

16. This difference of views on how the United States, Japan, and South Korea should respond to the October 2002 revelations of secret DPRK nuclear activities in violation of the 1994 Agreed Framework is found in chapter 5.

17. *Washington Post* January 20, 2003 (Vernon Loeb and Peter Slevin, "Overcoming North Korea's Tyranny of Proximity"), A16.

18. See, for example, Stephen M. Walt, "Rigor or rigor mortis? Rational choice and Security Studies," *International Security* 23.4 (Spring 1999), pp. 5–48; Chalmers Johnson, "A Disaster in the Making: Rational Choice and Asian Studies," *National Interest* 36 (Summer 1994), pp. 14–22; Robert Bates, "Area Studies and the Discipline: A Useful Controversy?" *PS: Political Science and Politics* (June 1997), pp. 166–69; Daniel Little, "Rational-Choice Models and Asian Studies," *Journal of Asian Studies* 50.1 (February 1991), pp. 35–52; Victor Cha, "Globalization and the Study of International Security," *Journal of Peace Research* 37.3 (May 2000), pp. 391–403; and Robert Bates, "Area Studies and Political Science: Rupture and Possible Synthesis," *Africa Today* 44 (April-June 1997), pp. 123–31.

19. Jack Snyder, "Richness, Rigor, and Relevance in the Study of Soviet Foreign Policy," *International Security* 9.3 (Winter 1984–1985), pp. 89–108.

20. Representative works include: Helen Louise Hunter, *Kim Il-Sung's North Korea* (Westport, CT: Praeger, 1999); Bruce Cumings, *Korea's Place in the Sun* (New York: Norton, 1997); Donald Oberdorfer, *The Two Koreas* (New York: Basic Books, 2001); Han S. Park, *North Korea: The Politics of Unconventional Wisdom* (Boulder, CO: Lynne Reiner, 2002); Marcus Noland, *Avoiding the Apocalypse: The Future of the Two Koreas* (Washington, D.C.: IIE, 2000); Dae-Sook Suh, *The Korean Communist Movement, 1918–1948* (Princeton: Princeton University Press, 1967); Chong-sik Lee and Robert Scalapino, *Communism in Korea* (Los Angeles: University of California Press, 1972); B.C. Koh, *The Foreign Policy Systems of North and South Korea* (Berkeley: University of California Press, 1984); Joseph Bermudez, *North Korea's Special Forces* (London: Jane's Publishing Company, Ltd., 1988); Dae-Sook Suh, *Kim Il Sung: The North Korean Leader* (New York: Columbia University Press, 1988); Bon-

Hak Koo, *The Political Economy of Self-Reliance: Juche and Economic Development, 1961–1990* (Seoul: Research Center for Peace and Unification, 1992); Koon Woo Nam, *The North Korean Communist Leadership, 1945–1965: A Study of Factionalism and Political Consolidation* (University, Alabama: The University of Alabama Press, 1974); Desmond Ball, *Signals Intelligence (SIGINT) in North Korea* (Canberra, Australia, Strategic and Defence Studies Centre, Australian National University, 1996); Hy-Sang Lee, *North Korea: A Strange Socialist Fortress* (Westport, Conn.: Praeger, 2001); Charles Armstrong, *The North Korean Revolution, 1945–1950* (Ithaca, New York: Cornell University Press, 2002); Adrian Buzo, *The Guerilla Dynasty: Politics and Leadership in North Korea* (Boulder, CO: Westview Press, 1999); Andrew Natsios, *The Great North Korean Famine* (Washington, D.C.: U.S. Institute for Peace, 2001); Song-Ji Choi, *Kim Jong-Il gwa hyondae pukhan chongch'isa* (Kim Jong-Il and Modern North Korea Political Thought) (Seoul: Korean Broadcasting Publishers, 2001); and Jong-hyon Shin ed., *Pukhanui t'ongil chongch'aek* (North Korean Unification Policy) (Seoul: Ulyumunhwasa, 1989). There is a growing body of work on North Korean defectors, see Kongdan Oh and Ralph Hassig, *North Korea through the Looking Glass* (Washington, D.C.: Brookings Institution, 2000); and Chol-Hwan Kang and Pierre Rigoulot, *The Aquariums of Pyongyang: Ten Years in a North Korean Gulag* (New York: Basic Books, 2001).

21. Leon Sigal, *Disarming Strangers: Nuclear Diplomacy with North Korea* (Princeton, N.J.: Princeton University Press, 1998); Nicholas Eberstadt, *The End of North Korea* (Washington, D.C.: AEI Press, 1999); Chuck Downs, *Over the Line: North Korea's Negotiating Strategy* (Washington, D.C.: AEI Press, 1999); Scott Snyder, *Negotiating on the Edge: North Korean Negotiating Behavior* (Washington DC: US Institute of Peace Press, 1999); and Joel Wit, Robert Gallucci, and Daniel Poneman, *Going Critical: The 1994 US-North Korea Nuclear Crisis* (Washington, D.C.: Brookings, forthcoming 2003).

22. The quality of works drops off substantially in this category. Among the more coherent and insightful efforts are Samuel Kim ed., *North Korea and Northeast Asia* (Lanham, MD: Rowman and Littlefield, 2002); Samuel Kim, ed., *North Korean Foreign Relations*

in the Post-Cold War Era; Han S. Park ed., *North Korea: Ideology, Politics, Economy* (Englewood Cliffs, NJ: Prentice Hall, 1996); David Albright ed., *Solving the North Korean Nuclear Puzzle* (Washington, D.C.: Institute for Science and International Security Press, 2000); Young W. Kihl, and Peter Hayes, eds. *Peace and Security in Northeast Asia: The Nuclear Issue and the Korean Peninsula* (Armonk, NY, M. E. Sharpe, 1997); Hazel Smith ed., *North Korea in the New World Order* (New York: St. Martin's Press, 1996); James Clay Moltz, Alexandre Mansourov eds., *The North Korean Nuclear Program* (New York: Routledge, 1999); and Dae-Sook Suh and Chae-Jin Lee eds., *North Korea After Kim Il Sung* (Boulder, CO: Lynne Rienner Publishers, 1998).

23. One exception to this was Obderdorfer, *The Two Koreas*.

24. Sigal, *Disarming Strangers*, pp. 241–42.

25. Two of the best overviews are Bruce Cumings, *Korea's Place in the Sun* (New York: W.W. Norton, 1997); and Oberdorfer, *The Two Koreas*.

26. These events are only highlighted here, and discussed in greater detail in the book.

27. Victor Cha and Michael O'Hanlon, " Clumsy U.S. Risks Ties to Seoul," *Los Angeles Times* (op-ed), December 11, 2002; William Safire, "Three-Ring Circus," *New York Times* (op-ed) January 2, 2003, A17; Richard V. Allen, "Seoul's Choice: The U.S. or the North, *New York Times* (op-ed) January 16, 2003, A29; and Dave Kang, "Two Countries, One Anxiety," *New York Times* (op-ed) December 22, 2002.

NOTES TO CHAPTER 1

1. *New York Times*, March 1, 1998 (Nicholas Kristof, "New Shape to Triangle Tying U.S. and Koreas"); and *Wall Street Journal* (op-ed), October 12, 1998 (Fred Ikle, "U.S. Folly May Start Another Korean War").

2. Press statement by Secretary of State Madeleine Albright, Pyongyang, October 24, 2000. http://secretary.state.gov/www/statements/2000/601024b.html

3. Events pursuant to the October 2002 nuclear revelations are referred to in this chapter, but are dealt with in full scope in chapter six.

4. The nuclear revelations of October 2002, and their relevance to this argument, are discussed in detail in chapter 5.

5. The first theory is based in the notion that DPRK threatening behavior represents a classic security dilemma. Insecurity, particularly after the loss of its cold war patrons in the Soviet Union and China (after Beijing's normalization with the ROK in 1992), drives the North to aggression, hence engagement will offer the security assurances that will mollify DPRK behavior. The last view calls for engagement because this is the only way to move Pyongyang away from traditional patterns of unpredictably aggressive behavior. Moreover, the regime's irrationality renders useless basic deterrence and defense strategies (which presume a degree of rationality on the part of the target state).

6. It should be emphasized that the use of preemptive war theory does not mean that North Korea will undertake a second attempt to overrun the peninsula. The "logic" of preemptive action is the valuable insight from this body of theory. The "act" need not be war, but could be a violent act of some sort (as described below).

7. Ashton Carter and William Perry, *Preventive Defense* (Washington, DC: Brookings, 1999), p. 14. The North Korea case also underscores a more general foreign policy problem highlighted in the new and burgeoning IR literature on theories of influence and reassurance which specify the conditions under which threats or rewards are more effective policy instruments. This literature originated in classic works by David Baldwin ("The Power of Positive Sanctions," *World Politics* 24 [October 1971], pp. 19–38 and "Thinking About Threats," *Journal of Conflict Resolution* 15.1 [1971], pp. 71–78), but has grown in the post-cold war era. See Janice Gross Stein, "Deterrence and Reassurance," in Philip Tetlock et al., eds., *Behavior, Society and Nuclear War* vol. 2 (New York: Oxford University Press, 1990), pp. 9–72; Richard New Lebow, *The Art of Bargaining* (Baltimore: Johns Hopkins University Press, 1996), ch.7; Thomas Milburn and Daniel Christie, "Rewarding in International Politics," *Political Psychology* 10.4 (1989), pp. 625–45; and Stephen

Rock, *Appeasement in International Politics* (Lexington: University Press of Kentucky, 2000). For two recent and useful additions, see George Shambaugh, *States, Firms, and Power* (NY: SUNY, 2000); and James Davis, *Threats and Promises* (Baltimore: Johns Hopkins, 2000).

8. To reiterate, although strategies of engagement and containment are often juxtaposed, I use the term "engagement" in a conditional sense, meaning engagement instruments that are used in conjunction with—not in lieu of—basic containment strategies. Thus, for example, characterizing U.S. policy toward North Korea as engagement does not necessarily entail an abandonment of deterrent measures. In this sense, the spectrum of policy choice really ranges from unconditional containment (i.e., an unadulterated "stick" policy) to conditional engagement (i.e., a containment-plus-engagement or carrot and stick policy).

9. To argue the appeal of engagement to both doves and hawks is not meant to be flip or irresponsible. On the contrary, a responsible policy prescription is one that is implementable across a wide spectrum of views, and the latter clearly exists in the case of North Korea given the regime's secrecy and the acute cognitive biases of those who observe it. In this regard, the implications of engagement are open-ended, but the point is that the policy still remains the best choice as it prevents the emergence of a more unstable situation tomorrow vis-à-vis DPRK assessments and preemptive logic (discussed below). This implication of the policy should be palatable to both doves and hawks. The argument's other implication is to recognize the need to move beyond old cold war templates and reexamine the nature of the DPRK threat. This is because what was successful during the cold war (containment-plus-isolation) may actually cause *more* instability today.

10. Jonathan Pollack and Chung Min Lee, *Preparing for Korean Unification : Scenarios and Implications* (Santa Monica, CA : RAND, 1999).

11. Robert Scalapino, *North Korea at a Crossroads*, Hoover Institution Essays on Public Policy, Stanford University, No. 73 (1997), pp. 16–17. Michael O'Hanlon contends that North Korea's war initiation would be an "unwise gamble" or an act of desperation." See

Michael O'Hanlon, "Stopping a North Korean Invasion: Why Defending South Korea is Easier than the Pentagon Thinks," *International Security* 22.4 (1998), p. 138.

12. Marcus Noland, "Why North Korea Will Muddle Through," *Foreign Affairs* 76.4 (1997), pp. 105–18; Byung-joon Ahn, "The Man Who Would Be Kim," *Foreign Affairs* 73.6 (1994), pp. 94–108; and Nicholas Eberstadt, "Hastening Korean Unification," *Foreign Affairs* 76.2 (1997), pp. 77–92.

13. For representative examples of these bodies of theory, see Jack Levy, "Declining Power and the Preventive Motivation for War," *World Politics* 40.1 (October 1987), pp. 82–107; and Dan Reiter, "Exploding the Powderkeg Myth: Preemptive Wars Almost Never Happen," *International Security* 20.2 (Fall 1995), pp. 5–34. Also see, Thomas Schelling, *The Strategy of Conflict* (Cambridge: Harvard University Press, 1960); Thomas Schelling, *Arms and Influence* (New Haven: Yale University Press, 1966); Glenn Snyder, *Deterrence and Defense: Toward a Theory of National Security* (Princeton: Princeton University Press, 1961); Robert Jervis, "Cooperation Under the Security Dilemma," *World Politics* 30 (January 1978); Stephen Van Evera, *The Causes of War* (Ph.D. diss., University of California, Berkeley, 1984); Jack Snyder, "Perceptions of the Security Dilemma in 1914," in Robert Jervis, Richard Ned Lebow, and Janice Gross Stein, *Psychology and Deterrence* (Baltimore: Johns Hopkins University Press, 1985), pp. 153–79; Emerson M.S. Niou and Peter C. Ordeshook, "Preventive War and the Balance of Power: A Game Theoretic Approach," *Journal of Conflict Resolution* 31.3 (Summer 1987), pp. 387–419; Randall Schweller, "Domestic Structure and Preventive War: Are Democracies More Pacific?" *World Politics* 44.2 (January 1992), pp. 235–69; Richard Ned Lebow, "Windows of Opportunity: Do States Jump Through Them?" *International Security* 9.1 (Summer 1984), pp. 147–186; Stephen Van Evera, "Offense, Defense, and the Causes of War," International Security 22.4 (Spring 1998), pp. 5–43; and Charles Glaser and Chaim Kaufmann, "What is the Offense-Defense Balance and How Can We Measure It?" *International Security* 22.4 (Spring 1998), pp. 44–82.

14. Most scholars see the primary difference between the two as the time factor. The motivation for preemption is an imminent attack measured in days, while for prevention, threats are measured in years. The former also tends to take the form of surprise attacks; although not all surprise attacks are preemptive. See Reiter, "Exploding the Powder Keg Myth," p. 7; also see Levy, "Declining Power and the Preventive Motivation for War"; Jervis, "Cooperation Under the Security Dilemma"; Richard K. Betts, *Surprise Attack: Lessons for Defense Planning* (Washington, D.C.: Brookings Institution, 1982); and Robert Axelrod, "The Rational Timing of Surprise," *World Politics* 31.2 (January 1979), pp. 228–246. For a slightly different distinction, see Van Evera, *Causes of War.*

15. On power transitions, see Robert Gilpin, *War and Change in World Politics* (Cambridge: Cambridge University Press, 1981). Also see A.F.K. Organski, *World Politics* (New York: Knopf, 1968), chapter 14; Joshua Goldstein, *Long Cycles: Prosperity and War in the Modern Age* (New Haven: Yale University Press, 1988); George Modelski, "The Long Cycle of Global Politics and the Nation-State," *Comparative Studies in Society and History* 20 (April 1978), pp. 214–235; William Thompson, *On Global War: Historical-Structural Approaches to World Politics* (Columbia: University of South Carolina Press, 1988); Paul Kennedy, *The Rise and Fall of the Great Powers: Economic Change and Military Conflict from 1500 to 2000* (New York: Random House, 1987); Jacek Kugler and A.F.K Organski, "The Power Transition: A Retrospective and Prospective Evaluation," in Manus I. Midlarsky, ed., *Handbook of War Studies* (Boston: Unwin Hyman, 1989), pp. 171–194; and Charles Kupchan, *The Vulnerability of Empire* (Ithaca: Cornell University Press, 1994).

16. Winston Churchill, *The Grand Alliance* (Boston: Houghton Mifflin, 1950), p. 603.

17. For applications to the Pacific War in 1941, see Bruce Russett, *Power and Continuity in World Politics* (San Francisco: Freeman, 1974), Chap. 13; and Scott Sagan, "The Origins of the Pacific War," *Journal of Interdisciplinary History* 18 (Spring 1988).

18. This was not the case during the early years of the cold war as both Koreas adhered to a "unification by force" policy (*sônggong t'ongil*

[literally, "unification by success"], or *pukchin t'ongil* ["march north"]). The threat of ROK-initiated violence decreased under the Third and Fourth Republics as Park Chung-hee dropped the *pukchin t'ongil* for a formula seeking to beat the North on the economic and diplomatic front through export-led growth, heavy/chemical industry development, and an omnidirectional foreign policy. Why North Korea did not preempt during the cold war is discussed below.

19. For economic data, see Bruce Cumings, *The Two Koreas*, Foreign Policy Association, Headline Series No. 269 (May/June 1984), pp. 65–66. The North Korean military grew from 300,000 to more than one million troops over the two decades. See Nicholas Eberstadt, "'National Strategy' in North and South Korea" *NBR Analysis* 7.5 (1996), pp. 10, 12.

20. See Oberdorfer's recounting of conversations between Hwang and Selig Harrison in *The Two Koreas*, p. 401.

21. Inter-Korean matters have been subsumed nominally under the Party Central Committee. See "The DPRK Report," No.14 (September/October 1998), ftp://ftp.nautilus.org/napsnet/RussiaDPRK/DPRK"Report"14.txt.

22. "The DPRK Report," No. 7 (May/June 1997), ftp://ftp.nautilus.org/napsnet/RussiaDPRK/DPRK"Report"7.txt. 1997. Also see Kim Jong-il's address at 50th anniversary commemoration ceremony of Kim Il-sung University (December 1996), reprinted in *Wolgan Choson* [Choson Monthly] April 1997.

23. *Nodong Sinmun* 27 December 2000 *FBIS-EAS*-2001–0117, 27 December 2000.

24. "Collection of Comrade Kim Jong Il's Works," p. 272 cited in *Vantage Point* 25.4 (April 2002), p. 52.

25. Eberstadt, "National Strategy," p. 23.

26. On the South Korean side, for example, the purpose of the Vance mission in 1969 was to communicate to the South that the U.S. would not support unilateral retaliation by the South in response to a series of North Korean provocations in 1968.

27. Personal interview, high-level Chinese foreign ministry official with Asia portfolio, Washington DC, October 1997.

28. See *Chosun Ilbo-Gallup Korea* polls, January 1, 2003 at http://www.gallup.co.kr/News/2003/release004.html.

29. For ROK plans to continue certain force modernization programs in spite of the economic crisis, see *Korea Herald*, June 8, 1998 ("Defense Ministry pushes destroyer plan"); *Korea Herald*, September 22, 1998 ("Defense Ministry Proposes First-Ever Budget Cuts"); Sally Harris, "Coping with Pressure: South Korea's Defense Restructuring," *Korean Journal of Defense Analysis* 12.2 (Winter 2000), pp. 207–30; and Victor Cha, "The Economic Crisis, Strategic Culture and the Military Modernization of South Korea," *Armed Forces & Society* 28.1 (Fall 2001).

30. On these arguments, see Schweller, "Domestic Structure and Preventive War"; Reiter, "Exploding the Powderkeg Myth," pp. 25–28; and Van Evera, "Offense, Defense, and the Causes of War," pp. 4–6.

31. For 2001 testimony on the improvements and augmentation to the DPRK military posture that has occurred at the same time that Pyongyang has sought detente with Seoul and the rest of the world, see the CINC UNC/CFC/USFK Posture Statement to US Congress (General Schwartz) available at http://www.korea.army.mil/pao/news.htm

32. "Flashpoint," *ABC News Nightline with Ted Koppel*, aired January 10, 2003. 11:35 PM EST. General James Clapper, Director of DIA (1991–94) and former chief of intelligence in Korea and Pacific commands, notes that the North's forward deployments may actually reflect a "best defense is a good offense" mentality to compensate for inferiorities in the relative military balance on the peninsula. In other words, the North does not necessarily believe that offense has the advantage but chooses to forward deploy because, as experienced in 1950, it would be incapable of sustaining supply routes with rear-area forces in the face of U.S. bombing runs (Clapper's analysis in Leon Sigal, *Disarming Strangers: Nuclear Policy with North Korea*: [Princeton: Princeton University Press, 1996], p. 21).

33. Examples of past DPRK activity that are consonant with this logic are detailed below.

34. Richard Halloran, "New Warplan Calls for Invasion of North

Korea," *Global Beat*, November 14, 1998, http://www.nyu.edu/globalbeat/asia/Halloran111498.html.

35. See Daniel Kahneman and Amos Tversky, "Prospect Theory: An Analysis of Decision Under Risk," *Econometrica* 47.2 (March 1979), pp. 263–91; and Amos Tversky and Daniel Kahneman, "Rational Choice and the Framing of Decisions," *Journal of Business* 59.4, part 2 (1986), S251-S278. For a good readable introduction, see Jack Levy, "An Introduction to Prospect Theory," *Political Psychology* 13.2 (1992), pp. 171–86. The applications to international relations and political choice have been fairly recent. See Janice Gross Stein, "International Co-operation and Loss Avoidance: Framing the Problem," in Stein, ed., *Choosing to Co-operate: How States Avoid Loss* (Baltimore: Johns Hopkins University Press, 1993), pp. 2–34; George Quattrone and Amos Tversky, "Contrasting Rational and Psychological Analyses of Political Choice," *American Political Science Review* 82.3 (September 1988), pp. 719–36; Levy, "An Introduction to Prospect Theory"; Kupchan, *Vulnerability of Empire*; Robert Jervis, "Political Implications of Loss Aversion," *Political Psychology* 13.2 (1992), pp. 187–204; Jack Levy, "Prospect Theory and International Relations: Theoretical Applications and Analytical Problems," *Political Psychology* 13.2 (1992), 283–310; Eldar Shafir, "Prospect Theory and Political Analysis: A Psychological Perspective," *Political Psychology* 13.2 (1992), pp. 311–22; and Y.Y.I. Vertzberger, *Risk Taking and Decision making* (Stanford: Stanford University Press, 1998). There have been even fewer applications of prospect theory to specific cases. See Barbara Farnham, "Roosevelt and the Munich Crisis: Insights from Prospect Theory," *Political Psychology* 13.2 (1992), pp. 205–35; Rose McDermott, "Prospect Theory in International Relations: The Iranian Hostage Rescue Mission," *Political Psychology* 13.2 (1992), pp. 237–63; Audrey McInerney, "Prospect Theory and Soviet Policy Toward Syria, 1966–1967," *Political Psychology* 13.2 (1992), pp. 265–82; Paul Huth, D.S. Bennett, and C. Gelpi, "System Uncertainty, Risk Propensity, and International Conflict Among the Great Powers," *Journal of Conflict Resolution* 36 (1992), pp. 478–517; Gregory Gause, "Prospect Theory and Iraqi War Decisions," paper presented at the

1997 APSA, Washington DC August 28–31, 1997; Davis, *Threats and Promises*; and Victor Cha, "Hawk Engagement and Preventive Defense on the Korean Peninsula," *International Security* 27.1 (Summer 2002), pp. 40–78.

36. On these points, see Levy, "Prospect Theory and International Relations," p. 285; and Robert Jervis, "Domino Beliefs and Strategic Behavior," in Jervis and Snyder, eds. *Dominoes and Bandwagons*, pp. 20–50. The endowment effect highlights the status quo bias of states. See Levy, "Prospect Theory and International Relations," p. 284; Robert Jervis, *The Meaning of the Nuclear Revolution* (Ithaca, NY: Cornell University Press, 1989), pp. 29–35; and Randall Schweller, "Neorealism's Status Quo Bias," *Security Studies* 5.3 (1996).

37. As experiments by Kahneman and Tversky have shown, individuals preferred certain gains to uncertain but larger ones (or breaking even), and uncertain losses (or breaking even) to smaller but certain losses. Both of these findings run contrary to the predictions of expected utility theory ("Prospect Theory," pp. 265–69).

38. Stein, "International Cooperation and Loss Avoidance," p. 14.

39. Reference points can either refer to the status quo or to an aspiration point (Levy, "Prospect Theory and International Relations, p. 285). Kahneman and Tversky generally see the reference point as chosen by the decisionmaker at the beginning of the problem. However, the act of encoding, as Levy argues, can be discrete, i.e. the reference point with respect to one's asset position at each choice; or cumulative, i.e. the reference point and encoding of the choice within a string of choices (Levy, "An Introduction to Prospect Theory," p. 177). For recent work that further develops the concept of reference point as a subjective process rather than as an objectively neutral point, see William Boettcher, "Framing Foreign Policy Problems: A Study of Truman's Decision to Intervene in Korea," paper presented at the International Studies Association meeting, March 1998.

40. This is not the first attempt to link propositions from prospect theory with those from preemptive/preventive theories of war; it is, however, a more specified drawing out of hypotheses. Links drawn between the two theories have been sketchy, emphasizing

200

how loss aversion calculations can create more destabilizing situations than can regular cost-benefit calculations. See Levy, "Prospect Theory and International Relations"; Jervis, *The Meaning of the Nuclear Revolution*, p. 171; Stein, "International Co-operation and Loss Avoidance," p. 21; and Jervis, "Political Implications of Loss Aversion." Authors have also shown how loss aversion contributes to cooperation (i.e., when leaders identify small but certain losses from defection and larger but uncertain losses from cooperation). See Stein, "International Co-operation and Loss Avoidance," p. 22; and Michael Mastanduno, "Framing the Japan Problem: The Bush Administration and the Structural Impediments Initiative," *International Journal*, Vol. 47, No. 2 (Spring 1992), pp. 235–264. Levy has studied how certain war situations (Franco-German, U.S.-Japan, U.S.-Iraq) were influenced by loss aversion. See Levy, "Declining Power and the Preventive Motivation for War"; and Levy, "Prospect Theory and International Relations," p. 287. Loss aversion has also been employed to explain the persuasiveness of the domino theory as a motivator of Cold War superpower confrontation. Jervis, "Domino Beliefs and Strategic Behavior."

41. See Van Evera, "Offense, Defense, and the Causes of War"; Schelling, *Arms and Influence*; Levy, "Declining Power and the Preventive Motivation for War," Jervis, "Cooperation under the Security Dilemma"; and Robert Jervis, *Perception and Misperception in International Politics* (Princeton, N.J.: Princeton University Press, 1976); and Schweller, "Domestic Structure and Preventive War."

42. Reiter's empirical study of interstate wars since 1816 shows the relative absence of preemptive war despite the existence of commonly accepted conditions for striking first. See Reiter, "Exploding the Powder Keg Myth."

43. If offense is perceived to have the advantage under the same conditions (i.e., cell 1), the outcome is indeterminate, although it is unlikely that preemptive action will take place because of the threat such action would have on current gains.

44. Levy, "Prospect Theory and International Relations," pp. 302–3.

45. For elaboration of prospect theory's insights for understanding

when preemptive or preventive actions can occur among similarly situated states, see Cha, "Hawk Engagement and Preventive Defense," pp. 56–58.

46. One of the difficulties of applying prospect theory to international conflict decisions is the operationalization of the decisional frame. As Gause states, analysts often define the frame by the choice made by the subject (see "Prospect Theory and Iraqi War Decisions"; also see Levy, "Prospect Theory and International Relations"; and Shafir, "Prospect Theory and Political Analysis"). As a second-best solution, I choose a set of indicators that appear to be a relatively reasonable set of variables by which any country might evaluate its current situation. The problem of operationalization is compounded for this project because of the paucity of reliable data on North Korean perceptions.

47. Arguably, the influx of food aid and economic assistance that came with the recent smile diplomacy by the DPRK may have moved the regime into cells 3 or 4, where they frame the status quo as neutral (i.e., not a daily losing one). Even if this were the case, the point remains that any backsliding would heighten the likelihood of DPRK action.

48. For the argument against preventive motivations for North Korean aggression during the cold war, see the next chapter, where David Kang argues counterfactually that if preventive motivations are applicable to North Korea, then Pyongyang should have attempted to close the window of vulnerability long before the current status quo. I argue that the cold war, while disadvantageous at times, was never viewed by the North in the domain of losses and thus preventive situations were not actualized. The post–cold war situation, as described above, is fundamentally different.

49. Cumings, *The Two Koreas*, pp. 65–66.

50. Oberdorfer, *Two Koreas*, pp. 100–01.

51. Respectively, these were the absence of U.S. retaliatory punishment for the January 1968 Blue House raid and *USS Pueblo* seizure; the Guam doctrine and Nixon's withdrawal of the 7th infantry division from Korea; the U.S. withdrawal from Vietnam in 1975 under Ford; and the 1977 Carter plan. See Victor Cha, *Alignment Despite*

Antagonism: The United States-Korea-Japan Security Triangle (Stanford: Stanford University Press, 1999).

52. The best account is in Oberdorfer, *Two Koreas*. Also see Dae-Sook Suh, *Kim Il-Sung: The North Korean Leader* (New York: Columbia University Press, 1988), chap. 6.

53. For good works on this period in South Korean domestic politics and relations with the United States, see William H. Gleysteen, *Massive Entanglement, Marginal Influence: Carter and Korea in Crisis* (Washington, D.C.: Brookings, 1999); John A. Wickham, *Korea on the Brink: From the "12/12 Incident" to the Kwangju Uprising, 1979–1980* (Washington, D.C.: National Defense University Press, 1999); and John K.C. Oh, *Korean Politics: The Quest for Democratization and Economic Development* (Ithaca, NY: Cornell University Press, 1999).

54. As cited in Oberdorfer, *Two Koreas*, p. 100. For these points generally, see pp. 96–101, 114–17.

55. Oberdorfer, *Two Koreas*, pp. 115–16.

56. "North Korea's Decline and China's Strategic Dilemmas," *USIP Special Report*, October 1997 (Washington, D.C.: U.S. Institute of Peace).

57. *Korea Herald*, February 6, 1998 ("DPRK Recalls 12 Ambassadors without Replacing Them"); and "The DPRK Report" No. 12 (March/May 1998), ftp://ftp.nautilus.org/napsnet/RussiaDPRK/DPRK"Report"12.txt

58. ROK National Assembly reports found that many more of the defectors in the 1990s were former government or party officials, and that the increase in numbers since 1993 do not include the unreported numbers (estimated between 2000–3000 annually) defecting through Russia and China (see *Kyodo Tsushin Nyusu Sokuho* 18 September 1998 cited in Narushige Michishita, "Two Alliance After Peace on the Korean Peninsula," A/PARC Working Paper, Stanford University, May 7, 1999).

59. Nicholas Eberstadt, "'National Strategy' in North and South Korea," *NBR Analysis* 7.5 (1996), pp. 14, 24.

60. Bruce Cumings, "Feeding the North Korea Myths," *The Nation* September 29, 1997, pp. 22–24.

61. *Nodong Sinmun* December 27, 2000, p. 2 ("The Sagacious Leadership that Keeps Strengthening the People's Regime") *FBIS-EAS-2001–0117* December 27, 2000.

62. *Chosun Ilbo* March 20, 1997 reprint of Kim Jong-il's 50th anniversary speech at Kim Il-sung university; and "The DPRK Report" No. 7 (May/June 1997), ftp://ftp.nautilus.org/napsnet/RussiaD-PRK/DPRK"Report"7.txt.

63. *Nodong Sinmun* January 9, 2001, p. 1 ("Let Us See and Solve all Problems from a New Viewpoint and a New Attitude.") *FBIS-EAS-2001–0118* January 9, 2001.

64. "Pyongyang Residents Ordered to Relocate," *Chosun Ilbo*, April 2, 1999; and "N. Korea Relocating 2 Million People," *Associated Press*, April 2, 1999.

65. *Jiji Tsushin Nyusu Sokuho* November 18, 1998 cited in Michishita, "Two Alliances."

66. *London Times*, November 23 and 30, 1997 ("North Korea Chokes on its Big Lie", and "Kim Shows Starving Nation No Mercy").

67. *Reuters*, June 15, 1998 (Defector: Famine Killed 2.5 Million N. Koreans").

68. The point here is not to deny that these acts took place in a general context of tensions, but that they were significantly more provocative and of a substantially different degree than the general level of tension might have predicted. In this sense, these acts were aberrations that were not easily explainable.

69. The North had been very dissatisfied with the larger role transferred to the South Koreans from the Americans in the MAC, which is the primary negotiation body for the armistice. To disrupt this, the North undertook clear armistice violations and refused to discuss these in the MAC, with the purpose of forcing the Americans to dialogue directly with them.

70. Jim Mann, "Hardliners Reap Benefits by Going to the Brink," *San Jose Mercury News*, December 30, 1994.

71. On the sunshine policy, see Chung-in Moon and David Steinberg eds., *Kim Dae-jung Government and Sunshine Policy* (Seoul: Yonsei University Press, 1999); and Hong Soon-young, "Thawing Korea's Cold War," *Foreign Affairs* (May/June 1999). On the Korea summit

and its aftermath, see Sung-joo Han, "The Evolving Inter-Korean Relationship," *Journal of East Asian Studies* 1.1 (February 2001), pp. 155–78; Park Jong-chul, "Challenges and Opportunities for the Two Koreas after the Summit," *Journal of East Asian Affairs* 14.2 (Fall 2000), pp. 301–27; Kwak Tae-hwan, "The Korean Peace Process," *International Journal of Korean Unification Studies* 9.1 (2000), pp. 1–30; and Scott Snyder, "The Inter-Korean Summit and Implications for US Policy," *Korean Journal of Defense Analysis* 12.2 (Winter 2000), pp. 53–70.

72. See Selig Harrison, "The Missiles of North Korea," *World Policy Journal* (Spring 2001); and Harrison, "Promoting a Soft Landing in North Korea," *Foreign Policy* 106 (Spring 1997), pp. 57–76.

73. Perhaps the two primary indicators of this are the food situation and Pyongyang's reduced diplomatic isolation. According to the World Food Program (WFP) food shortages across the provinces are less acute than they were in 1997–98. WFP DPR Korea Update , February 25, 2001, distributed by the World Food Program, Pyongyang. Moreover, the economy has stopped the free fall in growth rates, and the regime appears to have made a stable political transition after Kim Il-sung's death. See Doug Struck, "N. Korea Back From the Brink," *Washington Post*, September 5, 2000, p. A20.

74. In addition according to the WFP, because 20 percent of counties still remain inaccessible and Pyongyang has not allowed an international nutritional survey since 1998, there still is no reasonably accurate sense of how much the situation has improved (*WFP DPR Korea Update* 25 February 2001).

75. This statement came officially at Kim's Berlin Declaration (March 10, 2000); see Kongdan Oh, "North Korea's Engagement: Implications for South Korea," in National Intelligence Council and Library of Congress, *North Korea's Engagement: Perspectives, Outlook, and Implications* CR 2001–01 (May 2001).

76. Finally, even to concede that the recent improvements in the DPRK's food and economic situations are not transient, instead representing a new stable status quo and thereby putting Pyongyang in a less desperate situation than in the past, is to make, in effect, a similar argument. Such an argument acknowledges that the

status quo ex ante was indeed in the domain of gains for the DPRK and that engagement policies during the Kim-Clinton era were critical in pulling the North out of this situation and creating a stake for it in the new status quo.

77. Davis, *Threats and Promises*, p. 5.
78. See Hy-Sang Lee, *North Korea: A Strange Socialist Fortress* (Westport, CT: Praeger, 2001), pp. 171–228; and Eberstadt, *The End of North Korea*, pp. 70–75.
79. For a selection of these statements, see Eberstadt, *The End of North Korea*, pp. 83–84.
80. The larger nuclear withdrawal directive, applied to Korea, covered about forty W-33 artillery shells and sixty B-61 gravity bombs for U.S. F-16s based in South Korea. On this and other points, see Sigal, *Disarming Strangers*, p. 30.
81. For details of these agreements, see Young Whan Kihl, ed., *Korea and the World: Beyond the Cold War* (Boulder, CO: Westview Press, 1994); Byung Chul Koh, "The Inter-Korean Agreements of 1972 and 1992," *Korea and World Affairs* 16.3 (Fall 1992), pp. 463–82; and Dong-Won Lim, "Inter-Korean Relations Oriented toward Reconciliation and Cooperation," *Korea and World Affairs*, 16.2 (Summer 1992), pp. 213–23.

NOTES TO CHAPTER 2

1. Defense Intelligence Agency, as quoted in Patrick Hughes, Testimony before the Senate Select Committee on Intelligence, "Global Threats and Challenges to the United States and its Interests Abroad," February 5, 1997 (http://www.fas.org/irp/congress/1997_hr/s970205d.htm); Aaron Friedberg, "Loose Cannon," *New York Times Review of Books* (December 12, 1999), p. 23; Nicholas Eberstadt, "The Most Dangerous Country," *National Interest* 57 (Fall 1999), pp. 45–54; Fred Ikle, "U.S. Folly may Start Another Korean War," *Wall Street Journal* (October 12, 1998), p. A18; Amos Jordan, "Coping with North Korea," *Washington Quarterly* 21.1 (Winter 1998), pp. 33–46; *The Economist* "Sound the Alarm:

Defector Says North Korea Is Preparing for War," (April 26, 1997), p. 34.

2. Richard K. Betts, "Wealth, Power, and Instability: East Asia and the United States after the Cold War," *International Security* 18. 3 (Winter 1994), p. 66.

3. During the nuclear crisis, Hajime Izumi wrote "Given the past record, we cannot rule out the possibility of Pyongyang's taking some sudden, unanticipated action." Izumi, "North Korea and the Changes in Eastern Europe," *Korean Studies* 16 (1992), p. 8. Tong-Whan Park wrote that "One cannot rule out the possibility that Pyongyang may try to exploit a fluid international environment and unstable domestic situation, the result of which could well be a militarized dispute." Park, "Issues of Arms Control Between the two Korea," *Asian Survey* 32.4 (April 1992), p. 353. See also Kathleen C. Bailey, "North Korea: Enough Carrots, Time for the Stick," *Comparative Strategy* 13 (July/September 1994), pp. 277–82; Pan-Suk Kim, "Will North Korea Blink? Matters of Grave Danger," *Asian Survey* 34.3 (March 1994), pp. 258–72; Leonard S. Spector and Jacqueline R. Smith, "North Korea: the Next Nuclear Nightmare?" *Arms Control Today* 21.2 (March 1991), pp. 8–13; and John Curtis Perry, "Dateline North Korea: A Communist Holdout," *Foreign Policy* 80 (Fall 1990), pp. 172–191. On the 1980s, see Peter Polomka, "The Two Koreas: Catalyst for Conflict in East Asia?" *Adelphi Papers* 208 (London: International Institute for Strategic Studies, 1986); Young-Whan Kihl, "Korea's North-South Dialogue Rests on a Powder Keg," *Far Eastern Economic Review* (October 17, 1985), p. 64; and Young Choi, "The North Korean Buildup and its Impact on North Korean Military Strategy in the 1980s," *Asian Survey* 25.3 (March 1985), pp. 341–55. On North Korean moves following the 1979 assassination of Park Chung-hee, see John A. Wickham, *Korea on the Brink: from the "12/12 Incident" to the Kwangju Uprising, 1979–1980* (Washington, D.C.: National Defense University Press, 1999), pp. 30–32. Don Oberdorfer argues that Kim Il-sung was so confident of South Korean collapse after the Park's 1979 assassination that he saw no need to invade. Oberdorfer, *The Two Koreas: A Contemporary History* (New York: Addison-Wesley, 1998), pp. 96–

101. On the "missed opportunity" of 1961, see Wayne Kiyosaki, *North Korea's Foreign Relations: The Politics of Accommodation, 1945–75* (New York: Praeger, 1976), p. 79.

4. Norman Levin, "Global Detente and North Korea's Strategic Relations," *Korean Journal of Defense Analysis* 2.1 (Summer 1990), p. 42.

5. In 2001, New Hampshire's gross state product was $47.7 billion, while North Korea's GDP was estimated at $20 billion. (*Source: Northeast-Midwest staff calculations of data from the Department of Commerce, Bureau of Economic Analysis, September 2002*). And there are only trees and video rental stores in New Hampshire!

6. "The National Security Strategy of the United States" (The White House, September 17, 2002). For discussion of the strategy, see Michael O'Hanlon, Susan Rice, and James Steinberg, "The New National Security Strategy and Preemption" (m.s., Brookings Institute, 2002).

7. William Wohlforth, "Realism and the End of the Cold War," *International Security* 19.3 (Winter 1994), p. 99.

8. A small and growing group of scholars argue that North Korea is not as dangerous as believed. See Denny Roy, "North Korea and the Madman Theory," *Security Dialogue* 25 (1994), pp. 307–16; Leon Sigal, "The North Korean Nuclear Crisis: Understanding the Failure of the 'Crime and Punishment' Strategy," *Arms Control Today* (May 1997), pp. 3–13; David C. Kang, "Preventive War and North Korea," *Security Studies* 4.2 (Winter 1995), pp. 330–63; and David C. Kang, "Rethinking North Korea," *Asian Survey* 35.3 (March 1995), pp. 253–67.

9. David C. Kang, "Rolling with the Punches: North Korea and Cuba after the Cold War," *Journal of East Asian Affairs* 8.1 (Winter 1993).

10. Waltz (1993, 74). See also Layne 1993.

11. Thazhakuzhyil Paul, *Asymmetric Conflicts: War Initiation by Weaker Powers* (Cambridge: Cambridge University Press, 1994), p. 5.

12. Gilpin *War and Change*, p. 95.

13. Jack S. Levy, "Declining Power and the Preventive Motivation for War," *World Politics* 40.1 (October 1987), pp. 82–107; Alex Roberto Hybel, *The Logic of Surprise in International Conflict* (Lexington, MA: Lexington Books, 1986); Richard Ned Lebow, "Windows of

Opportunity: Do States Jump Through Them?" *International Security* 9.1. (Summer 1984), pp. 147–86; Randall L. Schweller, "Domestic Structure and Preventive War: Are Democracies More Pacific?" *World Politics* 44.2 (January 1992), pp. 235–69; Emerson Niou and Peter C. Ordeshook, "Preventive War and the Balance of Power: A Game-Theoretic Approach," *Journal of Conflict Resolution* 31.3 (Summer 1987), pp. 387–419; Robert Gilpin, *War and Change in World Politics* (Cambridge: Cambridge University Press, 1981); A.E.K. Organski and Jacek Kugler, *The War Ledger* (Chicago: University of Chicago Press, 1980); Indra De Soysa, John Oneal, and Yong-Hee Park, "Testing Power-transition Theory Using Alternative Measures of National Capabilities," *Journal of Conflict Resolution* 41 (August 1997), pp. 509–28; Douglas Lemke and Suzanne Werner, "Power Parity, Commitment to Change, and War," *International Studies Quarterly* 40 (1996), pp. 235–60; and Woosang Kim and James Morrow, "When Do Power Shifts Lead to War?" *American Journal of Political Science* 36 (1992), pp. 896–922.

14. Douglas Lemke, "The Continuation of History: Power Transition Theory and the End of the Cold War," *Journal of Peace Research* 34.1 (1997), pp. 23–36.

15. Douglas Lemke and William Reed, "Regime Types and Status Quo Evaluations: Power Transition Theory and the Democratic Peace," *International Interactions* 22.2 (1996), pp. 143–64; and Woosang Kim, "Alliance Transitions and Great Power War," *American Journal of Political Science* 34.4 (1991), pp. 833–50.

16. This has also been pointed out by Peter Hayes, who estimates that if one includes U.S. Army expenditures on both ground forces and part of the cost of the 7th fleet, combined South Korean-U.S. military spending in Korea was about $12 billion in 1986, four times what the north spent on defense that year. Peter Hayes, *Pacific Powderkeg* (Lexington, MA: Lexington Books, 1991), p. 166.

17. Young-sun Ha, "The Korean Military Balance: Myth and Reality," in William J. Taylor, Jr., et al., eds., *The Future of the South Korea-U.S. Security Relationship* (Boulder, CO: Westview Press, 1989).

18. Arms Control and Disarmament Agency, *World Military Expenditures and Arms Trade* (Washington D.C.: ACDA, various years).

19. Trevor N. Dupuy, *Attrition: Forecasting Battle Casualties and Equipment Losses in Modern War* (Fairfax, VA: HERO Books, 1990).

20. *Associated Press*, Sunday, January 14, 1996.

21. Author's personal interview with a U.S. military official, June 11, 1994. See also Kevin Sullivan, "U.S. Troops Train to Fight N. Korea." *Washington Post* (June 7, 1996), pp. A30.

22. Michael O'Hanlon, *Defense Planning for the Late 1990s: Beyond the Desert Storm Framework* (Washington, D.C.: Brooking Institution, 1995) p. 43.

23. Michael O'Hanlon, "Stopping a North Korean Invasion: Why Defending South Korea Is Easier Than the Pentagon Thinks It Is," *International Security* 22.4 (Spring 1998), p. 142.

24. Stuart Masaki, "The Korean Question: Assessing the Military Balance," *Security Studies* 4.2 (Winter 1995), pp. 365–425.

25. Oberdorfer, *The Two Koreas*.

26. Glenn Baek, "Bringing an End to Brinksmanship," *Washington Times* (November 15, 1998), p. B4.

27. On the security dilemma, see Robert Jervis, "Cooperation Under the Security Dilemma," *World Politics* 30.2 (1978), pp. 167–214.

28. Hakjoon Kim, "U.S.-South Korean Security Relations: A Challenging Partnership," *Korean Journal of Defense Analysis* 2.1 (Summer 1990), pp. 149–60; William Tow, "Reassessing Deterrence on the Korean peninsula," *Korean Journal of Defense Analysis* 3.1 (Summer 1991), pp. 179–218.

29. Jonathan Salant, "Powell says U.S. is Willing to Talk with North Korea," *Associated Press* (December 29, 2002); and Susan V. Lawrence, Murray Hiebert, Jay Solomon, and Kim Jung Min, "Time to Talk," *Far Eastern Economic Review*, January 23, 2003, pp. 12–16.

30. Department of Defense, "Nuclear Posture Review," submitted to Congress December 31, 2001, p. 16.

31. Roberto Suro, "Ex-Defense Officials Decry Missile Plan," *Washington Post* (May 17, 2000), p. A02; Victor D. Cha, "The Rationale for "Enhanced" Engagement of North Korea: After the Perry Policy Review," *Asian Survey* 39.6 (November/December 1999), p. 853.

32. Kenneth Waltz, "Nuclear Myths and Political Realities," *American Political Science Review* 84.3 (September 1990), pp. 731–45.

33. Bruce Cumings, "Spring Thaw for Korea's Cold War," *Bulletin of the Atomic Scientists* 48.3 (April 1992), pp. 14–23.

34. Nautilus Institute, *DPRK Report* No. 19 (July–August 1999).

35. Zachary S. Davis and Benjamin Frankel, eds., *The Proliferation Puzzle: Why Nuclear Weapons Spread* (London: Frank Cass, 1993); and Lewis A. Dunn, *Controlling the Bomb: Nuclear Proliferation in the 1980s* (New Haven: Yale University Press, 1982).

36. Andrew Mack, "North Korea and the Bomb." *Foreign Policy* 83 (Summer 1991), p. 93.

37. Young-Sun Song, *The Korean Nuclear Issue* (Canberra: Dept. of International Relations, Australian National University, 1991).

38. Spector and Smith, "North Korea: the Next Nuclear Nightmare?" p. 13.

39. Both quotes are from "Experts Challenge U.S. Claims of N. Korean Missile Threat," *Korea Times*, April 27, 2000.

40. "DPRK Warns U.S. of 'Unpredictable Consequences," *People's Korea* August 7, 1999, p. 1.

41. Hayes, *Pacific Powderkeg*, p. 158.

42. The one exception to this is the 1987 downing of the Korean airliner in an attempt to disrupt the Olympic games. This failed spectacularly.

43. Edward A. Olsen, "The Arms Race on the Korean Peninsula," *Asian Survey* 26.8 (August 1986), p. 851; Spector and Smith, "North Korea: the Next Nuclear Nightmare?" p. 8.

44. Perry, "Dateline North Korea."

45. James Pierce, "Remarks at the Second US-Korea Forum," Institute for Far Eastern Studies, Seoul, Korea, October 15, 1992.

46. Hazel Smith, "Bad, Mad, Sad or Rational Actor? Why the 'Securitization' Paradigm Makes for Poor Policy Analysis of North Korea," *International Affairs* 76.1 (January 2000), pp. 111–32.

47. Hak-joon Kim, "North Korea after Kim Il-song and the future of North-South Korean Relations," *Security Dialogue* 26.1 (March 1995); Byung-joon Ahn, "The Man Who Would Be Kim," *Foreign Affairs* 73.6 (November–December 1994), pp. 94–108; "*Vantage Point* 1996; ; and Jae-jean Suh and Byoung-lo Kim, "Prospects for

Change in the Kim Jong-il Regime," *Policy Studies Report*, Series No. 2 (Seoul: Research Institute for National Unification, 1994).

48. Oberdorfer, *The Two Koreas*; *Vantage Point* 1996; *Vantage Point* 1997.

49. Samuel S. Kim, "North Korea in 1999," *Asian Survey* 40.1 (January/ February 2000), pp. 152–54.

50. Nicholas Eberstadt, *Korea Approaches Unification* (London: M. E. Sharpe 1995), p. 132.

51. Kenneth Waltz, *Theory of International Politics* (Reading, MA: Addison-Wesley, 1979), p. 61.

NOTES TO CHAPTER 3

1. The Northern Limitation Line was unilaterally declared by the United Nations Command after the 1950–53 Korean war, and for the United States and ROK represents the de facto maritime border. The DPRK does not recognize the line and claims as its own the resource and fish-rich waters less than 12 miles away from its western coast, which are also less than 12 miles from South Korea-owned islands in the West Sea.

2. Victor D. Cha, "The Continuity Behind the Change in Korea," *Orbis* 44.4 (Fall 2000), pp. 585–98; and "Korea's Place in the Axis," *Foreign Affairs* (May/June 2002).

3. Chuck Downs, "Discerning North Korea's Intentions" in *Korea's Future*, p. 94.

4. Memorandum of Conversation with the Ambassador of the People's Republic of Hungary, Comrade Kadasch, on January 27, 1968, from 2:00 PM to 2:20 PM. MfAA, C 1091/70; translated by Karen Riechert; GDR Embassy in the DPRK, Pyongyang: January 29, 1968. Confidential. Obtained through the Cold War History Project, Woodrow Wilson Center, *Inside North Korea: Selected Documents from the Russian, East German, Hungarian, Czech, and Polish Archives* (March 8, 2003), ed. Kathryn Weathersby, Section 8 "The Crises of 1968" Document 4.

5. Memorandum of Conversation with the 1st Secretary of the Embassy

of the USSR in the DPRK, Comrade Zvetkov, and Comrade Jarck on July 26, 1968 between 1430 and 1615 in the USSR Embassy, MfAA, G-A 320; translated by Karen Riechert; Embassy of the GDR in the DPRK, Pyongyang, July 29, 1968. Confidential. Obtained through the Cold War History Project, Woodrow Wilson Center, *Inside North Korea: Selected Documents from the Russian, East German, Hungarian, Czech, and Polish Archives* (March 8, 2003), ed. Kathryn Weathersby, Section 8 "The Crises of 1968" Document 17.

6. I acknowledged in my opening statement that this potential may have decreased marginally in 2000–2001 as a result of US and ROK engagement with the North, but maintained that this new situation is far from permanent.

7. Speculation in the press that the United States might expand the war against terrorism to North Korea grew out of public statements at the end of 2001 by President Bush, defense secretary Rumsfeld, and undersecretary for arms control Bolton intimating a link between countries with WMD capabilities in defiance of the nonproliferation regime and terrorist regimes. See Donald Gregg, "Collateral Damage in Korea," *The Korea Society Quarterly* (Fall 2001), pp. 4–5.

8. For elaboration of the problems in Japan-DPRK dialogue, see Victor Cha, "Japan's Engagement Dilemmas with North Korea," *Asian Survey* (July/August 2001).

9. A financial scandal involving the pro-DPRK General Association of Korean Residents in Japan (Chongryun or Chosen Soren) revealed that the 1999 collapse of a credit union bank in Japan was tied to some 12.6 billion yen in shady loans extended to a senior member of Chongryun (Kang Yong Gwan, former chief financial officer for the Association). This revelation raised speculation that the credit union had been funneling money to the North Korean association on a regular basis as the association's other forms of income had dried up. The upshot was a police raid for the first time of Chongryun headquarters.

10. Hee-Sung Kim, "N.K. Patrol Ship Violates NLL Yet Again," *Joongang Ilbo* November 18, 2001; "Koreas Exchange Fire At Border, But No Casualties are Reported," *Associated Press* November 27, 2001; and "Legal Questions Raised over Shooting at Suspicious Ship," *Asahi Shimbun* December 25, 2001.

11. After the Korean war, the KPA also emphasized adequate logistics as a lesson of the war. Concerted efforts were made to maintain war reserves for all classes of supply for a minimum of six months for active forces and three months for reserve units.

12. Infantry divisions were reformed into mechanized infantry corps; armored divisions disappeared from the order of battle in the mid-1980s and were replaced by armored corps and a two-fold increase in the armored brigade count; and self-propelled artillery was reorganized into a multibrigade artillery corps.

13. North Korean special forces also underwent significant augmentation during this period as did conventional forces. In the latter case, between 1984 and 1992 for example, additions included more than 1,000 tanks, 2,500 infantry fighting vehicles; 6,000 artillery tubes and 2,700 multiple rocket launchers. For the latter, see Joseph Bermudez, *North Korean Special Forces* (Annapolis, Md.: Naval Institute Press, 1998).

14. Cited in *East Asian Strategic Review 2001* (Tokyo: NIDS 2001), p. 145.

15. The North did not modernize in ways dictated by an offensive doctrine given their capabilities. For example, they did not seek the next generation of mobile SAM systems beyond man-portable SA-7, SA-14, SA-16 (needed for maintaining tactical air defense capabilities). See Larry Niksch, "North Korea," in William Carpenter and David Wiencik eds., *Asian Security Handbook* (New York: M.E. Sharpe, 2000).

16. By the 1990s, the 30,000 km highway system (only 15 percent paved) and 5,000 km rail network might have been able to support initial combat operations during wartime, but could not support sustained operations because of rugged terrain, limited-east-west routes, easily targeted bridges and tunnels and other problematic chokepoints. See Office of the Secretary of Defense, *2000 Report to Congress: Military Situation on the Korean Peninsula September 12, 2000* available at www.defenselink.mil/news/Sep2000/korea09122000.html.

17. Bob Bateman, "Korean People's Army," unpublished paper, CSIS Working Group on Conventional Arms Control on the Korean Peninsula, p. 13.

18. For the best statement of the North's attempts at economic reform

(and the problems associated with such steps) see Marcus Noland, *Avoiding the Apocalypse* (Washington DC: IIE, 2001).

19. Kim Dae-jung's sunshine policy was historically unique in that it was the first unification policy in South Korea that explicitly removed absorption or victory of the South over the North as the ultimate objective. Instead, the purpose of engagement with the North became peaceful coexistence, representing a major change in ROK intentions on the peninsula.

20. Charles Armstrong, "Apocalypse Postponed? North Korea, Inter-Korean Relations and the Politics of Survival," paper presented at the conference on Inter-Korean Relations, Columbia University, May 2002.

21. Bernd Schafer, "Weathering the Sino-Soviet Conflict: The GDR and North Korea, 1949–1989," in *Inside North Korea: Selected Documents from the Russian, East German, Hungarian, Czech, and Polish Archives* edited by Kathryn Weathersby (Washington, D.C.: Woodrow Wilson Center, Cold War International History Project, DRAFT), p.8; and Oberdorfer, *The Two Koreas*, p. 25.

22. For the best statement of the argument, see Marcus Noland, "Why North Korea Will Muddle Through," *Foreign Affairs* 76.4 (July/August 1997), pp. 105–18.

23. For the first statement of this point with specific reference to Korea, see Byung-joon Ahn, "The Man Who Would Be Kim," *Foreign Affairs* 73.6 (1994), pp. 94–108.

24. Richard L. Armitage, "A Comprehensive Approach to North Korea," *Strategic Forum* No. 159 (March 1999), p. 4, http://www.ndu.edu/inss/strforum/forum159.html.

25. Elizabeth Rosenthal, "In North Korean Hunger, Legacy Is Stunted Children," *New York Times* December 16, 1998. For a fascinating memoir by a North Korean defector, see Chol-Hwan Kang and Pierre Rigoulot, *Aquariums of Pyongyang: Ten Years in the North Korean Gulag* (New York: Basic Books, 2001).

26. Nicholas Eberstadt, "Disparities in Socioeconomic Development in Divided Korea: Indications and Implications," *Asian Survey* 40.6 (November/December 2000), pp. 875–76.

27. For interesting observations on the American unwillingness to view

itself as capable of negotiating with pariah states, see Leon Sigal, *Disarming Strangers* (Princeton: Princeton University Press, 1998).

28. A key element of such an exit strategy is having China view U.S.-ROK-Japan engagement efforts as complete and undertaken in good faith.

29. Armitage, "A Comprehensive Approach to North Korea," p. 6.

30. Jack Rendler, "The Last Worst Place on Earth," in Sokolski, *Planning for a Peaceful Korea;* and Nicholas Eberstadt, *The End of North Korea* (Washington DC: AEI, 2000).

31. For an interesting account that highlights some of the problems encountered by former North Korean defectors trying to assimilate into southern society, see Young-chul Chang's *Tangsinûri kûroke chalnattsôyo?* (Seoul: Sahoe p'yông on, 1997).

32. Remarks by President Bush and President Kim Dae-jung in Press Availability—Seoul, Korea The Blue House, Seoul, Republic of Korea, February 20, 2002 available at http://www.whitehouse.gov/news/releases/2002/02/20020220-1.html

33. http://www.whitehouse.gov/news/releases/2002/01/20020129-11.html.

34. The implications of this argument for the 2003 nuclear crisis are covered in chapter 5. On DPRK negotiating tactics, see Scott Snyder, *Negotiating on the Edge: North Korean Negotiating Behavior* (Washington, D.C.: U.S. Institute of Peace, 1999); Chuck Downs, *Over the Line: North Korea's Negotiating Strategy* (Washington, D.C.: The AEI Press, 1999); and Victor Cha, "The Continuity Behind the Change in Korea," *Orbis,* 44.4 (Fall 2000), pp. 585–98.

35. Also implicit is the belief that the Clinton administration overestimated the North's vigilance and readiness to fight during the nuclear crisis in June 1994.

36. This strategy is elaborated in chapter 5.

NOTES TO CHAPTER 4

1. Michael O'Hanlon, "Stopping a North Korean Invasion: Why Defending South Korea Is Easier Than the Pentagon Thinks It Is,"

International Security 22.4 (Spring 1998), p. 142; Scott Sagan, "The Origins of the Pacific War," *Journal of Interdisciplinary History* 18.4 (Spring 1988), pp. 893–922.

2. For deeper discussion of North Korea's economy, see Marcus Noland, *Avoiding the Apocalypse* (Washington, D.C.: Institute for International Economics, 2000); and Nicholas Eberstadt, Disparities in Socioeconomic Development in Divided Korea: Indications and Implications," *Asian Survey* 40.6 (November/December 2000), pp. 867–93.

3. Yoon Deok-ryong and Park Soon-chan, "Capital needed for North Korea's Economic Recovery and Optimal Investment Policy," *Policy Analysis 01–08* (Seoul: Korea Institute for International Economic Policy, 2002) (in Korean).

4. See Ministry of Unification, "Data on North Korea, 2002); Heather Smith, "The Food Economy: the Catalyst for Collapse?" in Marcus Noland, ed., *Economic Integration of the Korean Peninsula* (Washington, D.C.: Institute for International Economics, 1997); and Nicholas Eberstadt, "The North Korean Economy in 2000," *The Korean Peninsula in the 21st Century: Prospects for stability and cooperation* Joint U.S.-Korea Academic Studies, Volume 11 (Washington, D.C.: Korean Economic Institute, 2001).

5. Marcus Noland, *Avoiding the Apocalypse*, p. 305. Noland gives a series of estimates for the costs of unification. See also James Williams, David von Hippel, and Peter Hayes, "Fuel and Famine: Rural Energy Crisis in the DPRK," *Policy Paper No. 46* (UCSD, Institute on Global Conflict and Cooperation, 2000).

6. Donald Gregg, "Kim Jong Il: The Truth Behind the Caricature," *Newsweek*, February 3, 2003, p. 13.

7. See Aidan Foster-Carter, "North Korea Caves in to the Market," *Asia Times* (August 6, 2002), http://www.asiatimes.com/atimes/Korea/DH06Dgol.html.

8. Quoted in a statement made in a meeting between Kim Yong-nam and Kenzo Oshima, UN Under Secretary General for Humanitarian Affairs, August 1, 2002.

9. "DPRK's Economic Measures Lead to Brisker Market, Better Life," *People's Daily*, Wednesday, October 30, 2002.

10. Park Suhk-sam, "Measuring and assessing Economic Activity in North Korea," *Korea's Economy 2002* (Washington, DC: Korea Economic Institute, 2002), p. 76.

11. Park Suhk-sam, "Measuring and Assessing Economic Activity in North Korea," p. 77–80.

12. "DPRK's Economic Measures Lead to Brisker Market, Better Life," People's Daily, Wednesday, October 30, 2002.

13. Park Suhk-sam, "Measuring and assessing Economic Activity in North Korea," p. 76.

14. Bank of Korea estimates, based on interviews with refugees and observations taken from North Korea. Cited in Park Suhk-sam, "Measuring and assessing Economic Activity in North Korea," p. 81.

15. Markku Heiskanen, "Eurasian Railways—Key To The Korean Deadlock?" Nautilus Institute Special Report, January 22, 2003, http://www.nautilus.org/fora/security/0232a%5Fheiskanen.html.

16. Ahn Byung-min, "Reconnection of the Kyonggi Railway: Effects and Future Prospects" (Seoul: The Korea Transport Institute, September 2000), cited in Hong Soon-jick, "North-South Economic Cooperation," *Korea's Economy 2001* (Washington, DC: Korea Economic Institute, 2001), p. 75.

17. Soo-Jeong Lee, "North Korea Proposes Reconciliation Talks with South Despite Nuclear Issue," *Associated Press*, January 16, 2003.

18. For the full text of the current and past DPRK Constitutions, see the Japanese-run *People's Korea* site (http://www.korea-np.co.jp/pk/).

19. For details, see Martin Williams, "North Korea to promote tech, science development" (http://www.idg.net/go.cgi?id = 456627).

20. For details, see Noland, *Avoiding the Apocalypse*, pp. 134–38.

21. Personal communication with Professor Ronald Duncan, Executive Director, National Centre for Development Studies, Asia Pacific School of Economics and Management, Australian National University. October 17, 2000.

22. Lee Joon-seung, "WCC Seeks Convergence of Biz Sector Interest, Inter-Korean Talks," Yonhap News, June 7, 2001.

23. *Jungang Ilbo* April 16, 2000 (http://www.joins.com/top.html).

24. N.a., "Samsung Group Chairman Wants to Visit North Korea," *Asia Pulse* May 3, 2000.

25. Telecom Cos. Moving Briskly to begin business in North Korea," *Korea Times* July 26, 2000.

26. Ministry of Unification, "Data on North Korea" (www.unikorea. go.kr).

27. Economist Intelligence Unit, *Country Report: China, North Korea* (London: Economist Intelligence Unit, 2000), p. 49.

28. See n.a., "Sinuiju Designated as H.K.-Type Special Zone: First Market Economy Experience in DPRK," *People's Korea*, September 28, 2002 (www.korea-np.co.jp/pk/184th_issue/2002092802.htm).

29. Yoon Deok-ryong, "Economic Development in North Korea: A Possible Time Line for North Korean Transformation," *Korea's Economy 2002* (Washington, D.C.: Korea Economic Institute, 2002), p. 73. Marcus Noland argues that the bureaucrats received extensive reeducation upon their return to Pyongyang. In conversations with the director of the ANU program, he said that ANU had closely monitored the North Korean bureaucrats' careers upon their return, and said that as of yet they did not seem to have suffered in terms of career progression. Noland, *Avoiding the Apocalypse*, p. 86, and personal communication.

30. Park Kyung-Ae, "The Pattern of North Korea's Track-Two Foreign Contacts," in, "The Korean Peninsula in the 21st Century: Prospects for Stability and Cooperation," *Joint U.S.-Korea Academic Studies* 11 (Washington, D.C.: Korean Economic Institute, September 2001), pp. 157–84.

31. Bradley Babson, remarks at the conference, "The North Korean System at the Dawn of the 21st Century." University of California, April 7, 2000.

32. Kenneth Quinones, remarks at the conference, "The North Korean System at the Dawn of the 21st Century." University of California, April 7, 2000.

33. *Jungang Ilbo*, June 15, 2000 (http://www.joins.com/top.html).

34. On war initiation by a weaker power, see T.V. Paul, *Asymmetric Conflicts: War Initiation by Weaker Powers* (New York: Cambridge University Press, 1994).

35. See Martin Wagner, "D.P.R.K. Extends Missile Pledge as U.S. Readies to Resume Talks," *Arms Control Today* (June 2001).

36. See Gary Samore, "U.S.-DPRK Missile Negotiations," *The Non-proliferation Review* (Summer 2002), pp. 16–20; and Alex Wagner, "D.P.R.K. Threatens to end Missile Moratorium, Nuclear Cooperation," *Arms Control Today* (March 2001).

37. Donald Gregg, "Kim Jong Il: The Truth Behind the Caricature," *Newsweek*, February 3, 2003, p. 13.

38. "N. Korea's Kim eyes better ties, ready to visit Japan," *Kyodo News Service*, September 14, 2002, http://home.kyodo.co.jp/printer_friendly.jsp?an = 20020914132, quoted in Leon Sigal, "North Korea Is No Iraq: Pyongyang's Negotiating Strategy," Nautilus Institute, December 23, 2002.

39. Marcus Noland, "North Korea and the South Korean Economy," paper prepared for the Roh Government Transition Team, Seoul, Korea, February 24, 2003 (http://www.iie.com/papers/noland0203.htm), p. 2.

40. Susan V. Lawrence, Murray Hiebert, Jay Solomon, and Kim Jung Min, "Time to Talk," *Far Eastern Economic Review*, January 23, 2003, p. 14.

41. See James Brooke, "China 'Looming Large' in South Korea as Biggest Player, Replacing the U.S.," *The New York Times*, January 3, 2003. On U.S.-Chinese relations, see Gerald Segal, "East Asia and the Constraintment of China," *International Security*, 20.4 (Spring 1996), pp. 107–35; Denny Roy, "Hegemon on the Horizon? China's Threat to East Asian Security," *International Security*, 19.1 (Summer 1994), pp. 149–68, p. 164; Nicholas D. Kristof, "The Rise of China," *Foreign Affairs*, 72.5 (November/December 1993), pp. 59–74; and Edward Friedman and Barrett McCormick, eds., *What If China Doesn't Democratize? Implications for War and Peace* (New York: M.E. Sharpe, 2000).

42. Susan V. Lawrence, Murray Hiebert, Jay Solomon, and Kim Jung Min, "Time to Talk," *Far Eastern Economic Review*, January 23, 2003, p. 13.

43. Akiko Yamamoto and Sachiko Sakamaki, "N. Korea's Neighbors Unmoved By Threats: Little Anxiety Felt in Seoul, Tokyo," *Washington Post*, Tuesday, February 11, 2003, p. A13.

44. James Cotton, "A New Initiative in Australia-North Korea Rela-

tions." *Policy Forum Online* #00–02 (Nautilus Institute, March 29, 2000), http://www.nautilus.org/newsletter/web/fora/security/0002d%5Fcotton.html.

NOTES TO CHAPTER 5

1. Unless otherwise cited, the following description of events is based on several not-for-attribution interviews with U.S. government officials and press reports.

2. For the State of the Union Address, see http://www.whitehouse.gov/news/releases/2002/01/20020129–11.html. For Bush's March 2001 remarks, see "Remarks by President Bush and President Kim Dae-Jung of South Korea," March 7, 2001, http://www.whitehouse.gov/news/releases/2001/03/20010307–6.html. Also see Bob Woodward, *Bush At War* (New York: Simon & Schuster, 2002), pp. 339–40.

3. For the June 2001 policy review, see "Statement by the President," June 13, 2001, *http://www.whitehouse.gov/news/releases/2001/06/20010611–4.html. http://www.whitehouse.gov/news/releases/2001/03/20010307–6.html* For Secretary of State Powell's remarks about picking up the threads of the Clinton administration's engagement policy, see "Press Availability with Her Excellency Anna Lindh, Minister of Foreign Affairs of Sweden," March 6, 2001, *http://www.state.gov/secretary/rm/2001/1116.htm*.

4. Aidan Foster-Carter, "No Turning Back?" *Comparative Connections* (July 2002) available at http://www.csis.org/pacfor/cc/0203Qnk_sk.html.

5. Marcus Noland, "West-Bound Train Leaving the Station: Pyongyang on the Reform Track," unpublished paper prepared for the Council on US-Korea Security Studies, Seoul, Korea, October 14–15, 2002 available at http://www.iie.com/papers/noland1002.htm.

6. Victor Cha, "Mr. Koizumi Goes to Pyongyang," *Comparative Connections* (October 2002), available at http://www.csis.org/pacfor/cc/0203Qjapan_skorea.html.

7. Comments by Assistant Secretary of States James Kelly at "Defining

the Future of US-Korean Relations" Roundtable hosted by the *Washington Post*, February 6, 2003, 3–530PM.

8. "US Followed the Aluminum,"*Washington Post*, October 18, 2002; and Seymour Hersh, "The Cold Test: What the Administration knew about Pakistan and the North Korean Nuclear Program," *The New Yorker*, January 27, 2002, http://www.newyorker.com/fact/content/?030127fa_fact

9. Ralph Cossa, "Trials, Tribulations, Threats and Tirades," *Comparative Connections* (January 2003), available at http://www.csis.org/pacfor/cc/0204Qus_skorea.html.

10. Inquiries by Chris Nelson of the *Nelson Report* and Barbara Slavin of *USA Today* prompted the administration to go public with the news. Some argue that the Bush administration deliberately withheld information about the program until after Congress authorized the use of military force against Iraq. Others argued that intelligence reports on the HEU program were delivered to the White House as early as November 2001, but that the September 11 attacks and war against terrorism took all high-level focus away from the assessment. See *Washington Post*, February 1, 2003 (Walter Pincus, "N. Korea's Nuclear Plans Were No Secret"), A1; and Ryan Lizza, "Nuclear Test," *The New Republic*, November 4, 2002), pp. 10–11.

11. *Washington Post*, January 31, 2003 (Walter Pincus, "Hints of North Korean Plutonium Output"), A13; and February 6, 2003 (Doug Struck, "Reactor Restarted, North Korea Says), A31.

12. *Washington Post* (op-ed), February 9, 2003 (Mary McGrory, "Fuzzy-Headed on North Korea"), B7.

13. *Washington Post*, January 16, 2003 (Richard Cohen, "Amateur Hour at the White House"), A19.

14. Ben Johnson, "Appeasing North Korea: the Clinton Legacy," *FrontPageMagazine.com*, January 3, 2003 available at http://www.frontpagemag.com/Articles/Printable.asp?ID = 5368. Also see Frank J. Gaffney, "North Korean Revisionism," *National Review Online* January 10, 2003 available at http://www.nationalreview.com/gaffney/gaffney011003.asp.

15. On the last point, see Cumings, "The Structural Basis of 'Anti-Americanism' in the Republic of Korea."

16. Walter Pincus, "North Korea's Nuclear Plans Were No Secret: U.S. Stayed Quiet as It Built Support on Iraq," *Washington Post*, February 1, 2003, p. A01.

17. Seymour Hersh, "The Cold Test: What the Administration Knew About Pakistan and the North Korean Nuclear Program," *The New Yorker*, January 27, 2003, p. 47.

18. The most well known of these situations is the "security dilemma," where one side's attempts to make itself safer provoke fears in the other side. The other side thus adjusts to counter, and both sides end up worse off. See Robert Jervis, "Cooperation under the Security Dilemma," *World Politics* 30.2 (1978), p. 105.

19. See, for example, Rose Brady, "The Road to Détente gets Steeper," *Businessweek* April 9, 2001.

20. For further discussion, see Moon J. Pak, "The Nuclear Security Crisis in the Korean Peninsula: Revisit the 1994 Agreed Framework," December 28, 2002, http://www.vuw.ac.nz/~caplabtb/dprk/Paknuclearcrisis.doc

21. See Jay Solomon, Alix Freedman, and Gordon Fairclough, "Troubled Power Project Plays Role in North Korea Showdown," *The Wall Street Journal*, January 30, 2002.

22. Wade Huntley and Timothy Savage, "The Agreed Framework at the Crossroads," *Policy Forum Online* #99–05A (Nautilus Research Institute, March 11, 1999).

23. All three citations are from Michael Gordon, "U.S. Toughens Terms for North Korea Talks," *New York Times*, July 3, 2001, p. A9.

24. Colin Powell, remarks at the Asia Society Annual dinner, June 10, 2002, quoted in Leon Sigal, "North Korea is No Iraq: Pyongyang's Negotiating Strategy," Nautilus Institute *Special Report*, December 23, 2002 (http://nautilus.org/for a/security/0227A_Siga.html).

25. Leon Sigal, "North Korea is No Iraq: Pyongyang's Negotiating Strategy," Nautilus Institute *Special Report*, December 23, 2002 (http://nautilus.org/for a/security/0227A_Siga.html).

26. Philip Shenon, "North Korea Says Nuclear Program can be Negotiated," *New York Times*, November 3, 2002, p. A1.

27. Jonathan Salant, "Secretary of State Powell says U.S. is willing to talk with North Korea," *Associated Press*, December 29, 2002.

28. Nautilus Institute, *DPRK Report* No. 19 (July–August 1999).

29. Ri Kang Jin, "Statement of the Korean Anti-Nuke Peace Committee," January 28, 2003.

30. Gregory Clark, "Pyongyang is the Real Victim," *Japan Times*, January 10, 2003, p. 5.

31. See Leon Sigal, "North Korea is No Iraq: Pyongyang's Negotiating Strategy," *Nautilus Institute Policy Forum Online* (December 23, 2002) available at http://www.nautilus.org/fora/security/0227A_Siga.htm

32. Avery Goldstein, *Deterrence and Security in the 21st Century: China, Britain, France and the Enduring Legacy of the Nuclear Revolution* (Stanford, CA: Stanford University Press, 2000); and Scott Sagan, "Why Do States Build Nuclear Weapons?" *International Security* 21.3 (Winter 1996–1997), pp. 54–86.

33. Personal phone interviews, South Korean government officials, January 9, 2003.

34. Personal conversation, U.S. government official, January 14, 2003.

35. Anthony Lake and Robert Gallucci, "Negotiating with Nuclear North Korea," *Washington Post*, November 6, 2002, A21; Jimmy Carter, "Engaging North Korea," *New York Times* October 27, 2002; Leon Sigal, "A Bombshell that's Actually an Olive Branch," *Los Angeles Times* October 18, 2002.

36 Comments by Joel Wit, "N. Korea Nuclear Threat," transcript of Lehrer NewsHour (Ray Suarez, Joel Wit, Henry Sokolski), aired January 10, 2003 available at PBS Online NewsHour *http://www. pbs.org/newshour/bb/asia/jan-june03/korea_1-10.html*; and comments by Wendy Sherman, "Defining the Future of US-Korean Relations," Joongang Ilbo-Washington Post seminar, Washington DC February 6, 2003.

37. Jonathan Power, "A Hawk on North Korea Wants Bush to be a Dove," February 5, 2003. http://www.transnational.org/forum/power/2003/02.01_NorthKorea.html

38. This is risky because the DPRK's response might also be to forward deploy even more aggressively in a "best-defense is strong-offense" strategy. For further discussion, see Henry Sokolski ed., *Planning for a Peaceful Korea* (Carlisle, PA: SSI, 2001), chp. 1.

39. Thanks to Tom Christensen for raising the point about the Party Congress.

40. *Washington Post* December 20, 2002 (Victor Cha, "Stay Calm on Korea").

41. *Choson Ilbo-Gallup Korea* polls, January 1, 2003, http://www.gallup.co.kr/news/2003/release004.html.

42. *Joongang Ilbo*, February 12, 2003.

NOTES TO CHAPTER 6

1. The United States has provided $620 million of food aid (a floursoy mix) since 1995, averaging around 68 percent of total WFP donations. This figure averages to 155,000 tons annually. In 2003, Secretary of State Powell announced that donations for the United States to North Korea would start at 40,000 tons (with the potential to top out at 100,000 tons).

2. Marcus Noland, *Avoiding the Apocalypse: The Future of the Two Koreas* (Washington, DC: IIE, 2001), ch. 8.

3. *International Herald Tribune* February 26, 2003 ("Tensions Weigh on South Korean Ratings, S&P say"), B1.

4. *Korea Times* February 26, 2003 (Cho Hyung-kwon, "KOSPI Drops Below 600 on Worries Over NK, Iraq"), p. 1.

5. Nicholas Eberstadt, "Introduction," in Richard Ellings and Nicholas Eberstadt eds., *Korea's Future* (Seattle, WA: National Bureau of Asian Research, 2001).

6. There is an emerging literature on hierarchy in various forms. See William Wohlforth, "The Stability of a Unipolar World," *International Security* 24.1 (Summer 1999), p. 13; David Lake, "Anarchy, hierarchy, and the variety of international relations," *International Organization* 50 (Winter 1996), pp. 1–33; Alexander Wendt and Daniel Friedheim, "Hierarchy Under Anarchy: Informal Empire

and the East German State," *International Organization* 49.4 (Autumn 1995), pp. 689–721; Douglas Lemke, *Regions of War and Peace* (Cambridge: Cambridge University Press, 2002); and Douglas Lemke and Suzanne Werner, "Power Parity, Commitment to Change, and War," *International Studies Quarterly* 40 (1996), pp. 235–260.

7. Aaron Friedberg, "Ripe for Rivalry," *International Security* 18.3 (Winter 1993–94), pp. 5–53; and Richard Betts, "Wealth, Power, and Instability," *International Security* 18.3 (Winter 1993–94), pp. 34–77.

8. See David C. Kang, "Culture and Hierarchy: The Chinese System and Stability in Asia," in John Ikenberry and Michael Mastanduno, eds., *International Relations Theory and the Asia-Pacific* (New York: Columbia University Press, 2003).

9. Economist Intelligence Unit, "Country Profile: China 2003" (London, The Economist Intelligence Unit, 2003).

10. See the discussion by Victor Cha, "Nuclear Weapons, Ballistic Missiles and Order in Asia," in Muthiah Alagappa ed., *Asian Security Order* (Stanford, CA: Stanford University Press, 2002).

11. For discussion of the normalization of ties, see Dan Sanford, *South Korea and the Socialist Countries: the Politics of Trade* (New York: St. Martin's Press, 1990). On military planning, see Ministry of Foreign Affairs, *Waegyo Baekso (Foreign Policy White Paper)* (Seoul: Ministry of National Defense, 2002).

12. There are a plethora of other scenarios to consider, but if one surveyed specialists about likely and potentially disturbing dynamics emerging from unification, few would disavow any of the trends listed above.

13. In 1969, the "Korea clause" stated that because Japan acknowledged that the defense of South Korea was critical to Japan's security, it would allow the United States unfettered access to bases in Japan in the event of a second Korean war. This agreement ran concurrent with the declaration of Nixon's Guam doctrine in the same year calling for Asian allies to bear the primary burden of defense.

14. Strictly speaking, Beijing will not approve of any future configurations in Asia that retain a U.S. military presence, but the choices

posed to Beijing will not be framed in such absolute terms, but rather in relative ones.

15. Ashton B. Carter and William J. Perry, *Preventive Defense: A New Security Strategy for America* (Washington, D.C.: Brookings Institution, 1999), p. 14.

16. Alliances serve the purpose not just of providing for one's security, but doing so in an efficient and relatively less costly manner than would otherwise be the case (i.e., self-help). In this vein, an alliance's success is measured by the extent to which it serves as a facilitator of power accretion and projection; operates as a unified command; enables common tactics and doctrine through joint training; promotes a division of security roles; facilitates cooperation in production and development of military equipment, and elicits political support among domestic constituencies. See William J. Perry, "Commentary," in Yoichi Funabashi, ed., *Alliance Tomorrow* (Tokyo, Japan: Tokyo Foundation Press, 2000).

17. Glenn Snyder, *Alliance Politics* (Ithaca, N.Y.: Cornell University Press, 1998).

18. "The Korean-American Relationship: Continuity and Change," Address before the Korean-American Society and the American Chamber of Commerce, January 23, 1998, Seoul (*napsnet@nautilus.org*). Also see public statements by Peter Tarnoff and Edward Royce in Bergsten and Sakong, *Korea-United States Cooperation*; and "Perspectives on U.S.-Korea Relations," *US-Korea Tomorrow* 1.1 (August 1998).

19. *Korea Herald*, November 23, 1998 ("Kim Dae-jung, Clinton in Agreement on Democracy, Free Market").

BIBLIOGRAPHY

Ahn, Byung-joon. "The Man Who Would Be Kim." *Foreign Affairs* 73.6 (November–December 1994), pp. 94–108.

Albright, David, ed. *Solving the North Korean Nuclear Puzzle.* Washington, DC: Institute for Science and International Security Press, 2000.

Allen, Richard V. "Seoul's Choice: The U.S. or the North." *New York Times,* January 16, 2003, p. A29.

Armitage, Richard L. "A Comprehensive Approach to North Korea." *Strategic Forum* No. 159 (March 1999). (http://www.ndu.edu/inss/strforum/forum159.html.)

Armstrong, Charles. "Apocalypse Postponed? North Korea, Inter-Korean Relations and the Politics of Survival." Paper presented at the conference on Inter-Korean Relations, Columbia University, May 2002.

Armstrong, Charles. *The North Korean Revolution, 1945–1950.* Ithaca, New York: Cornell University Press, 2002.

Axelrod, Robert. "The Rational Timing of Surprise." *World Politics* 31.2 (January 1979), pp. 228–46.

Babson, Bradley. Remarks at the conference, "The North Korean System at the Dawn of the 21st Century." University of California, Berkeley. April 7, 2000.

Baek, Glenn. "Bringing an End to Brinksmanship." *Washington Times,* November 15, 1998, p. B4.

Bailey, Kathleen C. "North Korea: Enough Carrots, Time for the Stick." *Comparative Strategy* 13 (July/September 1994), pp. 277–82.

Baldwin, David. "The Power of Positive Sanctions." *World Politics* 24 (October 1971), pp. 19–38.

Baldwin, David. "Thinking About Threats," *Journal of Conflict Resolution* 15.1 (1971), pp. 71–78.

Ball, Desmond. *Signals Intelligence (SIGINT) in North Korea.* Canberra,

228

Australia: Strategic and Defence Studies Centre, Australian National University, 1996.

Bateman, Bob. "Korean People's Army." unpublished paper, CSIS Working Group on Conventional Arms Control on the Korean Peninsula, Washington, DC.

Bates, Robert. "Area Studies and Political Science: Rupture and Possible Synthesis." *Africa Today* 44 (April–June 1997), pp. 123–31.

Bates, Robert. "Area Studies and the Discipline: A Useful Controversy?" *PS: Political Science and Politics* (June 1997), pp. 166–69.

Bermudez, Joseph. *North Korea's Special Forces*. London: Jane's Publishing Company, Ltd.,1988.

Bermudez, Joseph. *North Korean Special Forces*. Annapolis, MD: Naval Institute Press, 1998.

Betts, Richard K. *Surprise Attack: Lessons for Defense Planning*. Washington, DC: Brookings Institution, 1982.

Betts, Richard. "Wealth, Power, and Instability: East Asia and the United States After the Cold War." *International Security* 18 (1994), pp. 34–77.

Bosworth, Stephen. "The Korean-American Relationship: Continuity and Change," Address before the Korean-American Society and the American Chamber of Commerce, Seoul, Korea. January 23, 1998 (*napsnet@nautilus.org*).

Brady, Rose. "The Road to Détente Gets Steeper." *BusinessWeek* April 9, 2001.

Brooke, James. "China 'Looming Large' in South Korea as Biggest Player, Replacing the U.S." *The New York Times*, January 3, 2003, p. A3.

Buchanan, Patrick J. "The Great Equalizer." *The American Conservative*, February 10, 2003, p. 7.

Bush, George, and Dae-jung Kim. "Remarks by President Bush and President Kim Dae-Jung in Press Availability—Seoul, Korea The Blue House, Seoul, Republic of Korea," February 20, 2002 (http://www.whitehouse.gov/news/releases/2002/02/20020220-1.html).

Bush, George. "State of the Union Address." January 29, 2002, (http://www.whitehouse.gov/news/releases/2002/01/20020129-11.html).

Bush, George. "Remarks by President Bush and President Kim Dae-Jung of South Korea." March 7, 2001 (http://www.whitehouse.gov/news/releases/2001/03/20010307-6.html).

Buzo, Adrian. *The Guerilla Dynasty: Politics and Leadership in North Korea.* Boulder, CO: Westview Press, 1999.

Carter, Ashton B., and William J. Perry. *Preventive Defense: A New Security Strategy for America.* Washington, DC: Brookings Institution, 1999.

Carter, Jimmy. "Engaging North Korea." *New York Times* October 27, 2002, p. A21.

Cha, Victor and Michael O'Hanlon. "A Clumsy U.S. Risks Ties to Seoul." *Los Angeles Times*, December 11, 2002.

Cha, Victor D. "The Rationale for "Enhanced" Engagement of North Korea: After the Perry Policy Review." *Asian Survey* 39.6 (November/December 1999), pp. 845–66.

Cha, Victor D. "Japan's Engagement Dilemmas with North Korea." *Asian Survey* 41.4 (July/August 2001), pp. 549–63.

Cha, Victor D. "Korea's Place in the Axis." *Foreign Affairs* 81.3 (May/June 2002), pp. 79–92.

Cha, Victor. "Globalization and the Study of International Security." *Journal of Peace Research* 37.3 (May 2000), pp. 391–403.

Cha, Victor. "Hawk Engagement and Preventive Defense on the Korean Peninsula." *International Security* 27.1 (Summer 2002), pp. 40–78.

Cha, Victor. "Mr. Koizumi Goes to Pyongyang." *Comparative Connections* (October 2002), (http://www.csis.org/pacfor/cc/0203Qjapan_skorea.html).

Cha, Victor. "Stay Calm on Korea." *Washington Post*, December 20, 2002, p. A22.

Cha, Victor. "The Economic Crisis, Strategic Culture and the Military Modernization of South Korea." *Armed Forces & Society* 28.1 (Fall 2001), pp. 99–128.

Cha, Victor. *Alignment Despite Antagonism: The United States-Korea-Japan Security Triangle* (Stanford: Stanford Univ. Press, 1999.

Cha, Victor D. "The Continuity Behind the Change in Korea." *Orbis* 44.4 (Fall 2000), pp. 585–98;

Cha, Victor. "Nuclear Weapons, Ballistic Missiles and Order in Asia." In Muthiah Alagappa ed., *Asian Security Order.* Stanford, CA: Stanford University Press, 2002, pp. 458–98..

Chang, Jekuk. "Pyongyang's New Strategy of Frank Admission." Nautilus Institute Policy Forum Online PFO02–11A, 24 October 2002 http://nautilus.org/fora/security/0211A_Chang.html .

Chang, Young-chul. *Tangsindûli kûroke chalnattsôyo?* Seoul: Sahoe p'yông on, 1997.

Cho, Hyung-kwon. "KOSPI Drops Below 600 on Worries Over NK, Iraq." *Korea Times*, February 26, 2003, p. 1.

Choi, Song –Ji. *Kim Jong-Il gwa hyôndae pukhan chongch'isa (Kim Jong-Il and Modern North Korea Political Thought)*. Seoul: Korean Broadcasting Publishers, 2001.

Choi, Young. "The North Korean Buildup and Its Impact on North Korean Military Strategy in the 1980s." *Asian Survey* 25.3 (March 1985), pp. 341–55.

Chosôn Ilbo various issues.

Chosôn Ilbo-Gallup Korea polls, January 1, 2003, (http://www.gallup.co.kr/news/2003/release004.html).

CIA. *World Factbook 2002*. Washington, DC: Central Intelligence Agency, 2002.

CINC UNC/CFC/USFK Posture Statement to US Congress (General Schwartz) (http://www.korea.army.mil/pao/news\index.htm).

Clark, Gregory. "Pyongyang is the Real Victim." *Japan Times*, January 10, 2003, p. 5.

Cohen, Richard. "Amateur Hour at the White House." *Washington Post*, January 16, 2003, p. A19.

Cossa, Ralph. "Trials, Tribulations, Threats and Tirades." *Comparative Connections* (January 2003), (http://www.csis.org/pacfor/cc/0204Qus_skorea.html).

Cotton, James. "A New Initiative in Australia-North Korea Relations." Policy Forum Online #00–02, (Nautilus Institute, March 29, 2000).

Cox, Christopher. Hearing of the House International Relations Committee, October 13, 1999.

Cumings, Bruce. "Feeding the North Korea Myths." *The Nation* September 29, 1997, pp. 22–24.

Cumings, Bruce. "Spring Thaw for Korea's Cold War." *Bulletin of the Atomic Scientists* 48.3 (April 1992), pp. 14–23.

Cumings, Bruce. "The Structural Basis of Anti-Americanism in the Republic of Korea." paper presented at Georgetown University, January 30, 2003.

Cumings, Bruce. *Korea's Place in the Sun*. New York: Norton, 1997.

Cumings, Bruce. *The Two Koreas*, Foreign Policy Association, Headline Series No. 269 (May/June 1984), pp. 65–66.

Davis, James. *Threats and Promises: The Pursuit of International Influence*. Baltimore: Johns Hopkins, 2000.

Davis, Zachary S., and Benjamin Frankel, eds. *The Proliferation Puzzle: Why Nuclear Weapons Spread*. London: Frank Cass, 1993.

De Soysa, Indra, John Oneal, and Yong-Hee Park. "Testing Power-Transition Theory Using Alternative Measures of National Capabilities." *Journal of Conflict Resolution* 41 (August 1997), pp. 509–28.

Department of Commerce, Bureau of Economic Analysis, September 2002.

Department of Defense. "Nuclear Posture Review." (Submitted to Congress December 31, 2001).

Doug Struck, "N. Korea Back From the Brink," *Washington Post*, September 5, 2000, p. A20.

Downs, Chuck. "Discerning North Korea's Intentions." In Richard Ellings and Nicholas Eberstadt eds., *Korea's Future and the Great Powers*. Seattle: National Bureau of Asian Research, 2001.

Downs, Chuck. *Over the Line: North Korea's Negotiating Strategy*. Washington, DC: AEI Press, 1999.

Dunigan, James F. *How to Make War*. New York: Quill, 1983.

Dunn, Lewis A. *Controlling the Bomb: Nuclear Proliferation in the 1980s*. New Haven: Yale University Press, 1982.

Dupuy, Trevor N. *Attrition: Forecasting Battle Casualties and Equipment Losses in Modern War*. Fairfax, VA: HERO Books, 1990.

Eberstadt, Nicholas. "Disparities in Socioeconomic Development in Divided Korea: Indications and Implications." *Asian Survey* Vol. 40.6 (November/December 2000), pp. 867–93.

Eberstadt, Nicholas. "Hastening Korean Unification." *Foreign Affairs* 76.2 (1997), pp. 77–92.

Eberstadt, Nicholas. "'National Strategy' in North and South Korea." *NBR Analysis* 7.5 (1996), pp. 1–12.

232

Eberstadt, Nicholas. "The Most Dangerous Country." *National Interest* 57 (Fall 1999), pp. 45–54.

Eberstadt, Nicholas. "The North Korean Economy in 2000." In *The Korean Peninsula in the 21st Century: Prospects for Stability and Cooperation.* Joint U.S.-Korea Academic Studies, Volume 11. Washington, DC: Korean Economic Institute, 2001.

Eberstadt, Nicholas. "Introduction," In Richard Ellings and Nicholas Eberstadt eds., *Korea and the Major Powers.* Seattle, Wash.: National Bureau of Asian Research, 2001.

Eberstadt, Nicholas. *Korea Approaches Unification.* London: M.E. Sharpe 1995.

Eberstadt, Nicholas. *The End of North Korea.* Washington DC: AEI, 2000.

Economist Intelligence Unit. *Country Profile: China 2003.* London, The Economist Intelligence Unit, 2003.

Farnham, Barbara. "Roosevelt and the Munich Crisis: Insights from Prospect Theory." *Political Psychology* 13.2 (1992), pp. 205–35.

Foster-Carter, Aidan. "North Korea Caves in to the Market." *Asia Times,* August 6, 2002.

Foster-Carter, Aidan. "No Turning Back?" *Comparative Connections* (July 2002) (http://www.csis.org/pacfor/cc/0203Qnk_sk.html).

Friedberg, Aaron. "Loose Cannon." *New York Times Review of Books,* December 12, 1999, p. 23.

Friedberg, Aaron. "Ripe for Rivalry: Prospects for Peace in a Multipolar Asia." *International Security* 18 (1994), pp. 5–33.

Friedman, Edward, and Barrett McCormick, eds. *What If China Doesn't Democratize? Implications for War and Peace.* New York: M.E. Sharpe, 2000.

Gaffney, Frank J. "North Korean Revisionism." *National Review Online* January 10, 2003 (http://www.nationalreview.com/gaffney/gaffney 011003.asp.)

Gallucci, Robert, Joel Wit and Daniel Poneman, "Going Critical: The 1994 U.S.–DPRK Nuclear Negotiations." Forthcoming ms.

Gause, Gregory. "Prospect Theory and Iraqi War Decisions." paper presented at the 1997 APSA, Washington DC August 28–31, 1997.

Gilinsky, Victor. "Answering North Korea." *Washington Post*, October 18, 2002.

Gilinsky, Victor. "North Korea and the End of the Agreed Framework." *Heritage Foundation Backgrounder* No. 1605 (October 18, 2002).

Gilinsky, Victor. "North Korea as the Ninth Nuclear Power?" Nautilus Institute Policy Forum Online, PFO 02–10A, (October 22, 2002) http://nautilus.org/fora/security/0210A_Victor.html;

Gilman, Benjamin. Press release Sept 17, 1999. U.S. House of Representatives International Relations Committee. Accessed at http://www.nautilus.org/napsned/dir/9909/Sept. 17.html.

Gilpin, Robert. *War and Change in World Politics.* Cambridge: Cambridge University Press, 1981

Glaser, Charles, and Chaim Kaufmann. "What is the Offense-Defense Balance and How Can We Measure It?" *International Security* 22.4 (Spring 1998), pp. 44–82.

Gleysteen, William H. *Massive Entanglement, Marginal Influence: Carter and Korea in Crisis.* Washington, DC: Brookings, 1999.

Goldstein, Avery. *Deterrence and Security in the 21st Century: China, Britain, France and the Enduring Legacy of the Nuclear Revolution.* Stanford, CA: Stanford University Press, 2000.

Goldstein, Joshua. *Long Cycles: Prosperity and War in the Modern Age.* New Haven: Yale University Press, 1988.

Gordon, Michael. "U.S. Toughens Terms for North Korea Talks." *New York Times*, July 3, 2001, p. A9.

Gregg, Donald. "Kim Jong Il: The Truth Behind the Caricature." *Newsweek*, February 3, 2003, p. 13.

Gregg, Donald. "Collateral Damage in Korea." *The Korea Society Quarterly* (Fall 2001), pp. 4–5.

Ha, Young-sun. "The Korean Military Balance: Myth and Reality." In William J. Taylor, Jr., et al., eds., *The Future of the South Korea-U.S. Security Relationship.* Boulder, CO: Westview Press, 1989.

Halloran, Richard. "New Warplan Calls for Invasion of North Korea." *Global Beat* 14 (November 1998) (http://www/nyu/edu/globalbeat/asia/Halloran111498.html).

Hamilton, Lee. "Our Stake in Asia's Nuclear Future." *Washington Times*, May 13, 1998.

234

Han, Sung-joo. "The Evolving Inter-Korean Relationship." *Journal of East Asian Studies* 1.1 (February 2001), pp. 155–78.

Harris, Sally. "Coping with Pressure: South Korea's Defense Restructuring." *Korean Journal of Defense Analysis* 12.2 (Winter 2000), pp. 207–30.

Harrison, Selig. "The Missiles of North Korea." *World Policy Journal* (Spring 2001).

Harrison, Selig. "Promoting a Soft Landing in North Korea." *Foreign Policy* 106 (Spring 1997), pp. 57–76.

Hayes, Peter. *Pacific Powderkeg*. Lexington, MA: Lexington Books, 1991.

Heiskanen, Markku. "Eurasian Railways—Key To The Korean Deadlock?" Nautilus Institute Special Report, January 22, 2003.

Hersh, Seymour. "The Cold Test: What the Administration knew about Pakistan and the North Korean Nuclear Program." *The New Yorker*, January 27, 2002.

Hong, Soon-jick. "North-South Economic Cooperation." *Korea's Economy 2001*. Washington, DC: Korea Economic Institute, 2001.

Hong, Soon-young. "Thawing Korea's Cold War." *Foreign Affairs* (May/June 1999).

"Press Briefing with Secretary of State Madeleine Albright. Pyongyang, October 24, 2000. http://secretary.state.gov/www/statements/2000/601024b.html

Hughes, Patrick. "Global Threats and Challenges to the United States and its Interests Abroad," February 5, 1997. (http://www.fas.org/irp/congress/1997_hr/s970205d.htm).

Hunter, Helen Louise. *Kim Il-Sung's North Korea*. Westport, Conn.: Praeger, 1999.

Huntley, Wade, and Timothy Savage. "The Agreed Framework at the Crossroads." *Policy Forum Online* #99–05A, (Natuilus Research Institute, March 11, 1999).

Huth, Paul, D.S. Bennett, and C. Gelpi. "System Uncertainty, Risk Propensity, and International Conflict Among the Great Powers." *Journal of Conflict Resolution* 36 (1992), pp. 478–517.

Hybel, Alex Roberto. *The Logic of Surprise in International Conflict*. Lexington, Mass.: Lexington Books, 1986.

Hy-Sang Lee, *North Korea: A Strange Socialist Fortress* (Westport, Conn.: Praeger, 2001), pp. 171–228.

Ikle, Fred. "U.S. Folly May Start Another Korean War." *Wall Street Journal*, October 12, 1998, p. A18.

International Institute for Strategic Studies. *The Military Balance 1997–1998*. London: International Institute for Strategic Studies, 1998.

Izumi, Hajime. "North Korea and the Changes in Eastern Europe." *Korean Studies* 16 (1992), pp. 1–22.

Jervis, Robert. "Political Implications of Loss Aversion." *Political Psychology* 13.2 (1992), pp. 187–204.

Jervis, Robert. "Cooperation under the Security Dilemma." *World Politics* 30.2 (1978), pp. 77–108.

Jervis, Robert. "Domino Beliefs and Strategic Behavior." in Jervis and Snyder, eds. *Dominoes and Bandwagons*, pp. 20–50.

Jervis, Robert. *The Meaning of the Nuclear Revolution*. Ithaca, NY: Cornell University Press, 1989.

Johnson, Ben. "Appeasing North Korea: the Clinton Legacy." *FrontPageMagazine.com*, January 3, 2003 (http://www.frontpagemag.com/Articles/Printable.asp?ID = 5368).

Johnson, Chalmers. "A disaster in the making: rational choice and Asian studies." *National Interest* 36, (Summer 1994), pp. 14–22.

Joongang Ilbo, various issues.

Jordan, Amos. "Coping with North Korea." *Washington Quarterly* 21, no.1 (Winter 1998), pp. 33–46.

June 2001 policy review, "Statement by the President," June 13, 2001, http://www.whitehouse.gov/news/releases/2001/06/20010611–4.html.

Kahneman, Daniel, and Amos Tversky. "Prospect Theory: An Analysis of Decision Under Risk." *Econometrica* 47.2 (March 1979), pp. 263–91.

Kang, Chol-Hwan, and Pierre Rigoulot. *Aquariums of Pyongyang: Ten Years in the North Korean Gulag*. New York: Basic Books, 2001.

Kang, David C. "Preventive War and North Korea." *Security Studies* 4.2 (Winter 1995), pp. 330–63.

Kang, David C. "Rethinking North Korea." *Asian Survey* 35.3 (March 1995), pp. 253–67.

Kang, David C. "Rolling with the Punches: North Korea and Cuba after the Cold War." *Journal of East Asian Affairs* 8.1 (Winter 1994), pp. 18–55.

236

Kang, David C. "Culture and Hierarchy: the Chinese System and Stability in Asia." In Michael Mastanduno and John Ikenberry, eds., *International Relations Theory and the Asia-Pacific.* New York: Columbia University Press, 2003.

Kang, David C. "Two Countries, One Anxiety." *New York Times*, December 22, 2002.

Kelly, James. "Defining the Future of US-Korean Relations." Roundtable hosted by the Washington Post, February 6, 2003.

Kennedy, Paul. *The Rise and Fall of the Great Powers: Economic Change and Military Conflict from 1500 to 2000.* New York: Random House, 1987.

Kihl, Young W., and Peter Hayes, eds. *Peace and Security in Northeast Asia: The Nuclear Issue and the Korean Peninsula.* Armonk, NY: M. E. Sharpe, 1997.

Kihl, Young Whan, ed., *Korea and the World: Beyond the Cold War.* Boulder, CO: Westview Press, 1994.

Kihl, Young-Whan. "Korea's North-South Dialogue Rests on a Powder Keg." *Far Eastern Economic Review*, October 17, 1985, p. 64.

Kim, Hakjoon. "North Korea After Kim Il-song and the Future of North–South Korean Relations." *Security Dialogue* 26.1 (March 1995), pp. 21–42.

Kim, Hakjoon. "U.S.-South Korean Security Relations: A Challenging Partnership." *Korean Journal of Defense Analysis* 2.1 (Summer 1990), pp. 149–160.

Kim, Hee-Sung. "N.K. Patrol Ship Violates NLL Yet Again." *Joongang Ilbo*, November 18, 2001, p. 3.

Kim, Pan-Suk. "Will North Korea Blink? Matters of Grave Danger." *Asian Survey* 34.3 (March 1994), pp. 258–72.

Kim, Samuel, ed. *North Korean Foreign Relations in the Post-Cold War Era.* Oxford: Oxford University Press, 1998.

Kim, Samuel S. "North Korea in 1999." *Asian Survey* 40.1 (January/February 2000), pp. 152–54.

Kim, Samuel, ed. *North Korea and Northeast Asia.* Lanham, MD: Rowman and Littlefield, 2002.

Kim, Woosang and James Morrow. "When Do Power Shifts Lead to War?" *American Journal of Political Science* 36 (1992), pp. 896–922.

Kim, Woosang. "Alliance Transitions and Great Power War." *American Journal of Political Science* 34.4 (1991), pp. 833–50.

Kiyosaki, Wayne. *North Korea's Foreign Relations: the Politics of Accommodation, 1945–75*. New York: Praeger, 1976.

Koh, B.C. *The Foreign Policy Systems of North and South Korea*. Berkeley: University of California Press, 1984.

Koh, Byung Chul. "The Inter-Korean Agreements of 1972 and 1992." *Korea and World Affairs* 16.3 (Fall 1992), pp. 463–482.

Kongdan Oh, "North Korea's Engagement: Implications for South Korea," in National Intelligence Council and Library of Congress, *North Korea's Engagement: Perspectives, Outlook, and Implications* CR 2001–01. May 2001.

Koo, Bon-Hak. *The Political Economy of Self-Reliance: Juche and Economic Development, 1961–1990*. Seoul: Research Center for Peace and Unification, 1992.

Korea Herald, various issues.

Kristof, Nicholas D. "The Rise of China." *Foreign Affairs*, Vol. 72.5 (November/December 1993), pp. 59–74.

Kristof, Nicholas. "New Shape to Triangle Tying U.S. and Koreas." *New York Times*, March 1, 1998, p. A21.

Kugler, Jacek, and A.E.K. Organski. *The War Ledger*. Chicago: University of Chicago Press, 1980.

Kugler, Jacek, and A.F.K Organski. "The Power Transition: A Retrospective and Prospective Evaluation." In Manus I. Midlarsky, ed., *Handbook of War Studies*, pp. 171–194. Boston: Unwin Hyman, 1989.

Kupchan, Charles. *The Vulnerability of Empire*. Ithaca: Cornell, 1994.

Kwak, Tae-Hwan. "The Korean Peace Process." *International Journal of Korean Unification Studies* 9.1 (2000), pp. 1–30.

Lake Anthony, and Robert Gallucci. "Negotiating with Nuclear North Korea." *Washington Post*, November 6, 2002, p. A21.

Lake, David. "Anarchy, hierarchy, and the variety of international relations." *International Organization* 50.1 (Winter 1996), pp. 1–33.

Lawrence, Susan V., Murray Hiebert, Jay Solomon, and Kim Jung Min. "Time to Talk." *Far Eastern Economic Review*, January 23, 2003, pp. 12–16.

Lebow, Richard Ned. "Windows of Opportunity: Do States Jump

Through Them?" *International Security* 9.1. (Summer 1984), pp. 147–86.

Lebow, Richard Ned. *The Art of Bargaining*. Baltimore: Johns Hopkins Univ. Press, 1996.

Lee, Chong-sik and Robert Scalapino. *Communism in Korea*. Los Angeles, CA: University of California Press, 1972.

Lee, Hy-Sang, North Korea: *A Strange Socialist Fortress*. Westport, Conn.: Praeger, 2001.

Lee, Joon-seung. "WCC Seeks Convergence of Biz Sector Interest, Inter-Korean Talks." *Yonhap News*, June 7, 2001.

Lee, Soo-Jeong. "North Korea Proposes Reconciliation Talks with South Despite Nuclear Issue." *Associated Press*, January 16, 2003.

Lemke, Douglas and Suzanne Werner. "Power Parity, Commitment to Change, and War." *International Studies Quarterly* 40 (1996), pp. 235–60.

Lemke, Douglas and William Reed. "Regime Types and Status Quo Evaluations: Power Transition Theory and the Democratic Peace." International Interactions 22.2 (1996), pp. 143–64.

Lemke, Douglas. "The Continuation of History: Power Transition Theory and the End of the Cold War." *Journal of Peace Research* 34.1 (1997), pp. 23–36.

Lemke, Douglas. *Regions of War and Peace*. Cambridge: Cambridge University Press, 2002.

Levin, Norman. "Global Detente and North Korea's Strategic Relations." *Korean Journal of Defense Analysis* 2.1 (Summer 1990), p. 42.

Levy, Jack S. "Declining Power and the Preventive Motivation for War." *World Politics* 40.1 (October 1987), pp. 82–107.

Levy, Jack. "An Introduction to Prospect Theory." *Political Psychology* 13.2 (1992), pp. 171–86.

Levy, Jack. "Prospect Theory and International Relations: Theoretical Applications and Analytical Problems." *Political Psychology* 13.2 (1992), 283–310.

Lim, Dong-Won. "Inter-Korean Relations Oriented Toward Reconciliation and Cooperation." *Korea and World Affairs* 16.2 (Summer 1992), pp. 213–23.

Little, Daniel. "Rational-Choice Models and Asian Studies." *Journal of Asian Studies* 50.1 (February 1991), pp. 35–52.

Lizza, Ryan. "Nuclear Test." *The New Republic*, (November 4, 2002), pp. 10–11.

Loeb, Vernon and Peter Slevin. "Overcoming North Korea's Tyranny of Proximity." *Washington Post*, January 20, 2003, p.A16.

Mack, Andrew. "North Korea and the Bomb." *Foreign Policy* 83 (Summer 1991), p. 93.

Masaki, Stuart. "The Korean Question: Assessing the Military Balance." *Security Studies* 4.2 (Winter 1995), pp. 365–425.

Mastanduno, Michael. "Framing the Japan Problem: The Bush Administration and the Structural Impediments Initiative." *International Journal* 47.2 (Spring 1992), pp. 235–64.

McCain, John. "The Crisis in Korea." Statement on the Senate floor. 140 Cong. Rec. S7497; Date: 6/23/94. Text from Congressional Record. Available from: Lexis Nexis Congressional (online service). Bethesda, MD: Congressional Information Service.

McDermott, Rose. "Prospect Theory in International Relations: The Iranian Hostage Rescue Mission." *Political Psychology* 13.2 (1992), pp. 237–63.

McGrory, Mary. "Fuzzy-Headed on North Korea." *Washington Post*, February 9, 2003, p. B7.

McGrory, Mary. "Bush's Moonshine Policy." Washington Post (op-ed), December 29, 2002, p. B7.

McInerney, Audrey. "Prospect Theory and Soviet Policy Toward Syria, 1966–1967." *Political Psychology* 13.2 (1992), pp. 265–82.

Memorandum of Conversation with the 1st Secretary of the Embassy of the USSR in the DPRK, Comrade Zvetkov, and Comrade Jarck on July 26, 1968 between 1430 and 1615 in the USSR Embassy, MfAA, G-A 320; translated by Karen Riechert; Embassy of the GDR in the DPRK, Pyongyang, July 29, 1968. Confidential. Obtained through the Cold War History Project, Woodrow Wilson Center, In Kathryn Weathersby, ed., *Inside North Korea: Selected Documents from the Russian, East German, Hungarian, Czech, and Polish Archives* (March 8, 2003), Section 8 "The Crises of 1968" Document 17.

Memorandum of Conversation with the Ambassador of the People's Republic of Hungary, Comrade Kadasch, on January 27, 1968, from 2:00 PM to 2:20 PM. MfAA, C 1091/70; translated by Karen Riechert;

240

GDR Embassy in the DPRK, Pyongyang: 29 January 1968. Confidential. Obtained through the Cold War History Project, Woodrow Wilson Center, In Kathryn Weathersby, ed., *Inside North Korea: Selected Documents from the Russian, East German, Hungarian, Czech, and Polish Archives* (March 8, 2003), Section 8 "The Crises of 1968" Document 4.

Michishita, Narushige. "Two Alliance After Peace on the Korean Peninsula." A/PARC Working Paper, Stanford University, May 7, 1999.

Milburn, Thomas, and Daniel Christie. "Rewarding in International Politics." *Political Psychology* 10.4 (1989), pp. 625–45.

Ministry of Foreign Affairs. *Waegyo Baekso (Foreign Policy White Paper)*. Seoul: Ministry of National Defense, 2002.

Ministry of Unification. "Data on North Korea." Seoul, Korea: Ministry of Unification, 2002 (www.unikorea.go.kr).

Modelski, George. "The Long Cycle of Global Politics and the Nation-State." *Comparative Studies in Society and History* 20 (April 1978), pp. 214–35.

Moltz, James Clay and Alexandre Mansourov, eds. *The North Korean Nuclear Program*. New York: Routledge, 1999.

Moon, Chung-in, and David Steinberg eds. *Kim Dae-jung Government and Sunshine Policy*. Seoul: Yonsei University Press, 1999.

n.a. "DPRK Warns U.S. of 'Unpredictable Consequences." *People's Korea*, August 7, 1999), p. 1.

n.a. "DPRK's Economic Measures Lead to Brisker Market, Better Life." *People's Daily*, Wednesday, October 30, 2002.

n.a. "Experts Challenge U.S. Claims of N. Korean Missile Threat." *Korea Times*, April 27, 2000, p. 1.

n.a. "Kim Dae-jung, Clinton in Agreement on Democracy, Free Market." *Korea Herald*, November 23, 1998.

n.a. "Koreas Exchange Fire At Border, But No Casualties are Reported." *Associated Press* November 27, 2001.

n.a. "Legal Questions Raised over Shooting at Suspicious Ship." *Asahi Shimbun* December 25, 2001.

n.a. "Samsung Group Chairman Wants to Visit North Korea." *Asia Pulse*, May 3, 2000.

n.a. "Sinuiju Designated as H.K.-Type Special Zone: First Market Economy Experience in DPRK." *People's Korea*, September 28, 2002, (www.korea-np.co.jp/pk/184th_issue/2002092802.htm)

n.a. "Sound the alarm: Defector Says North Korea is Preparing for War." *The Economist*, April 26, 1997, p. 34.

n.a. "Telecom Cos. Moving Briskly to begin business in North Korea." *Korea Times*, July 26, 2000.

n.a. "Tensions Weigh on South Korean Ratings, S&P say." *International Herald Tribune*, February 26, 2003, p. B1.

n.a. "US Followed the Aluminum."*Washington Post*, October 18, 2002, p. A3.

Nam, Koon Woo. *The North Korean Communist Leadership, 1945–1965: A Study of Factionalism and Political Consolidation*. University, Alabama: The University of Alabama Press, 1974.

National Institute of Defense Studies. *East Asian Strategic Review 2001*. Tokyo: NIDS 2001.

National Unification Board. *The Economies of South and North Korea*. Seoul: National Unification Board, 1988.

Natsios, Andrew. *The Great North Korean Famine*. Washington, DC: U.S. Institute for Peace, 2001.

Nautilus Institute. *DPRK Report* No. 19 (July-August 1999).

Niksch, Larry. "North Korea." In William Carpenter and David Wiencik eds., *Asian Security Handbook*. New York: M.E. Sharpe, 2000.

Niou, Emerson and Peter C. Ordeshook. "Preventive War and the Balance of Power: A Game-Theoretic Approach." *Journal of Conflict Resolution* 31.3 (Summer 1987), pp. 387–419.

Nodong Sinmun, various issues.

Noland, Marcus. "North Korea and the South Korean Economy." paper prepared for the Roh Government Transition Team, Seoul, Korea, February 24, 2003 (http://www.iie.com/papers/noland0203.htm).

Noland, Marcus. "West-Bound Train Leaving the Station: Pyongyang on the Reform Track." unpublished paper prepared for the Council on US-Korea Security Studies, Seoul, Korea, October 14–15, 2002 (http://www.iie.com/papers/noland1002.htm).

Noland, Marcus. "Why North Korea Will Muddle Through." *Foreign Affairs* 76.4 (July/August 1997), pp. 105–18.

242

Noland, Marcus. *Avoiding the Apocalypse: The Future of the Two Koreas.* Washington, DC: International Institute for Economics, 2001.

Oberdorfer, Don. *The Two Koreas: A Contemporary History.* New York: Addison-Wesley, 1998.

Office of the Secretary of Defense. *2000 Report to Congress: Military Situation on the Korean Peninsula September 12, 2000* (www.defenselink.mil/news/Sep2000/korea09122000.html.)

Oh, John K.C. *Korean Politics: The Quest for Democratization and Economic Development.* Ithaca, NY: Cornell University Press, 1999.

Oh, Kongdan and Ralph C. Hassig. *North Korea through the Looking Glass.* Washington, DC: Brookings Institution, 2000.

O'Hanlon, Michael, Susan Rice, and James Steinberg. "The New National Security Strategy and Preemption." Brookings Institute, 2002.

O'Hanlon, Michael. "Stopping a North Korean Invasion: Why Defending South Korea Is Easier than the Pentagon Thinks it Is." *International Security* 22.4 (Spring 1998), pp. 135–70.

O'Hanlon, Michael. *Defense Planning for the Late 1990s: Beyond the Desert Storm Framework.* Washington, DC: Brooking Institution, 1995.

Olsen, Edward A. "The Arms Race on the Korean Peninsula." *Asian Survey* 26.8 (August 1986), pp. 851–67.

Organski, A.F.K. *World Politics.* New York: Knopf, 1968.

Pak, Moon J. "The Nuclear Security Crisis in the Korean Peninsula: Revisit the 1994 Agreed Framework." December 28, 2002 (http://www.vuw.ac.nz/~caplabtb/dprk/Paknuclearcrisis.doc).

Park, Han S. *North Korea: The Politics of Unconventional Wisdom.* Boulder. CO: Lynne Reiner, 2002.

Park, Han S., ed. *North Korea: Ideology, Politics. Economy.* Englewood Cliffs, NJ: Prentice Hall, 1996.

Park, Jong-Chul. "Challenges and Opportunities for the Two Koreas after the Summit." *Journal of East Asian Affairs* 14.2 (Fall 2000), pp. 301–27.

Park, Kyung-Ae. "The Pattern of North Korea's Track-Two Foreign Contacts," In Joint U.S.-Korea Academic Studies, Vol. 11, pp. 157–184. Washington, DC: Korean Economic Institute, September 2001.

Park, Suhk-sam. "Measuring and Assessing Economic Activity in North

Korea." In *Korea's Economy 2002*. Washington, DC: Korea Economic Institute, 2002.

Park, Tong-Whan. "Issues of Arms Control Between the Two Koreas." *Asian Survey* 32.4 (April 1992), p. 353.

Paul, T.V. *Asymmetric Conflicts: War Initiation by Weaker Powers*. Cambridge: Cambridge University Press, 1994.

Perry, John Curtis. "Dateline North Korea: A Communist Holdout." *Foreign Policy* 80 (Fall 1990), pp. 172–191.

Perry, William J. "Commentary." In Yoichi Funabashi, ed., *Alliance Tomorrow*. Tokyo, Japan: Tokyo Foundation Press, 2000, pp. 265–69.

Pincus, Walter. "Hints of North Korean Plutonium Output." *Washington Post*, January 31, 2003, p. A13.

Pincus, Walter. "N. Korea's Nuclear Plans Were No Secret." *Washington Post*, February 1, 2003, p. A01.

Pollack, Jonathan, and Chung Min Lee. *Preparing for Korean Unification : Scenarios and Implications*. Santa Monica, CA : RAND, 1999.

Polomka, Peter. " The Two Koreas: Catalyst for Conflict in East Asia?" Adelphi Papers 208. London: International Institute for Strategic Studies 1986.

Powell, Colin. "Press Availability with Her Excellency Anna Lindh, Minister of Foreign Affairs of Sweden." March 6, 2001 (*http://www.state. gov/secretary/rm/2001/1116.htm*).

Power, Jonathan. "A Hawk on North Korea Wants Bush to be a Dove." February 5, 2003. http://www.transnational.org/forum/power/2003/ 02.01_NorthKorea.html

Quattrone, George, and Amos Tversky. "Contrasting Rational and Psychological Analyses of Political Choice." *American Political Science Review* 82.3 (September 1988), pp. 719–36.

Quinones, Kenneth. Remarks at the conference, "The North Korean System at the Dawn of the 21st Century." University of California, Berkeley. April 7, 2000.

Reiter, Dan. "Exploding the Powderkeg Myth: Preemptive Wars Almost Never Happen." *International Security* 20.2 (Fall 1995), pp. 5–34.

Rendler, Jack. "The Last Worst Place on Earth." In Henry Sokolski, ed., *Planning for a Peaceful Korea*. Carlisle, PA : Strategic Studies Institute, U.S. Army War College, 2001.

Ri, Kang Jin. "Statement of the Korean Anti-Nuke Peace Committee." January 28, 2003.

Rock, Stephen. *Appeasement in International Politics*. Lexington: University Press of Kentucky, 2000.

Rohrbacher, Dana. "U.S. Policy Toward North Korea." Hearings of the U.S. House International Relations Committee, March 24, 1999. Available from: Lexis Nexis Congressional (online service). Bethesda, MD: Congressional Information Service.

Rosenthal, Elizabeth. "In North Korean Hunger, Legacy is Stunted Children." *New York Times*, December 16, 1998.

Roy, Denny. "Hegemon on the Horizon? China's Threat to East Asian Security." *International Security*, Vol. 19.1 (Summer 1994), pp. 149–68.

Roy, Denny. "North Korea and the Madman Theory." *Security Dialogue* 25 (1994), pp. 307–16.

Rumsfeld, Donald. Report of the Commission to Assess the Ballistic Missile Threat to the United States, Executive Summary Pursuant to Public Law 201 104th Congress 15 July 1998 (available at http://www.fas.org/irp/threat/missile/rumsfeld/index.html).

Russett, Bruce. *Power and Continuity in World Politics*. San Francisco: Freeman, 1974.

Safire, William. "Three-Ring Circus." *New York Times*, January 2, 2003, p.A17

Sagan, Scott. "The Origins of the Pacific War." *Journal of Interdisciplinary History* 18 (Spring 1988).

Sagan, Scott. "Why Do States Build Nuclear Weapons?" *International Security* 21.3 (Winter 1996–1997), pp. 54–86.

Salant, Jonathan. "Powell Says U.S. is Willing to Talk with North Korea." *Associated Press*, December 29, 2002.

Samore, Gary. "U.S.-DPRK Missile Negotiations." *The Nonproliferation Review* (Summer 2002), pp. 16–20

Sanford, Dan. *South Korea and the Socialist Countries: the Politics of Trade*. New York : St. Martin's Press, 1990.

Scalapino, Robert. *North Korea at a Crossroads*. Hoover Institution Essays on Public Policy, Stanford University.73 (1997), 16–17.

Schafer, Bernd. "Weathering the Sino-Soviet Conflict: The GDR and North Korea, 1949–1989." In Kathryn Weathersby, ed., *Inside North*

Korea: Selected Documents from the Russian, East German, Hungarian, Czech, and Polish Archives. Washington, DC: Woodrow Wilson Center, Cold War International History Project.

Schelling, Thomas .*The Strategy of Conflict.* Cambridge: Harvard University Press, 1960.

Schelling, Thomas. *Arms and Influence.* New Haven: Yale University Press, 1966.

Schweller, Randall. "Domestic Structure and Preventive War: Are Democracies More Pacific?" *World Politics* 44.2 (January 1992), pp. 235–69.

Schweller, Randall. "Neorealism's Status Quo Bias." *Security Studies* 5.3 (1996).

Segal, Gerald. "East Asia and the Constrainment of China." *International Security* 20.4 (spring 1996), pp. 107–35.

Shafir, Eldar. "Prospect Theory and Political Analysis: A Psychological Perspective." *Political Psychology* 13.2 (1992), pp. 311–22.

Shambaugh, George. *States, Firms, and Power.* NY: SUNY, 2000.

Shenon, Philip. "North Korea Says Nuclear Program Can Be Negotiated." *New York Times*, November 3, 2002, p. A1.

Sherman, Wendy. "Defining the Future of US-Korean Relations." *Joongang Ilbo Washington Post* seminar, Washington D.C., February 6, 2003.

Shin, Jong-hyon ed. *Pukhanui t'ongil chongch'aek (North Korean Unification Policy).* Seoul: Ulyumunhwasa, 1989.

Sigal, Leon. "The North Korean Nuclear Crisis: Understanding the Failure of the 'Crime and Punishment' Strategy." *Arms Control Today* (May 1997), pp. 3–13.

Sigal, Leon. "A Bombshell that's Actually an Olive Branch." *Los Angeles Times* October 18, 2002, p. A18.

Sigal, Leon. "North Korea is No Iraq: Pyongyang's Negotiating Strategy." Nautilus Institute *Special Report*, December 23, 2002, (http://nautilus.org/fora/security/0227A_Siga.html).

Sigal, Leon. *Disarming Strangers: Nuclear Diplomacy with North Korea.* Princeton, N.J.: Princeton University Press, 1998.

Smith, Hazel, ed. *North Korea in the New World Order.* New York: St. Martin's Press, 1996.

Smith, Hazel. "Bad, Mad, Sad or Rational Actor? Why the 'Securitization' Paradigm Makes for Poor Policy Analysis of North Korea." *International Affairs* 76 no. 1 (January 2000), pp. 111–32.

Smith, Heather. "The Food Economy: the Catalyst for Collapse?" In Marcus Noland, ed., *Economic Integration of the Korean Peninsula*, Washington, DC: Institute for International Economics, 1997.

Snyder, Glenn. *Alliance Politics*. Ithaca, N.Y.: Cornell University Press, 1998.

Snyder, Glenn. *Deterrence and Defense: Toward a Theory of National Security*. Princeton: Princeton University Press, 1961.

Snyder, Jack. "Perceptions of the Security Dilemma in 1914." In Robert Jervis, Richard Ned Lebow, and Janice Gross Stein, *Psychology and Deterrence*, pp. 153–79. Baltimore: Johns Hopkins University Press, 1985.

Snyder, Jack. "Richness, Rigor, and Relevance in the Study of Soviet Foreign Policy." *International Security* 9.3 (Winter 1984–1985), pp. 89–108.

Snyder, Scott. "The Inter-Korean Summit and Implications for US Policy." *Korean Journal of Defense Analysis* 12.2 (Winter 2000), pp. 53–70.

Snyder, Scott. *Negotiating on the Edge: North Korean Negotiating Behavior*. Washington DC: US Institute of Peace Press, 1999.

Solomon, Jay, Alix Freedman, and Gordon Fairclough. "Troubled Power Project Plays Role in North Korea Showdown." *The Wall Street Journal*, January 30, 2002, p. A1.

Song, Young-Sun. *The Korean Nuclear Issue*. Canberra: Dept. of International Relations, Australian National University, 1991.

Spector, Leonard S. and Jacqueline R. Smith. "North Korea: The Next Nuclear Nightmare?" *Arms Control Today* 21.2 (March 1991), pp. 8–13.

Stein, Janice Gross, "Deterrence and Reassurance,"in Philip Tetlock et al., eds., *Behavior, Society and Nuclear War* vol. 2 (New York: Oxford University Press, 1990), pp. 9–72;

Stein, Janice Gross. "International Co-operation and Loss Avoidance: Framing the Problem." in Stein, ed., *Choosing to Co-operate: How States Avoid Loss*, pp. 2–34. Baltimore: Johns Hopkins University Press, 1993.

Struck, Doug. "Reactor Restarted, North Korea Says." *Washington Post*, February 6, 2003, p. A31.

Suh, Dae-Sook and Chae-Jin Lee, eds. *North Korea After Kim Il Sung*. Boulder, CO: Lynne Rienner Publishers, 1998.

Suh, Dae-Sook. *Kim Il Sung: The North Korean Leader*. New York: Columbia University Press, 1988.

Suh, Dae-Sook. *The Korean Communist Movement, 1918–1948*. Princeton, N.J.: Princeton University Press, 1967.

Suh, Jae-jean, and Byoung-lo Kim. "Prospects for Change in the Kim Jong-il Regime." *Policy Studies Report*, Series No. 2 (Seoul: Research Institute for National Unification, 1994).

Sullivan, Kevin. "U.S. Troops Train to Fight N. Korea." *Washington Post*, June 7, 1996, p. A30.

Suro, Roberto. "Ex-Defense Officials Decry Missile Plan." *Washington Post*, May 17, 2000, p. A02.

Tenet George J. "Worldwide Threats to U.S. National Security." Testimony of Director, Central Intelligence Agency, Senate Armed Services Committee, February 2, 1999

Thatcher, Margaret. "Advice to a Superpower." *New York Times*, February 11, 2002.

The Secretariat for the President. *The 1980s: Meeting A New Challenge: Selected Speeches of President Chun Doo Hwan*. Seoul: Korea Textbook Co, 1984.

Thompson, William. *On Global War: Historical-Structural Approaches to World Politics*. Columbia: University of South Carolina Press, 1988.

Tow, William. "Reassessing Deterrence on the Korean peninsula." Korean Journal of Defense Analysis 3.1 (Summer 1991), pp. 179–218.

Tversky, Amos, and Daniel Kahneman. "Rational Choice and the Framing of Decisions." *Journal of Business* 59.4, part 2 (1986), pp. S251–S278.

United States Institute for Peace. "North Korea's Decline and China's Strategic Dilemmas," *USIP Special Report*, October 1997. Washington, DC: US Institute of Peace.

Van Evera, Stephen. "Offense, Defense, and the Causes of War." International Security 22.4 (Spring 1998), pp. 5–43.

Van Evera, Stephen. *The Causes of War*. Ph.D. diss., University of California, Berkeley, 1984.

Vantage Point various issues.

Vertzberger, Y.Y.I. *Risk Taking and Decision making*. Stanford: Stanford University Press, 1998

Wagner, Alex. "D.P.R.K. Threatens to End Missile Moratorium, Nuclear Cooperation." *Arms Control Today* (March 2001).

Wagner, Martin. "D.P.R.K. Extends Missile Pledge as U.S. Readies to Resume Talks." *Arms Control Today* (June 2001).

Walt, Stephen M. "Rigor or rigor mortis? Rational choice and security studies." *International Security* 23.4 (Spring 1999), pp. 5–48.

Waltz, Kenneth. "Nuclear Myths and Political Realities." *American Political Science Review* 84.3 (September 1990), pp. 731–45.

Waltz, Kenneth. *Theory of International Politics*. Reading, MA: Addison-Wesley, 1979, p. 61.

Wendt, Alexander, and Daniel Friedheim. "Hierarchy Under Anarchy: Informal Empire and the East German State." *International Organization* 49.4 (Autumn 1995), pp. 689–721

Wickham, John A. *Korea on the Brink: from the "12/12 Incident" to the Kwangju Uprising, 1979–1980*. Washington, DC: National Defense University Press, 1999.

Williams, James, David von Hippel, and Peter Hayes. "Fuel and Famine: Rural Energy Crisis in the DPRK." Policy Paper No. 46. UCSD, Institute on Global Conflict and Cooperation, 2000.

Williams, Martin. "North Korea to Promote Tech, Science Development." (http://www.idg.net/go.cgi?id = 456627).

Wit, Joel. "N. Korea Nuclear Threat." Transcript of *Lehrer NewsHour* (Ray Suarez, Joel Wit, Henry Sokolski), aired January 10, 2003 available at PBS Online NewsHour *http://www.pbs.org/newshour/bb/asia/jan-june03/korea_1–10.html;*.

Wohlforth, William. "Realism and the End of the Cold War." *International Security* 19.3 (Winter 1994), p. 99.

Wohlforth, William. "The Stability of a Unipolar World." *International Security* 24.1 (Summer 1999), pp. 5–41.

Woodward, Bob. *Bush At War*. New York: Simon & Schuster, 2002.

Yamamoto, Akiko, and Sachiko Sakamaki. "N. Korea's Neighbors Unmoved By Threats: Little Anxiety Felt in Seoul, Tokyo." *Washington Post*, Tuesday, February 11, 2003, p. A13.

Yang, Sung Chul. *The North and South Korean Political Systems*. Boulder, CO: Westview Press, 1994.

Yoon, Deok-ryong, and Park Soon-chan. "Capital needed for North Korea's Economic Recovery and Optimal Investment Policy." *Policy Analysis 01–08*. Seoul: Korea Institute for International Economic Policy, 2002.

Yoon, Deok-ryong. "Economic Development in North Korea: A Possible Time Line for North Korean Transformation." *Korea's Economy 2002*. Washington, DC: Korea Economic Institute, 2002.

Index compiled by Fred Leise